The Great
Year-Round
Turkey
Cookbook

The Great Year-Round Turkey Cookbook

ANITA BORGHESE

STEIN AND DAY/*Publishers*/New York

MY SINCERE THANKS TO:

Mr. Kenneth L. Klippen *of the National Turkey Federation, Reston, Virginia;* Mr. Robert L. Hogue *of the American Poultry Historical Society; and* The Schultz family *and all the tender turkeys at Schultz's Turkey Farm, Croton Falls, New York*

Instruction Drawings by Yaroslava Mills

Decorative Drawings by Dorothy Zahra Hurley

Copyright © 1979 by Anita Borghese
All rights reserved.
Designed by David Miller
Printed in the United States of America
Stein and Day/*Publishers*/Scarborough House
Briarcliff Manor, N.Y. 10510

Library of Congress Cataloging in Publication Data

Borghese, Anita.
    The great year-round turkey cookbook.

    Includes index.
    1. Cookery (Turkeys) I. Title.
TX750.B67   641.6'6'592   79-13605
ISBN 0-8128-2673-6

To my dear friend and buddy, RUTH,
who really knows her turkeys

Contents

The Great
Year-Round
Turkey
Cookbook

1

Turkey,
The All American Bird

... they were hypnotized by the uncarved, lus-
ciously glazed turkeys and the excellent aromas
rising from dishes of okra and corn, onion fritters
and hot mince pies.

—TRUMAN CAPOTE,
The Thanksgiving Visitor

What do a fifty-cent piece, a hobo's bundle, a play that closes after only one performance, and the most flavorful poultry in America have in common? Nothing, one might suppose. But the fact is, they're all turkeys—or are called turkeys.

Not only is turkey a toothsome part of America's diet, but it is also a popular ingredient of our language, for it has lent its name to a variety of objects, persons and situations that have become commonplace in our conversation. In addition, the turkey has special significance in our culture and heritage because of its traditional role in Thanksgiving festivities, but perhaps even more importantly, because it is truly an American bird and one of our few surviving original inhabitants.

So American is it, in fact, that if Benjamin Franklin had had his way there'd be a turkey instead of an eagle atop every flagpole in our land today. As he put it in a letter written to one Sarah Bache in 1784, "I wish the bald eagle had not been chosen as the representative of our country; he is a bird of bad moral character ... The turkey is a much more respectable bird, and withal a true original native of America." At one time the fifty-cent piece was called a "turkey," a whimsical reference, actually, to a less-than-grand eagle engraved on one side of the coin. This turnabout in bird names would no doubt have pleased Franklin very much, but unfortunately it never did help the turkey to get to the top of the flagpole.

How well the turkey qualifies as a bona fide American is quite impressive. More than a million years ago, perhaps even when sheets of glacial ice still covered some parts of Europe and North America, this noble bird was a firmly established resident of North America, where it ranged all the way from the Rocky Mountains eastward to the Atlantic coast and from what is now southern Maine to Mexico. There's no doubt that the turkey originated in our hemisphere, for the two surviving types as well as the one extinct type of this ancient bird were never found anywhere else in the world.

Indians of North America were intimately acquainted with the wild turkey more than a thousand years ago, for carbon-14 datings have shown that the birds were kept in captivity in parts of the southwest, where they were probably domesticated for use as food, clothing in the form of blankets woven from feathers, and even as pets for children.

Columbus may have been the first European to see a wild turkey, when on his fourth voyage to the New World he discovered some islands off the coast of Honduras where natives supplied him with a variety of foods that included turkey. He referred to the bird as *gallina de la tierra,* which means "fowl of the land," a name commonly used for the turkey soon afterwards.

There was for some time a great deal of confusion in settling on the name turkey for our native bird, and in the process *gallina de la tierra* fell by the wayside. The turkey was long involved in a case of mistaken identity with the guinea fowl and its family, which date back to the days of ancient Greece. The guinea fowl was brought from Africa by Meleager, King of Macedonia, and the Greeks gave it the name *meleagris.* When the guinea fowl was exported to Europe by way of the Turkish dominions it assumed the name "turkey". Later when the American bird was discovered it was thought to be a species of the guinea fowl, or "turkey", and so it was tagged not only with that bird's Latin name, *meleagris,* but also with its common name, turkey. To further complicate matters, the turkey was also confused at one time or another with the peacock, due, no doubt, to their common habit of spreading their tail feathers in courting display, and also due to the fact that as the peacock was moved westward into Europe it brought with it such names as *togi* from India and *togei* from Malabar. When the true identity of the American bird was realized, it was apparently too late to change the name, and so the dust and feathers having long since settled, our bird remains a turkey for all time.

In Mexico the Aztecs domesticated the turkey, and during the reign of Montezuma it was a cheap and plentiful source of meat. It must have been raised in great numbers, since at one point Montezuma demanded that every person in a certain part of his domain pay as a tribute to him one turkey every twenty days. The bird was used not only in his kitchens but also to feed his vast menagerie of eagles, falcons, and other hunting birds. Cortés, during his conquest of Mexico, enjoyed turkey not only in the form of food at his dining table, but also in the form of treasure when he was presented with six beautifully wrought golden figures of turkeys by Montezuma's ambassadors.

The explorer may have had his turkey roasted or prepared in a casserole with chilies, tomatoes and ground pumpkin seeds. In Mexico City, according to a letter he wrote, there was a street where game of all kinds, including wild turkey, was sold. Cooked turkey was available too in markets, but it's uncertain how it was prepared, and turkey eggs were also for sale. In a history written during the 1600s it is mentioned that during special festivals a giant-sized tamale was made by encasing an entire turkey in a mat made of palm leaves before it was cooked.

In Yucatán the first Spaniards to taste turkey had theirs roasted. They probably had ocellated turkey, a colorful bird with "eye" markings on its tail feathers similar to those of the peacock. This species of wild turkey was indigenous to Yucatán and was never domesticated. It could only be caught by trapping, and there's reason to believe that usually only the aristocracy and priesthood were privileged to eat it.

Europeans are indebted to the Spaniards, who took home some of the turkeys which the Indians had domesticated in Mexico. As early as 1511 turkeys were being imported into Spain by royal decree for breeding. The birds thrived in their new home across the ocean and were soon introduced to Italy where they were familiar food by 1552. They were also taken across the channel to England, where, twenty-five years later, they were popular items on the bill of fare at Christmas time. The turkey found its way into France, too, and in 1570 was the *pièce de résistance* at the wedding feast of King Charles IX and Elisabeth, daughter of Maximilian II, who found the bird much to her liking. It's uncertain by what route the turkey arrived in France, whether by way of Spain or directly from the New World where the Jesuits raised the birds. For some time turkeys in France were called *jésuites,* and the Jesuits did, in fact, introduce a breeding stock of the birds at Bourges which apparently fared well and spread to other parts of France. The French took to the bird with great enthusiasm, especially when it was reported that turkey meat was an aphrodisiac. At the same time the eating of turkey eggs was said to cause leprosy. It seems safe to assume that most people shunned the eggs, leaving them to hatch into turkeys that could then be transformed into dinners of delight.

When the colonists came to America in the 1600s they brought along domesticated turkeys from England, thus completing the round trip of domesticated turkeys from the New World to the Old and back again.

These birds, with wild American turkeys, served as foundation stock for the establishment of domesticated turkey varieties in the Colonies. The birds traveled still further west when an English sea captain took some of them to the Hawaiian Islands in the eighteenth century. The Spanish transferred some turkeys from Mexico or Central America to Peru, and over the years the turkey has been introduced to many lands on nearly every continent. Ultimately, we are indebted to the Aztecs for the domestication of the turkey, which made it possible for the bird to be raised all over the world.

While the domesticated bird is the one with which most of us in the United States are familiar, one does wonder about the "real" American turkey—the wild turkey, the role it played in the lives and diets of American Indians, explorers, and settlers, and its place in our country today.

Long before settlers began to arrive along our eastern seaboards, Coronado was busy exploring the area of what we now know as Arizona. He was searching for Cibola, a city reputed to be rich in gold, but found instead a small pueblo where the Cibolans lived a simple ungilded life. A chronicler of the journey revealed the delight of the Spaniards, nevertheless, in finding turkeys there when he wrote, "There we found something we prized much more than gold or silver: namely plentiful maize and beans, turkeys larger than those in New Spain . . . ." New Spain was the name given to Mexico, and the reference was to the turkeys raised by the Aztecs. So, it would appear from this report at least, that turkeys north of the border grew on a grander scale than did those south of it.

The Pueblos were the only American Indians to carry on large scale husbandry of the turkey, and diggings have unearthed pens of various kinds in which they were kept. Most of the Indians east of the Great Plains hunted the wild turkey, and it was a common food for them. It was, however, on the taboo list of foods for the Apaches, as well as for the Cheyennes, who feared that eating turkey would endow them with the turkeylike characteristic of fleeing at the first sign of danger. Although it did not appear on Apache dinner plates, the turkey did appear in their mythology as a beneficent figure who brought them corn, and it was also a symbol of fertility.

Eastern Indians occasionally kept turkeys, but never actually domesticated them. They raised captured wild baby turkeys and used some as decoys for attracting other birds. It was unnecessary for them to raise turkeys since they were so plentiful in all the forests and woodlands at the time. Wild turkeys were considered such easy hunting, in fact, that many Indians left the job to their children, who sometimes used blowguns to kill their prey.

Some Indians cooked wild turkey by placing the whole bird, complete with feathers, in hot coals to cook. When it was finished the charred outside was pulled away to reveal succulent roasted meat within. Turkey was also preserved by smoking, and could be carried on the trail and refreshed by boiling.

American colonists quickly learned how to hunt wild turkeys by trapping them in nets set under such places as oak trees where the birds came to eat acorns, or by hunting them with guns. Pioneers learned to imitate the calls of turkeys, just as the Indians did, and this skill helped to provide them with many a turkey dinner.

The settlers also used wild turkey eggs when they could find them, as well as the fat from turkeys as a substitute for butter. Sometimes turkey meat was salted down for winter use, or the breast meat was dried and used as a bread substitute or pounded down into a sort of flour.

Wild turkeys were so plentiful that people began to shoot them just for special parts, such as breast meat or giblets. Colonists in New England reported great flocks of wild turkeys passing in front of their doors, and it was said that the creatures were so abundant in Kentucky that it was a poor sportsman who could not shoot a dozen in a day.

The turkeys retaliated by feasting upon the settlers' cornfields and trampling the crops to get their fill of grains whenever they could. But it was a losing battle. Wild turkeys were hunted mercilessly from the Eastern seaboard to the west. They became a readily marketable, abundant food item at giveaway prices. William Penn wrote that in his colony 30-pound wild turkeys could be bought for a shilling apiece. Delaware Indians were recorded as having sold them for the equivalent of about five cents each around 1650. By 1818 they were selling at five for a dollar in Illinois, and were brought to market by the wagonload. They were even given away during the early settlement of Kentucky.

A visitor from England in the days of colonial Virginia reported that turkey was served at every dinner he ate, and sometimes as many as three or four turkeys appeared on the same table, although one can only speculate whether the turkeys he ate were wild or domesticated. But wild turkey became common fare throughout the east and midwest, and was a standard item on the daily menu at most inns.

Inevitably the bird became increasingly scarce as it was hunted without regard for the future, and land cleared for agriculture, building, and timber robbed it of its natural habitat. Fortunately this unhappy state of affairs has reversed itself in our time, and as we will see in Chapter 12, the wild turkey is thriving once again in nearly every state of the Union, including some where it never originally existed.

The domesticated turkey is thriving too and gaining in popularity each year as more people become acquainted with the versatility of turkey cuts and the availability of a wide variety of turkey products.

Most people don't confine themselves to turkey just for winter holiday meals any longer, because of the reputation it has earned for being delicious (no other generally marketed poultry has a more distinctive flavor), nutritious (low in saturated fats and higher in protein content than any other poultry), easy to prepare (almost never a pinfeather to be found), economical (probably the best buy of any meat or poultry in America), and readily available (the turkey industry now offers a year-round array of turkey products).

Turkeys have always been delicious, but they haven't always been the chunky-statured, clean-looking, full-breasted birds that we buy today. We have modern technology to thank for producing such gustable, well-shaped turkeys through genetic breeding. In the late 1800s there were at least five distinct turkey varieties in the United States, and most of our modern turkeys were developed from two of these varieties, the Bronze and the White Holland. The Bronze contributed a greater size and the White Holland evidenced various refinements such as a neater appearance when dressed. Most of the turkeys raised commercially nowadays have the light coloring of the White Holland variety. There are really no pure varieties of turkeys any longer, except for those raised by turkey fanciers as a hobby. And because of so much crossbreeding to develop strains of turkeys with special characteristics, the term used today to describe types of turkeys is not "variety," but "breed."

The ideal combination that breeders continue to work for is a strain where the male grows as fast and as large as possible, and the female lays as many eggs as possible, with all of the birds having full dimpled (heart-shaped) breasts and disease free constitutions. One of the many breeding marvels of recent times is the Beltsville turkey, which was developed by the U. S. Department of Agriculture at Beltsville, Maryland, to fill the need for full-breasted but smaller sized turkeys for everyday eating and for small families. Six varieties of turkeys, including one imported from Scotland, were used to produce the bird, and from the Beltsville other strains of small white turkeys have emerged. The Beltsville itself as a pure strain probably no longer exists, but extinction of pure strains simply means progress in the world of turkey raising, and production of better turkeys for our dinner tables.

Perhaps the only cause for nostalgia concerning the turkey-breeding days gone by are the turkey shows that once took place. These contests were held so that breeders could show off their birds of fine feather, compete for prizes awarded to the turkeys that most closely met the standards of perfection for each variety, and compare notes and news of the ins and outs of turkey raising. When meat quality and quantity became more important than the color of plumage, the shows gradually faded away, so that today only a few are held in the United States each year.

Turkeys began their current ascent to dinner table popularity when they became a major farm enterprise in the 1940s. That was due to the development of very desirable strains of turkeys, knowledge of better turkey care, demand for turkeys by the armed forces during World War II, favorable prices, and the fact that meat rationing didn't apply to turkeys during the war. Increased year-round eating of turkey, introduction of new turkey products, a growing export program, and favorable pricing compared to other meats have brought the turkey to the rank of a major meat in America's markets today.

Before we go on to buying, storing and cooking the elegant bird, and to the recipes themselves, let's follow the life of a turkey from egg to packaged poultry. The best way to learn about this is to visit a turkey farm to see the turkey lifestyle firsthand. At a turkey farm you'll immediately see that, for the most part, domesticated turkeys live their lives segregated from one another. The breeding stock lives apart from the stock being raised for market, the males live apart from the females, and the poults (baby turkeys) live apart from the grownups.

After spending some time looking at the turkeys and asking pertinent questions one has to say, quite fairly, that domesticated turkeys don't have anywhere near as much fun as their wild counterparts. Their sex life, first of all, is severely restricted because their heavy full-breasted conformation and short legs make mating virtually impossible, and for this reason all commercial turkey procreation is accomplished through artificial insemination. Second, these turkeys can't do much in the way of flying because they're too heavy and compact in shape to get very far off the ground. Third, turkeys never get to hatch their eggs and raise a family, so are deprived of the joys of motherhood. At the same time a baby turkey can't benefit from the care and attention it would receive from its mother, nor can it learn anything from her, because it never sees her.

On large turkey farms the birds spend their entire lives indoors. On small turkey farms they're usually more fortunate because they get to go outdoors on fine days and enjoy themselves in the fresh air and sunshine, even though their enjoyment is at the expense of the farmer who has to keep a sharp lookout for dogs, various wild animals, and hawks, all intent on attacking the defenseless birds. But the farmer is ultimately rewarded, for the outdoor life helps to produce a turkey with a better flavor and finer "finish," or appearance of flesh. Out of doors, sandy soil is the best kind for turkeys to walk on, and indoors their pens are usually carpeted with ground corn shavings, sugar cane shavings, or peanut shells. The days of wire mesh as cage flooring for turkeys has passed because today's birds are too weighty to walk on wire mesh, which would hurt their feet, cause them to lie down, and as a result ruin their breasts.

Turkeys are fed ample diets of meal consisting mostly of corn, soybeans, oats, fish meal, vitamins and minerals. There are special diets, too, for special needs. Toms, for example, receive low fat diets if they're being raised for breeding.

Turkeys have often been accused, rather unfairly I think, of being not too bright. If one considers the choice of activities left to a turkey after its food and drink have been supplied and don't need to be sought out, when its sex life and family life are nil, when it is in a state of confinement and can't fly about in the trees, and when it hasn't been able to learn any of the things, such as means of survival, that it would be taught at its mother's knee, so to speak, one realizes there really isn't much for the bird to do except get into mischief or stand around looking bored, just as humans are wont to do when left with too much idle time to fill. It has been found that probably because the domesticated bird no longer needs to rely on its wits to survive, the brain of a farm turkey is actually smaller in size than that of a wild one. Thus man, having made the turkey's intellect somewhat less than it should be, ought rightly to look at the bird with sympathetic understanding.

In spite of the life that it must inevitably lead, the domesticated turkey is, after all, a nice bird and an interesting one to watch. It has curiosity about human beings, and provided people don't descend upon it *en masse* or do things to frighten it, a turkey will generally come to take a look at a visitor outside its pen and say something by way of greeting. Turkeys, in fact, have a lot to say. Hens make a variety of sounds that include a kind of gurgling noise, one that is almost akin to a bark, and another that sounds like "awk". Occasionally when you remove an egg from the nest of a hen who would like to sit on the egg and hatch it, the bird will make a hissing sound to show its displeasure. Tom turkeys are great show-offs and do lots of gobbling, often in chorus, with heads bobbing up and down in unison like a row of stage performers. Little turkeys become very vocal by the time they're about three weeks old and peep long and noisily.

Turkey life starts, of course, with eggs, which are considerably larger than chicken eggs, tan in color, and speckled prettily all over with brown. A hen lays perhaps three dozen eggs in a clutch, about one egg a day. If you've ever wondered why you never see a turkey egg for sale it's because they're used for hatching and there simply aren't any extras to be used for food since a hen doesn't keep laying on a year-round basis. Those who have eaten turkey eggs (double yolk eggs, for instance, which can't be hatched) say that they taste very much like chicken eggs.

The eggs are collected daily from the laying hens and placed in incubators for about 28 days. During that time the temperature and humidity are controlled, and the eggs are turned every four hours, all in simulation of ideal conditions were a hen hatching the eggs herself. The poults peck their way out of the eggs with the help of a special tooth called an egg tooth attached to their beaks. The process takes from one to two days and the babies emerge damp and fatigued from their work. Within a day the egg teeth drop off, the birds are dry and fluffy, and look very much like baby chicks with long necks.

Each week's brood of newly hatched birds is kept separate, and one can observe the marked growth between poults say one week, three weeks and five weeks old, during which time they will grow tall and gangly-legged. After they attain their height they grow broader, and generally in 22 weeks a hen will have reached 14 pounds in weight, and in 26 weeks a tom will weigh from 22 to 26 pounds, or about a pound a week. Some toms attain a weight of perhaps 40 pounds, but not all breeds grow so large. It takes about three pounds of feed to produce about one pound of turkey, so one can appreciate the fact that feed is the greatest part of a turkey farmer's expense.

Another big expense is processing the turkeys and marketing them, so some farms join together in cooperatives that share such operations. There are some small farms, scarcer now with increased competition, that have their own processing plants or dressing houses as they are sometimes called, where the operation is just as efficient and clean as the larger plants, but slower and on a smaller scale. Regardless of size of operation the processing is under strict government inspection for wholesomeness at all times, and any questionable product is immediately destroyed, so that one can buy turkey products with complete confidence.

In the processing plant the turkeys are slaughtered and moved along in assemblyline fashion through a variety of machines and apparatus where they are defeathered, eviscerated, cleaned, and so forth. The greatest wonder of turkey processing, to the eye of the uninitiated at least, is the feather picking machine, which consists of a drum with whirling rubber fingers of various sizes that almost magically denude a turkey of its feathers in a matter of seconds. These machines vary in size and speed and while one operating in a small processing plant might defeather 600 turkeys a day, one in a giant operation could handle as many as 1,000 in an hour.

Giblets are cleaned and packaged and the birds are chilled and packaged in ready-to-cook form, or some of the whole birds are further processed into turkey parts, boned turkey meat, rolled roasts, and other forms convenient for cooking. Most of the turkey products are quickly frozen by blast freezing and held in freezer units for distribution to retail outlets.

It's apparent that we've come a long way from the days of our grandparents when turkeys were sold complete with innards, heads, feet, and plenty of pinfeathers. Then the birds were hung by the legs from hooks, and butchers took them down to be poked, prodded and otherwise examined by prospective buyers.

Selecting and carrying home the Christmas turkey was a special annual event of that time and a pleasureful task which, by tradition, was performed by the man of the house, especially among the more affluent families. In New York's finest market, the Fulton Market, gentlemen and ladies too would be found on Christmas Eve searching for the finest freshly-killed turkey which would later be well stuffed with oysters for the holiday meal. There were literally mountains of turkeys from which to choose and those who could afford the most tender and well-fattened birds might make their selection from among a group of birds artfully displayed on beds of evergreens or even with paper roses adorning their breasts. The less prosperous would buy their turkeys from stalls set up out-of-doors so that tiers of dangling turkeys lined the streets. While these conditions may not have been the most desirable from a sanitary standpoint, the weather was cold enough to allay fear of spoilage, but those who had reservations could always purchase their birds "on the hoof" and deal with the complete process of making them oven ready at home.

Whether he bought live or fresh killed birds, the buyer, who always had to bargain before coming to a mutually acceptable price with the butcher, was left with the problem of getting them home. While this presented something of a challenge when transporting a live turkey, the usual way to wrap the dressed birds was to pop them into a cloth sack, and the buyer headed off to hearth and home with the strange bundle in tow.

Today, most of us buy our turkeys ready for the oven, and we may have lost some of the romance involved in turkey buying over the years. We've more than made up for it, though, in safety, convenience, proportion of meat to bone in the bird, ease of preparation, and the saving of time and energy, not to mention the fact that now every day of the year can be turkey-eating day.

2

Before and After Cooking Turkey

BUYING, STORING, CUTTING UP, AND BONING TURKEY, AND GENERAL INFORMATION ABOUT THE RECIPES AND INGREDIENTS

Birds ready cooked do not fly into your mouth.
—Proverb

Before you head for the market to buy turkey you might like to know what a smart thing you're doing from a nutritional standpoint. Turkey meat in general, and its white meat in particular, is higher in protein and lower in fat than any other poultry or red meat. All turkey meat is extremely rich in niacin, which is needed by every living cell in your body. It's also high in riboflavin and is a good source of thiamine, other B vitamins, and iron.

Whether you're on a weight loss diet or not, it's nice to know that turkey meat is lower in calories than any meat, and if you're concerned with keeping saturated fats and cholesterol intake at a minimum you'll be happy to know that turkey is very low in saturated fats and lowest in cholesterol of all popular poultry and red meats. This assumes, by the way, that you eat the flesh only and pass up the skin. Light turkey meat is lower in fat than the dark, while the dark meat contains more iron, thiamine and riboflavin than the light, but either kind is one of the wisest choices you can make at the meat counter.

An interesting thing to note about turkey is that it's highest of all meats and poultry in its content of the the amino acid lysine. This may not sound very interesting in itself, but consider that grains are deficient in lysine, and if you put turkey and a grain product such as bread together, you end up with more usable protein than either of the foods could supply alone. A turkey sandwich, for instance, or a roast turkey with bread in its stuffing, supply you with really super protein.

Even if you don't want to think about its nutritional merits, choose turkey because its meat has more personality than chicken and as much versatility as any red meat, as you'll see from the recipes in the following chapters.

Buying Turkey

Whether you're buying a breast, parts, a boneless roast or a whole bird, there are two symbols you'll want to look for, one for wholesomeness and the other for quality or grade when you make your selection of turkey. If the turkey or turkey parts are frozen you'll find the symbols printed on the wrapper, or if they're fresh you'll find them on a tag attached to the wing. The circular symbol or mark, which says "Inspected for Wholesomeness by U.S. Department of Agriculture," followed by the number of the processing plant, is your assurance that the turkey was government inspected both when alive and at the time of evisceration and packaging, and that it was a healthy bird and was processed under sanitary conditions.

While the inspection for wholesomeness is mandatory, the grading of turkey and other poultry is optional. Although the producer is not obliged to grade his turkeys, you'll find that most of the time he does. The grades are A, B, and C. Look for a shield-shaped symbol or mark on the wrapper or wing tag that says "USDA Grade A." The A is large and easy to spot. It means that the government poultry grader has examined the turkey for conformation, amount of fat, and any defects such as torn skin or discoloration, and has found it to be of the highest grade; that is, full-breasted, full-fleshed and meaty all over, with attractive appearance and good finish. Turkey graded B is still good quality, but it is not as meaty and full and may have some minor dressing defect. The grade is usually not shown on the labels or tags of this class of turkey, so one can pretty much assume if there isn't a shield of quality the grade is B. Grade C is seldom seen in retail outlets since most of it is sold to commercial food processors for making processed foods. Grade C turkeys are less meaty than Grade A and do not have adequate fat coverage as do the other grades. They may also have crooked bones, which would not give them a nice appearance for the table, but this would not affect their edibility.

Whether you buy parts or whole turkeys, the age and sex of the bird is often specified in a general way, such as "young turkey breast," "young turkey thighs," "young hen turkey," or "young tom turkey." Sex sometimes omitted, but you know it's still a young bird if it's called a "turkey fryer-roaster" or "young turkey." There is little, if any, discernible difference in flavor, texture, or appearance of these birds, and it's doubtful if anyone can tell whether he's eating a male or female bird. There is really no advantage in seeking out one in preference to the other. When the birds become a little older they may be called simply "turkey," or when mature "mature turkey," or "yearling turkey," but fully mature turkeys, which tend to have rather coarse skin and hardened breastbones, are seldom found for retail purchase.

It's difficult to estimate the exact age of a turkey because size is not necessarily an indication of age. Different breeds grow to different sizes and a hen turkey of one breed may weigh only five pounds whereas one of the same age but a different breed may weigh several pounds more. Males, too, are heavier than females of the same age in their own breed. In any case, one can be virtually certain that any turkey or turkey parts on the market today are of tender age and texture, since there is sufficient demand for the older birds for commercial purposes to preclude their being distributed to butcher shops and supermarket poultry cases.

Other things to look for besides grading to guide you in selecting a whole turkey are conformation and finish. Look for a short, broad high-breasted bird. If it's not covered by a plastic wrapping that you can't see through, look for a dimpled breast where the meat is bulging up on either side of the center of the breastbone. The legs of the bird should be short and stocky, and the skin should look fine and unblemished.

You will notice that many frozen turkeys on the market have a solution (3 percent of their weight) injected into their breasts; the purpose of the liquid is to baste the white meat internally as it roasts. This interior basting solution is said to contribute flavor and texture to the turkey, but I have found that uninjected turkeys are equally tender and flavorful. The ingredients used in the basting solution usually include vegetable oil, water, salt, sugar in some form, an emulsifier such as sodium phosphate (which is also used in evaporated milk), vegetable protein, and flavoring. Some brands also contain coloring or other ingredients. There are staunch supporters of pre-basted turkeys, just as there are those who feel that pre-basting is objectionable. My experience has been that even when people engage in a taste test they usually aren't able to tell whether the turkey they're eating has been pre-basted or not. Whichever you choose to buy for roasting do remember that all turkeys, whether pre-basted or not, need to be basted in the usual way if they are to have a beautiful evenly browned skin.

Although they're not in every town and city in the United States, there are still many live poultry farms and shops where you can select your own turkey and have it freshly killed and eviscerated. The live turkeys, as well as the premises, are government inspected to assure you of healthy birds and clean surroundings. You can judge the cleanliness of the surroundings yourself, too, and watch the defeathering and evisceration if you want to. You pay for a freshly killed turkey according to its weight before it's killed, and there's between 1½ and 2½ pounds of waste, depending on the size turkey you select.

The price per pound as sold is about the same as for frozen or fresh turkey, but ultimately it costs a little more per pound because you're paying for the head, feet, feathers, and so on. The feet, of course, can be taken home to add to your soup pot. One thing that you don't pay for when buying a fresh or fresh killed turkey is basting liquid, which makes up 3 percent of the weight of most frozen whole turkeys.

If you buy a fresh killed turkey, plan to buy it the day before you plan to cook it. Rigor mortis, which sets in after the bird is killed, passes after about twelve hours. Then the turkey can be cooked. If cooked during rigor it will be tough, regardless of the cooking method. The best way to care for a freshly killed turkey when you get it home is to plunge it into cold salted water along with a few handfuls of ice cubes for about 20 minutes. Then drain it well, set it on a plate, wrap it well in plastic wrap or aluminum foil, and refrigerate it. It's perfectly safe to keep it for two days before cooking it.

What about the economics of buying turkey? It is, without question, your best buy. It has more usable meat and edible protein per-pound than any other poultry or meat. While other prices have soared, turkey has the distinction of selling at a lower price per pound today than it did fifteen years ago. If you compare the amount of cooked meat from whole birds of the three most popular kinds of poultry, you find that even a small turkey yields 46 percent meat, whereas a chicken yields 41 percent and a duckling 22 percent. Since the larger the turkey the greater the ratio of meat to bone, one can see that the proportion of turkey meat becomes progressively higher as the weight of the bird increases, and the amount of bone decreases. For this reason there are several possibilities to consider when buying turkey in order to get the best possible buy.

One money saving suggestion is instead of buying a small turkey, buy *half* of a turkey that's twice as large. Chances are that you'll pay the same price per pound, or perhaps less, and you'll end up with more meat.

Another idea is to buy a large bird and cut it up into various parts for making many different dishes. For example, the thighs can be cut into cubes, ground up as you would grind hamburger, or cooked whole in a variety of ways. The wings can be frozen and kept until you buy your next turkey, at which time you can put them together and have four wings to cook. The breast meat is easily boned off and can be sliced into cutlets and used much as you would cook veal cutlets. Or the whole breast sections can be put together for a boneless white meat roast. If you want to have a breast with the bone in you can have it simply by separating the breast from the back of the turkey after the wings and legs have been removed. Bones and odds and ends such as wing tips make excellent soup or stock. Recipes for using each part will be found by consulting the index or table of contents, and instructions for the actual cutting up of a whole uncooked turkey follow later in this chapter.

Still another idea in turkey economics is to buy a large turkey purposely to have lots of leftover meat for the making of many taste-laden main dishes, soups, salads, sandwiches, hors d'oeurves, appetizers, and more, included in this book.

Storing Turkey

Most turkey and turkey parts available today are frozen. Whole turkeys are wrapped in snug, vacuum-packed bags sealed at one end with a metal clip. Parts such as wings, necks, tails, drumsticks, thighs, cutlets, and ground meat come similarly packaged, or they may be on meat trays wrapped in transparent plastic wrap. Unless you plan to cook them within a day or two, any of these products should be placed in the freezer immediately upon arriving home from marketing. The freezer should be kept at 0°F. (−18°C.) or colder and the turkey should be kept solidly frozen. Whole birds and dark meat parts should be kept in the freezer no longer than a few months, and ground meat should be stored for as short a time as possible.

Fresh turkey should be wrapped loosely in aluminum foil or plastic wrap, placed on a plate or tray, and stored in the refrigerator at 38°F. (3°C.) or slightly lower. It should be used within one or two days of the date of purchase. If you buy a whole fresh bird remove the giblets and wrap them separately before storing. As mentioned above, if you buy a freshly killed bird wait twelve hours or more before cooking it.

Once turkey has been cooked it should be used within two days. Whatever you feel will not be used within that time should be packaged as soon after cooking as possible in airtight packages and frozen. If you have a roast turkey, remove all the stuffing and place it in a separate container in the refrigerator. Gravy, broth, and sauces should also be stored separately in covered containers with as little airspace in them as possible, and they should be used as soon as possible. These foods are quite perishable and, like the turkey, should be used within a day or two, or frozen immediately after cooling. Cooked and frozen turkey should be used within three months and stock, broth, and gravy within one month. A final word of caution—never leave cooked turkey, or any poultry, meat or other protein product for that matter, sitting out at room temperature for more than an hour or an hour and a half to prevent any possible bacterial growth. Store it, well wrapped, in the coldest part of your refrigerator, usually the top shelf. Don't wait until the end of a meal before thinking about putting away leftovers. Do it as soon as you clear the main course from the table, if not before.

Thawing Turkey

There are two good ways to thaw a whole turkey or turkey parts, but the best one, in my experience, is to thaw them in the refrigerator. This method results in a gradual temperature change where the surface of the bird remains cold while the balance of the bird thaws. Do not, as is sometimes recommended, puncture or open the wrapper in which the turkey has been packaged. Set the wrapped bird on a tray or shallow roasting pan in the refrigerator until it is completely thawed. This will take 48 hours, more or less, for a medium sized bird (up to 12 pounds), 3 days for a larger bird (up to 16 pounds) and 4 or 5 days for very large birds. Change the position of the bird occasionally for even thawing. Turkey parts packaged in a single layer will thaw overnight in the refrigerator.

The other thawing method, which is also a quicker one, is to place a whole turkey in its water-tight unpunctured plastic wrapping in a deep roasting pan set on a rack in the kitchen sink. Don't place the turkey directly in the sink, because, should the wrapper have an unseen puncture you'll risk contaminating your turkey should your sink be less than sterile. Cover the turkey as deep as possible with cold water and either allow a small stream of cold water to run over the turkey or change the water and add fresh cold water frequently for several hours until the turkey is thawed. Occasionally change the position of the turkey in the pan. A 12-to-14 pound turkey will thaw in 6 to 7 hours by this method. As a general guide you can figure one half hour thawing time per pound of turkey. This is not a suitable method for thawing turkey parts unless they're packaged in tight-fitting wrappers similar to the way whole frozen turkeys are packaged.

At one time it was a common practice to thaw a whole turkey by placing it in a brown paper bag and allowing it to thaw at room temperature, but this is no longer recommended because of the possibility that the surface temperature of the turkey skin will rise above 40°F. (4°C.) thus making it susceptible to bacterial contamination.

Regardless of which method you choose for defrosting turkey or turkey parts, do check frequently, and as soon as the thawing seems complete, which can best be judged by pushing the skin in various places to see if it gives to pressure, or while a few ice crystals still remain in the turkey, proceed with the cooking. Cook the turkey completely at one time. Don't, for example, roast a turkey partially and refrigerate it to finish roasting the following day. This is important from the standpoint of food safety.

Turkey lends itself to many methods of cooking which include sautéeing, braising, roasting, steaming, baking, spit-roasting or barbecuing, outdoor kettle cooking, and so on. Recipes using all these methods are included in this book. And of course there are numerous recipes for utilizing leftovers. These employ various kinds of cooking, and some, such as salads and sandwiches, require no cooking at all.

Cutting Up and Boning Turkey

TOOLS OF THE TRADE

Pinfeather picker. Before you cut up or bone your turkey you'll want to make sure all the pinfeathers are removed. Most birds today have no pinfeathers at all, but occasionally, particularly when you buy a wild turkey or a freshly killed one, there may be some pinfeathers to remove. The best tool for removing them is a strawberry huller or pinfeather picker, an inexpensive gadget that's built like tweezers with large rounded tips that hold the pinfeathers tightly while you pull them out.

Boning knife. A boning knife is the ideal tool for cutting up or boning turkey. Whatever knife you use should have a narrow flexible blade, and should be of quality that will allow it to be honed to razor sharpness. Carbon steel or stainless steel knives from Germany and France are often of the best quality and are likely to give the best results. That will make your work easier and more satisfying.

Poultry shears. While not a necessity, poultry shears are often handy for taking apart both uncooked and cooked turkey. They should be made of stainless steel with handles that feel comfortable in your grip. Ideally, the springs should be enclosed to keep the shears as clean as possible, and the blade should be slightly curved. If there is a rounded notch in one of the blades it will help you when you cut through at joints and bones.

Carving knives. These are not used in cutting up or boning turkey, but will be discussed in Chapter 5, which includes several methods for carving cooked turkey.

Cutting board. A wooden cutting board, chopping block, or other clean unpainted flat wooden surface is preferable to polyethylene boards or counter tops for cutting up, boning and carving turkey. The turkey does not stay as firmly in place on a polyethylene board, and most of these boards are too small to be practical as work surfaces. A counter top can be marred if used as a cutting board, and a knife edge can be damaged by hitting into it. With a wooden board the turkey stays where you put it while you're working with it, and wood is kind to knife edges. Whatever surface you work on, do be sure it's clean before you use it, and clean it well with soap and water, rinse it, and dry it after using. This is a general kitchen rule, of course, that should be followed regardless of what kind of poultry, meat or fish you may be working with.

How to cut up a whole turkey in order to use the various parts. Cutting up a turkey is very similar to cutting up a chicken, except that it is a larger bird whose joints are somewhat more closely knit than those of a chicken, so that there is a little less space between them in which to insert a knife. For this reason it requires a little more effort to cut up a turkey, but it is not difficult to do. Lay the turkey on a clean wooden cutting board.

First remove each wing by slitting the skin where it connects to the body, cutting around the flesh to expose the ball socket, and cutting the wing from the body. Cut off the wing tip at the joint, and plan to use it in making stock or soup. If you wish, cut the remaining sections of the wing apart at the joint. When separated they are easier to handle in cooking and the larger of the two parts is often called a "drummette" when you buy it in packages of turkey parts. These two wing parts are light meat, juicy, and give you the best of two worlds in turkey meat.

Second, remove each leg by slashing the skin between the thigh and the body, cutting through the flesh to the joint, and cutting the leg from the body. If you want to separate the thigh and drumstick cut through diagonally at the joint.

Next, with the turkey breast side up, separate the breast from the back by removing the back, cutting diagonally between the breast and back with one hand while pulling the breast up with the other. If there is a metal trussing wire for holding the legs in place while roasting, remove it. Next, if you plan to use the back for stock or a similar purpose, remove the "oysters," the meaty little circles on either side of the lower backbone, and use them with some of the other parts. They're too succulent to end up in the soup pot. Cut off the tail and add it to the stock pot group. The breast with bone intact can be used as is, can be boned out as directed below, or can be cut into serving pieces. To do this turn the breast skinside down. Place the blade of a cleaver inside the

HOW TO BONE A TURKEY BREAST
LEAVING THE SKIN INTACT

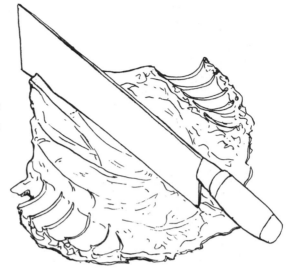

Cleaver in position to slit
center bone

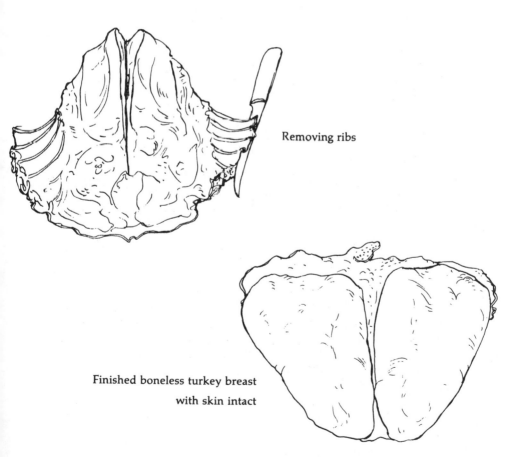

Removing ribs

Finished boneless turkey breast
with skin intact

turkey at the center of the breast bone, running from top to bottom. Hit the back edge of the cleaver with a rubber mallet to cut the breast in half. Using the mallet and cleaver cut each breast piece crosswise into two or three pieces, depending on the size of the turkey breast.

How to bone a turkey breast leaving the skin intact (see illustrations). Decide whether you need the skin intact or not, depending on what recipe you expect to follow. If you want to leave the skin intact place the breast on a clean wooden cutting board skin side down. With a knife or cleaver lightly slit the center bone lengthwise in the center. Do this by holding the knife or cleaver in position and tapping lightly with a rubber mallet. Press the turkey open to lie as flat as possible. If part of the ribs are attached, insert the point of a sharp narrow knife under one of the ribs, cutting lightly around it. Lift and pull the bone up while cutting against the bone and away from your hand. Pull off ribs one at a time, or loosen all the ribs and remove. Set aside the bones for the stock pot. Feel the turkey flesh in various places to see if there are any other bones besides the breast bone. If there are, slit the turkey flesh and extract the bones, cutting toward the bone and pulling the flesh away from the bone. Beginning at the tail end of the breast bone cut the flesh away from the bone by pulling on the flesh with one hand while cutting toward the bone and away from your hand with the knife. Do one complete side of the breast, taking care not to cut through the turkey skin which holds the breast meat together. Then do the other side of the turkey breast and remove the breast bone. Reserve for the stock pot. Where feasible, pull up or peel back any visible tendons or membranes in the flesh and cut them off.

How to bone a turkey breast to use the meat for cutlets or other purposes. Lay breast on a clean wooden cutting board. Pull the skin off the turkey breast and discard. Remove one side of the breast at a time, starting at the tail end of the breast bone. Cut the flesh away from the bone, following the contour of the bone, pulling on the flesh with one hand while cutting toward the bone and away from the hand with the knife. The breast bone and any ribs or meat attached to it can be added to parts for making stock.

How to cut a boneless turkey breast into cutlets. Lay one breast section on a clean wooden cutting board with the side that previously had the skin facing down. Lift out the filet and slice lengthwise into ¼-inch thick slices (or slice according to recipe directions). Slice the remaining piece of breast in the same manner. Repeat with the other breast section. If the recipe directs, flatten each cutlet by placing between two sheets of waxed paper or plastic wrap and smacking with the broad side of a cleaver or the flat side of a wooden meat mallet.

How to make a boneless white meat turkey roast. Follow directions for "How to bone a turkey breast to use the meat for cutlets or other purposes," but do not pull off the skin. Rather, try to leave as much skin as possible on the breast meat, including the neck skin. Pat the meat and skin well with paper towels to dry thoroughly. Lay one breast section on the cutting board with the skin side down. Set the other section, skin side up, on top of the first section so that the large end of one is on top of the small end of the other. Wrap any excess skin around the breast and tuck in any loose pieces of meat to make as compact a shape as possible. Tie lengthwise with string in two or three places without tightening the string, which would pull the roast out of shape. Then tie crosswise, fairly tightly, about every inch or so. Trim the ends of the strings. Use in recipes calling for boneless turkey roast. Cut off and remove the strings after cooking.

How to bone a turkey to get as much boneless meat as possible to be cut into pieces, ground, or otherwise used as directed in recipes (see illustrations). Lay the turkey on a clean wooden cutting board. Make an incision down the entire back of the turkey. Loosen the skin and peel it back from the body on either side, cutting with knife where necessary. Remove each wing by slitting the skin where it attaches to the body, cutting around the flesh to expose the ball socket, and cutting the wing from the body, leaving as much meat as possible on the breast. Remove each leg by slashing the skin between the thigh and the body, cutting through the flesh to the joint, and cutting the leg from the body. Separate the thigh and drumstick by cutting through diagonally at the joint. Pull the skin off each thigh. Remove the bone from each thigh by cutting through to the bone and cutting the meat away from the bone. Starting just beyond the "oyster" at the end of the turkey's back, cut away the breast meat from both sides of the turkey by following the contour of the bones. When all the flesh has been carved from both sides up to the ridge of the breast bone, cut through any cartilage and remove the meat from the carcass. Use the wings and drumsticks for "bone-in" recipes and the thigh bones, tail and carcass for the stock pot.

After you've cut up or boned turkey. If you aren't going to use the bones and trimmings immediately, wrap them tightly and refrigerate for making stock within a day, or freeze them and use them within a week or two. If you aren't going to use all the parts you've cut up right away,

HOW TO BONE A TURKEY TO GET AS MUCH BONELESS MEAT AS POSSIBLE TO BE CUT INTO PIECES, GROUND, OR OTHERWISE USED AS DIRECTED IN RECIPES

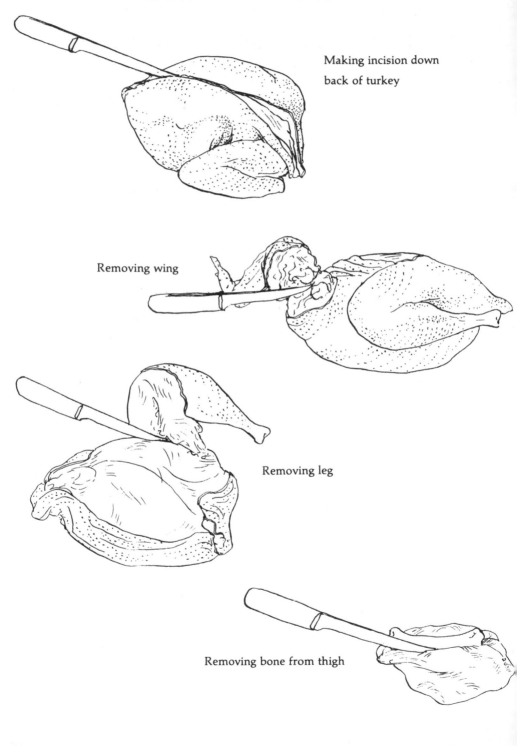

Making incision down
back of turkey

Removing wing

Removing leg

Removing bone from thigh

wrap them tightly and refrigerate to be cooked within a day, or freeze them and use them within a few weeks. If you work with previously frozen turkey and plan to refreeze part of it, it would be best to do the boning or cutting up before the turkey has completely defrosted. Wash knives and cutting board or other cutting surface well with soap and water, rinse with clear water, and wipe dry.

About the Recipes and Ingredients

The recipes. Please read a recipe all the way through before starting to cook in order to avoid any surprises about procedures or time of preparation.

The temperatures. All temperatures are given in degrees Fahrenheit, followed by degrees Centigrade (Celsius) in parentheses.

Margarine and butter. These can be used interchangeably, but are shown in order of preference in each recipe. If a recipe calls only for butter, however, it is preferable to use butter from the standpoint of flavor. All margarine referred to is the type that lists liquid vegetable oil (corn, safflower, or soybean) as the first ingredient on the package. This type margarine has an unsaturated to saturated fat ratio of 2 to 1 or better; that is, on the nutritional information panel on the package it will state that the margarine contains at least two grams of polyunsaturates for every one gram of saturates. Any other margarine can be used in the recipes if you wish, but the type described is more desirable nutritionally.

Vegetable oil. Safflower, sunflower, soybean, corn, wheat germ, sesame, or high grade peanut oil, or any combination of these oils, are suggested. Soybean and wheat germ oils tend to foam up when heated in a skillet and are best used in combination with other oils for sautéeing. Olive oil is called for where a special flavor is preferred. Coconut oil is not suggested as it lends too much coconut flavor to the food with which it is used. It's also very high in saturated fats, which most people prefer to avoid as a general rule.

Eggs. All eggs used in the recipes are medium size.

Garlic. All garlic cloves in the recipes are medium size unless otherwise specified. They should be peeled, the bases trimmed, and any bruised spots removed before using.

Vegetables and fruits. Any vegetable or fruit should be washed, dried if necessary, and trimmed before it is used in a recipe.

Mushrooms. All mushrooms used in the recipes are fresh mushrooms unless otherwise specified, and should be wiped or washed, and patted dry. Stems should be trimmed before using.

Parsley. All parsley used in the recipes is fresh parsley. Please don't substitute dried parsley, which is almost flavorless.

Grated orange rind or grated lemon rind. Use a sharp grater or lemon zester and grate or scrape off only the colored part of the rind, which is called the zest. Don't use any of the white part, which tends to have a bitter taste.

Spices. All spices used in the recipes are ground spices unless otherwise specified. Any whole spices, such as peppercorns or juniper berries, should be removed from the prepared dish before it is served.

Peppercorns. All peppercorns used in the recipes are dried black peppercorns, unless the recipe specifies dried white peppercorns or some other type. White peppercorns are milder in flavor and lighter in color than the black. Green peppercorns, which are sometimes called for, are unripe peppercorns which come packed in brine or vinegar, are soft in texture, and are much milder than dried peppercorns. Szechuan peppercorns, which are called for in a few recipes, are dried peppercorns, reddish brown in color, partially split open, and have a hotter flavor than black peppercorns.

Bay leaves. Use imported bay leaves if possible, as they are superior to the domestic kind. The label on the back of the herb bottle will usually state the country of origin. After cooking a dish always remember to remove the bay leaf before serving.

Turkey parts. Wash turkey parts and pat thoroughly dry with paper towels before proceeding with any recipe.

Turkey stock or chicken broth. Turkey stock or chicken broth is called for in quite a few of the recipes. You can either use turkey stock you've made (see index for recipes), or chicken broth, either homemade or canned.

Salt. Many of the recipes in this book call for salt to taste, rather than a specific amount. In most cases this is because the recipe also calls for another ingredient, such as stock or broth, which already contains salt. It's best to taste before adding any salt to a recipe of this kind, since it may not require any additional salt.

Bread crumbs. Unless otherwise mentioned, when bread crumbs are called for the bread from which they are made should be several days old and quite dry. If it is not, lay the slices out and let them dry in the air, turning them over when they have dried on one side. Include the crusts. If you wish, you can put the bread slices in a very low oven to dry them out. When dry crumble the bread into very small pieces with your fingers. This is the type of bread crumbs used in the stuffing recipes.

Converting to metric measures: In the event you wish to convert any of the recipes to metric measurements please refer to the following conversion table. All figures are approximations.

When you know (U.S.)	Multiply by	To find (Metric)
	WEIGHT	
ounces	28	grams
pounds	0.45	kilograms
	VOLUME	
teaspoons	5	milliliters
tablespoons	15	milliliters
fluid ounces	30	milliliters
cups	0.24	liters
pints	0.47	liters
quarts	0.95	liters

3

A Bird of Parts

*It was a turkey! He could never have stood upon
his legs, that bird! He would have snapped 'em off
short in a minute, like sticks of sealing wax.*
—CHARLES DICKENS, *A Christmas Carol*

Part 1—Turkey Breast (Bone In)

Turkey breast is great for family or company dinners since it's easy to carve and serve, and there's hardly anyone who doesn't love it. Use a turkey breast that you have cut from a whole turkey according to directions in Chapter 2, or buy a frozen turkey breast to make any of the recipes in this section. For white-meat turkey fans the readily available frozen breasts are the answer to a prayer in supplying slice after slice of tender breast meat.

The breasts range in size from as little as three pounds to as much as twelve or fifteen pounds. When you buy frozen turkey breast it may be called "prime young turkey breast" or simply "young turkey breast." You'll see that turkey breasts have either a portion of wing meat and a portion of back and neck skin attached, or ribs, or even all of these parts attached. None of the parts needs to be removed and are all cooked with the breast in one piece.

The recipes that follow range from the simple Turkey LePard to the more complicated Mardi Gras Turkey Glacé for a buffet party, and an elegant Truffled Turkey Breast with Sauce Périgourdine for a very special occasion sit-down dinner.

BRAISED TURKEY BREAST DIJON WITH LEEKS

2 bunches leeks	1 teaspoon salt
2 1½-inch-thick slices cabbage	6 peppercorns
(about half of a medium size	1 cup dry white wine
cabbage)	1 or 2 tablespoons Dijon mustard,
1 4-pound turkey breast (bone in)	depending on strength of
3¾ cups chicken broth	mustard
Generous pinch of ginger	3 tablespoons cornstarch

Trim base of leeks and cut off all but 1 inch of the top green part. Cut leeks in half lengthwise without cutting all the way through at the bottom. Wash well under cold running water, using a vegetable brush, and make sure that all sand is removed. Arrange in a large pot with the cabbage slices. Wash turkey breast under cold running water. Arrange, breast side down, on top of the vegetables. Add chicken broth, ginger, salt, peppercorns and wine. Bring to boil. Lower heat, cover tightly, and simmer 45 minutes. Turn turkey breast side up. Cover and continue to simmer 30 more minutes, or until meat thermometer inserted in thickest part of breast registers 170° to 175°F. (77° to 79°C.), or until tender when pierced with a sharp-tined fork.

Remove turkey breast from pot and set on a wooden carving board. Allow to stand 15 minutes before carving. Meanwhile remove vegetables from pot and drain. Keep warm. Discard the peppercorns. Remove ⅓ cup of the liquid from the pot and cool it quickly. Boil down the remaining liquid over high heat until it is reduced to 2 cups. Stir in the mustard.

Carve the turkey breast into slices. Cut the vegetables into serving size portions. Arrange the vegetables on a heated serving platter. Arrange the turkey slices over the vegetables. Combine the cornstarch with the ⅓ cup cooled liquid. Add to the reduced liquid and heat, stirring, until slightly thickened. Taste and adjust seasoning if necessary. Pour the liquid over the turkey slices and vegetables and serve immediately.

Makes 6 to 8 servings.

MARDI GRAS TURKEY GLACE

A perfect party buffet dish because it's served cold, looks beautiful with its creamy coating decorated with gay flowers all glazed and shining, and has a delicate delicious flavor.

For the turkey breast:
1 5½ pound turkey breast (bone in)
1¾ cups chicken broth
1 small chopped carrot
2 slices onion
1 bay leaf
¼ teaspoon thyme
6 to 8 peppercorns

For the coating sauce:
¾ cup strained broth in which
  turkey was cooked
½ cup heavy cream
1 tablespoon finely chopped onions
2 tablespoons finely chopped carrot
¼ teaspoon tarragon

Pinch of thyme
White pepper to taste (preferably
  freshly ground)
2 teaspoons plain gelatin
2 tablespoons dry vermouth

For the aspic and glaze:
1 envelope plain gelatin
3 tablespoons dry vermouth
1 10½ ounce can beef broth
  (bouillon)

For the decorating:
Pimientos or black truffle slices
Thin slices of lemon zest
Gherkins

For the turkey breast: Wash the turkey breast and place it in a heavy top-of-stove casserole or cocotte. Add chicken broth. Bring to simmer, skimming until no more particles rise to the surface. Add carrot, onion slices, bay leaf, thyme, and peppercorns. Reduce heat, cover, and simmer for 1½ hours or until thermometer inserted in thickest part of breast registers 170° to 175°F. (77° to 79°C.), or until tender when pierced with a sharp-tined fork. Remove casserole from heat. Allow to stand uncovered 30 minutes. Transfer turkey breast from casserole to a wire rack set on a plate. Break any bubbles that may have formed under the skin. Cover loosely and refrigerate until cold, about 1½ hours. Meanwhile strain the broth from the casserole into a saucepan and boil it down rapidly to about 1 cup. Pour into a small bowl, cool, and refrigerate until fat has risen to the surface and can be removed easily.

For the coating sauce: Remove fat from surface of the strained boiled-down broth in which the turkey was cooked. Measure ¾ cup of the broth and place it in a saucepan. Add the heavy cream, onions, carrots, tarragon, thyme and white pepper. Bring to a simmer, stirring. Lower heat and simmer until reduced to a generous cup, stirring occasionally. Meanwhile soften gelatin in the vermouth. Add to the saucepan and stir until completely dissolved. Strain through a fine strainer into a small bowl, making sure that none of the herbs have come through the strainer into the sauce. Allow to stand until completely cool.

For the glazing: Remove the chilled turkey breast from the refrigerator. Trim off any unsightly or protruding parts. If the turkey breast does not set straight and tends to tilt to one side you may need to turn the breast over and remove the underneath parts of the turkey breast and use them as props where necessary to keep the breast upright. Pat the breast thoroughly dry with paper towels. Set it on a wire rack over a platter. Spoon the coating sauce over the turkey, making sure all visible parts are covered. Set the rack on a plate and place it in the refrigerator for 15 minutes or until the first coating has set. Meanwhile, pour the coating sauce from the platter back into the bowl. Cover the sauce and keep it cool, but do not put it in the refrigerator. Wash and dry the platter.

Remove the turkey breast from the refrigerator and give it a second application of the coating sauce, following the same procedure as before. Chill, and give additional coatings, following the same procedure, until the coating sauce is used up. There should be enough for 4 coats.

For the aspic: While the coated turkey breast is setting after the final application of coating sauce, soften gelatin in the vermouth. In a saucepan heat the beef broth to boiling. Remove from heat and add the gelatin, stirring until completely dissolved. Allow to stand until completely cool. Cover and set aside.

For the decorating: While coating is setting prepare the decorations. Cut pieces of pimiento or slices of black truffles into flower petal shapes. Cut lemon zest into round pieces to resemble centers of flowers. Cut gherkins into various size strips to resemble stems and leaves.

When the last coating has set decorate the turkey breast with the cut-out flowers, centers, stems and leaves in an attractive way. Set the turkey breast on the wire rack over a clean platter and spoon aspic all over. Chill turkey breast until aspic has set. Meanwhile pour remaining aspic, including that in the platter, into a shallow pan and refrigerate until set.

To serve: Place the turkey breast in the center of a chilled serving platter. Cut off with scissors any of the coating that has congealed as drippings near the bottom of the turkey breast. Remove the aspic from the shallow pan and chop it. Arrange the chopped aspic around the turkey on the platter. Place on buffet. Slice to serve.

Makes 12 or more servings.

HARLEQUIN TURKEY BREAST

Making Harlequin Turkey Breast will give you not only a roast turkey breast with meat on one side and a scrumptious filling on the other, but also the bonus of half a raw turkey breast which you can later slice into cutlets and use to make another turkey dish.

1 5-to-6 pound turkey breast	¼ pound drained crumbled feta
1 pound fresh spinach	cheese
½ cup finely chopped onions	1 egg, beaten
2 tablespoons vegetable oil	2 tablespoons lemon juice
(preferably olive)	Freshly ground pepper to taste
¼ cup chopped parsley	Melted margarine or butter
½ teaspoon dill weed	

Wash spinach well, remove and discard stems, and dry the leaves thoroughly. Chop leaves and place in a bowl. Sauté the onion in oil until soft. Add to the spinach. Add the parsley, dill weed, feta, egg, lemon juice and pepper, and combine thoroughly.

Starting on the bottom of the turkey breast pull the skin away from the turkey up one side to the ridge of the breast bone. Do not break or cut through the skin. With a boning knife bone out the breast meat from the exposed side. Wrap and refrigerate for another use.

Preheat the oven at 325°F. (163°C.). Spoon the spinach mixture onto the boned-out side of the turkey breast. Cover the filling with the loose turkey skin and secure the ends of the skin with poultry pins. Place the turkey breast in a roasting pan just large enough to fit, and if necessary brace up the sides of the turkey with wads of aluminum foil so that it remains upright, or place it in a v-shaped rack and set in the roasting pan. Brush with melted margarine or butter.

Roast about 2 hours, or until the meat thermometer inserted in thickest part of breast registers 170° to 175°F. (77° to 79°C.), or until tender when pierced with a sharp-tined fork, basting with margarine or butter every 20 minutes. Remove from oven and set on a wooden carving board. Allow to stand 15-20 minutes before carving. Carve slices of breast meat and spoon out filling from under skin and serve together.

If desired make Turkey Pan Gravy (*see index*) while turkey breast is resting on carving board.

Makes 4 to 6 servings.

TURKEY LePARD

2 tablespoons margarine or butter	2 cups turkey stock or chicken broth
2 tablespoons vegetable oil	1 3-pound turkey breast (bone in)
2 cups sliced onions	½ pound mushrooms, sliced
1 teaspoon salt	2 tablespoons cornstarch mixed with 3 tablespoons water
Freshly ground pepper to taste	
¼ teaspoon of thyme	1 cup half and half (milk and cream dairy product)
1 bay leaf	
2 tablespoons paprika, or to taste	

In a medium sized top-of-stove casserole, Dutch oven, or cocotte, melt 1 tablespoon margarine or butter. Add 1 tablespoon vegetable oil and sauté onions until soft and lightly browned. Stir in salt, pepper, thyme, bay leaf and paprika. Add turkey stock or chicken broth and bring to boil. Place turkey breast in center of casserole, lower heat, cover, and simmer over low heat about 45 minutes, or until thickest part of turkey breast is tender when pierced with a sharp-tined fork or reaches an interior temperature of 170° to 175° (77° to 79°C.), basting several times with the pan liquid.

Meanwhile sauté the mushrooms in 1 tablespoon margarine or butter and 1 tablespoon vegetable oil over high heat until brown. Set aside. When turkey breast is tender remove from casserole and set on a wooden carving board. Allow to stand 15 to 20 minutes before carving. Meanwhile add cornstarch mixture to casserole and cook, stirring constantly, over high heat until mixture thickens. Cook several minutes more. Lower heat and stir in the half and half. Cook several minutes longer. Stir in the mushrooms.

Slice the turkey breast and arrange the slices on a heated serving platter. Spoon some of the sauce over the slices and serve the remaining sauce in a heated sauce boat.

Makes about 6 servings.

BRAISED GINGER-SCALLION
TURKEY BREAST

4 teaspoons finely chopped fresh
  ginger root or canned green
  ginger root
½ cup thinly sliced scallions,
  including some of green part
1 teaspoon Szechuan peppercorns
1 5-pound turkey breast (bone in)

1 tablespoon margarine or butter
1 tablespoon vegetable oil,
  preferably peanut oil
1 cup turkey stock or chicken broth
2 tablespoons cornstarch combined
  with 2 tablespoons cold water

Combine ginger root, scallions and peppercorns. Rub and pat all over turkey breast. Wrap tightly in aluminum foil and refrigerate 24 hours.

Scrape ginger, scallions and peppercorns from turkey breast and reserve. In a heavy top-of-stove casserole or Dutch oven brown the turkey breast lightly in margarine or butter and oil. Add the turkey stock or chicken broth and bring to simmer. Add the ginger, scallions and peppercorns. Lower heat, cover, and simmer 2 hours or until meat thermometer inserted in thickest part of breast registers 170° to 175°F. (77° to 79°C.), or until tender when pierced with a sharp-tined fork. Remove turkey breast and set on a wooden carving board. Allow to stand 15 to 20 minutes before slicing. Meanwhile add cornstarch mixture to casserole and cook, stirring constantly, until thickened. Cook a few minutes longer.

To serve, slice the turkey breast and arrange slices on a heated serving platter. Spoon some of the sauce over the slices and serve the remaining sauce in a heated sauce boat.

Makes 8 servings.

CLAY BAKER TURKEY BREAST
WITH VEGGIES

1 4 to 5 pound turkey breast (bone in)

1 pound green beans, ends removed, cut in half crosswise

2 medium tomatoes, peeled and chopped

½ pound mushrooms, trimmed and sliced

1 cup chopped onions

1 teaspoon basil

½ teaspoon thyme

1 teaspoon oregano

2 teaspoons salt

Freshly ground pepper to taste

¼ cup margarine or butter, melted

2 tablespoons cornstarch mixed with ¼ cup cold water

Soak clay baker in water 10 to 15 minutes, or according to manufacturer's instructions. Remove from water. Rub the turkey breast with 1 teaspoon salt. Place in the baker. In a bowl combine the green beans, tomatoes, mushrooms, onions, basil, thyme, oregano, 1 teaspoon salt and pepper. Toss and arrange around, under, and over the turkey breast. Pour melted margarine or butter over all. Place lid on baker.

Place baker in center of cold oven. Turn on oven at 400°F. (204°C.). Bake 1½ to 2 hours, or until meat thermometer inserted in thickest part of breast registers 170° to 175°F. (77° to 79°C.), or until tender when pierced with a sharp-tined fork, basting once or twice during baking with juices that have exuded from the turkey and vegetables. Remove turkey breast from baker and set on a wooden carving board. Allow to stand 15 minutes before carving. Drain juices from baker into a saucepan and add the cornstarch mixture. Heat over medium flame until thickened, stirring constantly. Slice the turkey breast and arrange it with the vegetables on a heated serving platter. Pour the sauce over all, or serve it separately in a heated sauce boat.

Makes 6 to 8 servings.

TRUFFLED TURKEY BREAST WITH SAUCE PERIGOURDINE

For the turkey:
1 ⅞-ounce can black truffles
¼ cup Madeira wine
1 5½ pound turkey breast (bone in)
4 tablespoons or more softened
    butter
2 tablespoons flour
Freshly grated nutmeg to taste
2 or 3 tablesppons melted butter

For the sauce:
3 tablespoons butter (1 of them
    softened)

¼ cup finely chopped onions
¼ cup finely chopped carrots
1 tablespoon finely chopped parsley
Generous pinch of thyme
1 small bay leaf
2 tablespoons flour
½ cup dry white wine
1 cup canned beef bouillon (not
    consommé)
1 teaspoon tomato paste
Freshly ground pepper to taste
Salt to taste

For the turkey: Drain truffles, reserving liquid for use in the sauce.
Place truffles in a small cup and cover with Madeira wine. Cover and
allow to sit at room temperature several hours or overnight.

Remove half of the truffles from the Madeira. Cut 12 thin slices of
truffle and put the remaining truffles back in the Madeira. Rinse and pat
the turkey breast thoroughly dry with paper towels. Work a finger under
the turkey skin in a few places on each side of the turkey breast and
insert half the truffle slices here and there in each side being careful not
to loosen skin any more than necessary. The best method is to insert 3 of
the slices on each side working from the neck skin area, and the other 3
slices up from the lower edge of the breast on each side. Combine 3
tablespoons softened butter with the flour and nutmeg and spread this
mixture over the skin of the turkey. Set the turkey breast on a piece of
buttered aluminum foil the size of the bottom of the turkey breast.
Butter enough parchment paper to wrap the entire turkey breast, overlapping ends so turkey is completely enclosed. Wrap plastic wrap all

around to keep the parchment paper in place. Set on a plate and refrigerate several hours or overnight.

An hour before ready to cook the turkey breast remove from the
refrigerator. Remove plastic wrap.

Preheat oven at 325°F. (163°C.). Place turkey breast in the parchment
paper on a rack in a roasting pan. Roast for 1 hour. Remove the parchment paper from the turkey breast and place the breast in the roasting
pan without the rack. Continue to roast, brushing every 15 minutes with
melted butter for 1 hour, or until meat thermometer inserted in thickest
part of breast registers 170° to 175°F. (77° to 79°C.) or until tender when
pierced with a sharp-tined fork. Remove turkey breast from roasting pan
and place on wooden carving board. Allow to stand 15 to 20 minutes
before carving.

For the sauce: Prepare sauce while turkey breast is roasting. Melt 2
tablespoons butter in a small heavy saucepan. Add the onions, carrots,
parsley, thyme and bayleaf and cook over low heat, stirring, until onions
become soft and slightly brown, about 12 minutes. Add flour and cook,
stirring, 2 or 3 minutes. Add wine, bouillon, tomato paste, and pepper,
and bring to simmer. Lower flame and simmer 10 to 15 minutes, or until
reduced to 1 cup. Remove from heat. Remove bay leaf.

Add the reserved Madeira and the reserved truffle liquid. Cut the
remaining truffles into small pieces and add them to the saucepan.
Transfer the sauce to the roasting pan after turkey breast has been
removed, and heat over medium heat until simmering. If too thick add a
little boiling water until of proper consistency. Taste and adjust seasoning, adding salt if necessary. Swirl in 1 tablespoon softened butter and
remove from heat.

To serve, slice the turkey breast so that not more than one slice of
truffle is in each slice. Arrange slices on heated platter and spoon some
of the sauce over them. Pour the remaining sauce into a heated sauce
boat.

Makes about 14 servings.

TURKEY BREAST A LA GRECQUE

1 4 to 4½ pound turkey breast (bone
   in)
1 garlic clove, cut in half
2 teaspoons salt, or to taste
Freshly ground pepper to taste

1 teaspoon oregano
8 cups ¼-inch thick sliced peeled
   potatoes
⅓ cup olive oil

Preheat oven at 325°F. (163°C.). Rub turkey breast all over with cut
garlic. Sprinkle underside of turkey with salt and place in shallow baking
pan. Arrange potato slices all around the turkey breast. Drop the garlic
halves among the potatoes. Sprinkle the turkey breast and potatoes with
salt, pepper and oregano. Pour the olive oil over the turkey breast and
potatoes. Bake about 2 hours or until meat thermometer inserted in
thickest part of turkey breast registers 170° to 175°F. (77° to 79°C.) or
until tender when pierced with a sharp-tined fork, basting every 20
minutes with pan drippings.

Set turkey breast on wooden carving board and allow to stand 15
minutes before carving. Serve with the potato slices.

Makes 6 to 8 servings.

Part 2—Turkey Drumsticks

Turkey drumsticks can be bought either fresh or frozen in your
supermarket poultry section. The drumsticks vary in weight so that you
may get a package of two drumsticks that weighs about two pounds, or it
may weigh as much as three or four pounds. For this reason most of the
recipes in this section call for a certain number of pounds of drumsticks,
rather than for a number of pieces.

Drumsticks are inexpensive, easy to cook and good for everyday
dinners. Since there are a number of tendons in each drumstick that are
best removed before serving, most of the drumstick recipes call for
carving off the meat and discarding the bones and tendons before serving. This is a quick and easy process that makes the eating much more

enjoyable. Another reason for carving the meat off the bones is that one drumstick is often much too large for one serving.

Besides regular turkey drumsticks another product you'll find is smoked turkey drumsticks. These generally come in see-through vacuum packages containing two drumsticks each. They are displayed either with other turkey products, or more often with other cured meat products, since they require refrigeration but not freezing. You'll find a recipe for using them as a main dish in this chapter, and two recipes using them in soups in Chapter 9 *(see index)*.

LEMON DRUMSTICKS WITH CHICKPEAS

⅓ cup plus 1 tablespoon vegetable oil
½ cup lemon juice
1 garlic clove, mashed
1 teaspoon salt
Freshly ground pepper to taste
1½ teaspoons dried mint
3 pounds turkey drumsticks

Flour
1 tablespoon margarine or butter
1 cup turkey stock or chicken broth
1 15-ounce can chickpeas, drained, or 1½ cups cooked drained chickpeas
2 tablespoons cornstarch combined with 2 tablespoons cold water

In a shallow glass or ceramic bowl or baking dish combine ⅓ cup vegetable oil, the lemon juice, garlic, salt, pepper, and mint. Place the drumsticks in the bowl or baking dish and turn them over to coat both sides. Cover and refrigerate 8 hours or more, basting occasionally.

Remove drumsticks from marinade and pat dry with paper towels. Dust with flour. Sauté in the remaining 1 tablespoon vegetable oil and the margarine or butter until brown on all sides. Add the marinade along with the turkey stock or chicken broth and the chickpeas. Bring to a boil. Lower heat, cover and simmer 1½ hours or until tender when pierced with a sharp-tined fork, turning drumsticks over after they have cooked 45 minutes.

Remove drumsticks and cut into serving slices, discarding tendons and bones. Arrange on a heated serving platter. Add cornstarch mixture to skillet and heat, stirring, until mixture thickens. Simmer a few minutes and pour the sauce with the chickpeas over the drumstick slices.

Makes 4 servings.

MUSTARD-BRAISED DRUMSTICKS WITH NEW POTATOES

3 pounds turkey drumsticks
1 cup chopped onions
1 tablespoon margarine or butter
1 tablespoon vegetable oil
¼ cup prepared mustard (use a
  flavorful mustard such as
  Pommery mustard, mild to
  medium hot Dijon, Zatarain's
  creole mustard, or Savora
  mustard)

3 cups turkey stock or chicken
  broth
1 teaspoon rosemary
Salt to taste
Freshly ground pepper to taste
2¼ to 2½ pounds small new
  potatoes, scrubbed
2 tablespoons cornstarch combined
  with 2 tablespoons cold water,
  or ¾ cup sour cream

In a top-of-stove casserole or heavy skillet large enough to hold the drumsticks and potatoes in a single layer, brown the drumsticks and onions in margarine and butter and the vegetable oil. Combine the mustard with ½ cup of the turkey stock or chicken broth. Set aside.

When drumsticks are browned add the remaining turkey stock or chicken broth to the casserole. Bring to boil. Stir in the mustard mixture along with the rosemary, salt, and pepper. Bring to boil, stirring. Lower heat, cover, and simmer 45 minutes. Turn drumsticks over. Arrange the potatoes around the drumsticks in the casserole so that the potatoes are in the liquid. Simmer, covered, 45 minutes more, or until drumsticks are tender when pierced with a sharp-tined fork, turning the potatoes over once during cooking. Remove the drumsticks and the potatoes and boil down the liquid by about one third. Use either the cornstarch mixture or the sour cream to thicken the sauce. If using the cornstarch mixture stir in and cook, stirring constantly, until mixture thickens. Simmer a few minutes longer. If using sour cream remove casserole from heat. Stir in the sour cream. Return to stove set at lowest heat and heat for a few minutes but do not allow to boil.

Slice the meat from the drumsticks and discard tendons and bones. Arrange drumstick slices down the center of a heated serving platter. Arrange the potatoes on the sides. Pour the mustard sauce over the turkey slices.

Makes 4 servings.

TURKEY DRUMSTICKS WITH PRUNE-TOMATO SAUCE

3 pounds turkey drumsticks
2 tablespoons vegetable oil
1 tablespoon margarine or butter
1 cup chopped onions
1 garlic clove, minced
1 8-ounce can tomato sauce

1 cup red wine
6 ounces (about 1¼ cups) pitted
   prunes
¼ teaspoon allspice
1 teaspoon salt
Freshly ground pepper to taste

In a top-of-stove casserole or heavy skillet brown the drumsticks on all sides in 1 tablespoon vegetable oil and the margarine or butter. Remove the drumsticks. Add the onions and garlic to the casserole along with the remaining tablespoon of vegetable oil, and sauté until onions are lightly browned. Add the tomato sauce, wine, prunes, allspice, salt and pepper to the casserole and bring to boil, stirring. Put the drumsticks back into the casserole, lower heat, cover and simmer 1½ hours or until tender when pierced with a sharped-tined fork, stirring occasionally and turning the drumsticks over after 45 minutes.

Remove drumsticks and slice off meat, discarding tendons and bones. Arrange slices on a heated serving platter. Meanwhile boil down the sauce over high heat, breaking up the prunes, until thickened. Spoon the sauce over the turkey slices.

Makes 6 servings.

BRAZILIAN DRUMSTICKS

2½ to 3 pounds turkey drumsticks
2 tablespoons vegetable oil
3 cups 1-inch raw potato cubes
2 celery ribs, sliced
¾ cup chopped green pepper
1 garlic clove, minced
1 cup beef broth
1 cup red wine

1 tablespoon instant coffee powder
⅛ teaspoon ground cloves
1 teaspoon cinnamon
1 teaspoon salt, or to taste
Freshly ground pepper to taste
3 tablespoons cornstarch mixed
      with 3 tablespoons cold water

In a top-of-stove casserole or Dutch oven brown drumsticks in the vegetable oil. Add the remaining ingredients, except the cornstarch mixture, and bring to simmer. Lower heat, cover, and simmer 1½ hours or until tender when pierced with a sharp-tined fork, turning once during cooking. Remove drumsticks and slice off meat, discarding tendons and bones. Add cornstarch mixture to casserole and heat until thickened, stirring constantly. Simmer a minute or two. Arrange drumstick slices on a heated platter and pour the sauce over them.

Makes 4 servings.

Note: This dish cannot be made ahead, as the potatoes will discolor.

SMOKED TURKEY DRUMSTICKS WITH HORSERADISH SAUCE

2½ pounds smoked turkey drumsticks
1 bay leaf
1 slice onion
4 or 5 peppercorns

½ cup sour cream
2 tablespoons horseradish, or to taste
Freshly ground pepper to taste

Cover drumsticks with boiling water in a large saucepan. Add the bay leaf, onion slice and peppercorns. Bring to boil, lower heat and simmer 40 minutes or until tender when pierced with a sharp-tined fork. Remove drumsticks from the water.

Combine the sour cream, horseradish and pepper. Slice the meat from the drumsticks, discarding tendons and bones. Arrange the drumstick slices on a heated serving platter. Serve the sauce separately in a heated sauceboat.

Makes 4 servings.

TURKEY DRUMSTICKS IN WINE SAUCE WITH MUSHROOMS

4 small turkey drumsticks
⅓ cup plus 1 tablespoon flour
    (preferably whole wheat flour)
1 teaspoon salt
Freshly ground pepper to taste
1 teaspoon paprika
½ cup margarine or butter, melted

4 slices bacon, cut up
1 cup chopped onions
¼ pound mushrooms, sliced
1 garlic clove, finely minced
¾ cup beef broth
1 cup red wine

Preheat oven at 325°F. (163°C.). Combine ⅓ cup flour with the salt, pepper and paprika and dust the drumsticks with the mixture. Arrange the drumsticks in a greased baking dish into which they just fit comfortably in a single layer. Pour melted margarine or butter over the drumsticks. Bake 1 hour, turning the drumsticks over after 30 minutes, and basting once or twice.

• Meanwhile sauté the bacon in a skillet over low heat until the fat runs out. Add the onions and sauté until soft. Add the mushrooms and garlic and sauté over medium heat until lightly browned. Add the remaining 1 tablespoon of flour and cook a minute, stirring. Add the beef broth and red wine. Raise the heat and bring mixture to boil, stirring. Lower heat, cover, and simmer until the drumsticks have baked 1 hour. Pour the mixture over the drumsticks, cover the baking dish with aluminum foil, and bake 30 minutes longer, or until tender when pierced with a sharp-tined fork. Arrange drumsticks on a heated serving platter or individual serving plates and spoon sauce over them.

Makes 4 servings.

TURKEY A LA MODE

2½ to 4 pounds turkey drumsticks	4 or 5 peppercorns
1½ cups thinly sliced carrots	1 teaspoon thyme
1 cup chopped onions	2 allspice berries
1 rib celery, sliced	1 bay leaf
1 garlic clove, smashed	2 tablespoons vegetable oil
3 cups red wine	1¾ cups beef broth
¼ cup olive oil	3 tablespoons cornstarch
1 teaspoon salt	¼ cup Port or Madeira wine

Place drumsticks in a glass or a ceramic casserole or similar container into which they will just fit comfortably. An oval-shaped deep casserole is ideal. Add carrots, onions, celery, garlic, wine, olive oil, salt, peppercorns, thyme, allspice berries, and bay leaf. Stir and spoon mixture over the drumsticks. Cover and refrigerate 24 to 48 hours, turning drumsticks over several times.

Remove drumsticks from the marinade and pat dry with paper towels. Brown on all sides in the vegetable oil in a Dutch oven or top-of-stove casserole. Remove the drumsticks. Pour out and discard the oil in which drumsticks were browned. Strain the marinade and pour it into the Dutch oven. Bring to boil slowly, skimming off particles as they rise to the surface. When no more particles rise to the surface add the beef broth and bring to boil again. Boil down rapidly for 10 minutes. Return the drumsticks to the Dutch oven. Cover and simmer gently for 2 hours, or until tender when pierced with a sharp-tined fork, turning after 1 hour.

Remove drumsticks. Combine cornstarch and Port or Madeira and stir into the Dutch oven. Cook, stirring, until slightly thickened. Simmer a few minutes longer.

Slice meat from drumsticks and discard tendons and bones. Arrange slices on a heated serving platter and pour the sauce into a heated sauce boat.

Makes 4 to 6 servings.

TURKEY MOLE

2½ to 3 pounds turkey drumsticks
Turkey stock or chicken broth to
    cover
1 slice onion
1 teaspoon salt
3 tablespoons vegetable oil
1 tablespoon sesame seeds
⅛ teaspoon anise seed (or ground
    anise)
⅛ teaspoon coriander seed (or
    ground coriander)
⅛ teaspoon cinnamon

1 green pepper, seeded, and cut up
1 large garlic clove, cut up
¼ cup shelled roasted peanuts
½ teaspoon salt
Freshly ground pepper to taste
1 small hot red pepper, seeded, and
    cut up, or ¼ teaspoon red
    pepper flakes (or more to taste)
½ cup toasted dry bread, broken up
½ of an 8-ounce can tomato sauce
1 1-ounce square unsweetened
    chocolate, chopped

Place the drumsticks in a top-of-stove casserole with enough turkey stock or chicken broth to just cover. Add the onion slice and salt and bring to boil. Cover, lower heat, and simmer 30 minutes or until almost tender. Remove the drumsticks and boil down the broth to 1 cup. Strain and reserve.

Pat the drumsticks dry with paper towels. Brown on all sides in a skillet in 2 tablespoons of the vegetable oil. Put the sesame seeds, anise seeds, coriander seeds and cinnamon through an electric blender or a grinder until pulverized. Add the green pepper, garlic, peanuts, salt, pepper and red pepper and grind again. Add the dry bread and tomato sauce and grind again. Sauté the mixture in a top-of-stove casserole in the remaining tablespoon of vegetable oil for 5 minutes, making certain the mixture does not scorch or burn. Add the chocolate and stir until melted. Add the reserved broth and heat. Add the drumsticks, cover, and simmer 30 minutes.

Makes 4 servings.

TURKEY A LA OSSO BUCO

3 medium size carrots
2 ribs celery, chopped
2 medium size onions, chopped
2 or more tablespoons butter or
   margarine
2 or more tablespoons vegetable oil
2½ to 3 pounds turkey drumsticks
1 tablespoon flour
1 teaspoon salt

Freshly ground pepper to taste
1 8-ounce can tomato sauce
½ cup dry white wine
½ cup turkey broth or chicken stock
¼ teaspoon rosemary
Pinch of thyme
Grated zest of 2 lemons
1 small garlic clove, finely minced
2 tablespoons chopped parsley

In a top-of-stove casserole or Dutch oven sauté the carrots, celery, and onions in 1 tablespoon butter or margarine and 1 tablespoon vegetable oil until lightly browned. Remove the vegetables. Dust the drumsticks with combined flour, salt, and pepper. Sauté the drumsticks, adding 1 tablespoon margarine or butter and 1 tablespoon vegetable oil, or more if necessary, until nicely browned on all sides.

Return the vegetables to the casserole and add the tomato sauce, wine, turkey stock or chicken broth, rosemary, and thyme. Bring to boil, reduce heat, cover, and simmer 1 to 1¼ hours, or until drumsticks are tender when pierced with a sharp-tined fork, turning now and then during cooking.

Combine lemon zest, garlic, and parsley. Stir into the casserole and cook 5 minutes, uncovered, spooning the sauce over the drumsticks.

Slice the meat from the drumsticks, removing and discarding tendons and bones. Arrange the slices on a heated serving platter and spoon the sauce over them.

Makes 4 servings.

TURMERIC TURKEY DRUMSTICKS

¼ cup flour (preferably whole
  wheat flour)
1 teaspoon tumeric
½ teaspoon salt
¼ teaspoon nutmeg
Freshly ground pepper to taste

2½ to 3 pounds turkey drumsticks
1 tablespoon margarine or butter
1 tablespoon vegetable oil
1–1½ cups turkey stock or chicken
  broth
1 teaspoon tarragon

Combine the flour, turmeric, salt, nutmeg, and pepper, and dust the drumsticks with the mixture. Sauté the drumsticks in a large skillet in the margarine or butter and the vegetable oil until browned on all sides. Sprinkle any remaining flour mixture into the skillet and cook for a few seconds, stirring. Add the turkey stock or chicken broth and the tarragon, stirring, and continue to stir gently until mixture is smooth and comes to a boil. Reduce heat, cover, and simmer until tender when pierced with a sharp-tined fork.

Slice meat from drumsticks, discarding tendons and bones. Arrange on heated serving platter and spoon the sauce over the meat.

Makes 4 servings.

TURKEY ALFREDO

4 turkey drumsticks weighing about
  4 pounds
⅓ cup plus 2 tablespoons flour
1 teaspoon salt
Freshly ground pepper to taste
3 or more tablespoons margarine or
  butter
1 or more tablespoons vegetable oil
½ cup or more turkey stock or
  chicken broth
½ pound medium-wide (fettuccine
  size) egg noodles

¼ cup grated onion
¼ pound mushrooms, sliced
1 cup finely diced ham (about ¼
  pound)
1 garlic clove, finely minced
½ teaspoon thyme
1 teaspoon tarragon
1 cup red wine
¼ cup water
2 cups half and half (milk and
  cream dairy product), or 1½ cups
  milk and ½ cup heavy cream

Rub the drumsticks with combined ⅓ cup flour, the salt, and pepper. Slowly sauté the drumsticks in 1 tablespoon margarine or butter and 1 tablespoon vegetable oil in a large skillet for about 30 minutes until browned on all sides, adding more margarine or butter and vegetable oil if necessary. Add ½ cup turkey stock or chicken broth, lower heat, cover tightly, and simmer 30 minutes.

Meanwhile cook noodles in boiling salted water according to package directions until barely tender. Drain. Transfer to a large buttered casserole. Remove the drumsticks from the skillet and nestle them among the noodles, reserving liquid in the skillet.

Preheat oven at 350°F. (177°C.). Sauté the onion, mushrooms, ham, garlic, thyme and tarragon in a skillet in 2 tablespoons margarine or butter for about 5 minutes, stirring. Add the liquid from the large skillet, including any browned particles that may have adhered to the skillet. Bring to simmer. Add the red wine and bring to simmer. Combine the remaining 2 tablespoons flour with the water and add to the mushroom mixture, stirring until thickened. Add the half and half and cook until the mixture simmers. Pour over the turkey and noodles. Cover tightly and bake 1¼ hours or until drumsticks are tender when pierced with a sharp-tined fork, turning them over once during cooking and spooning the noodles and sauce mixture over them. If necessary add up to 1 cup heated turkey stock or chicken broth during baking if the dish becomes too dry. Arrange on heated serving platter, or serve in casserole.

Makes 4 or more servings.

Part 3—Turkey Thighs

Of all the turkey parts the thighs are perhaps the most versatile, and for lovers of dark meat, the most luscious. Thighs are always generous in size so you get a lot of meat in proportion to the single bone they contain. Thighs come fresh or frozen, usually packaged in pairs. What you can do with them is almost limitless. You can grind up the meat and use it as you would ground beef, running it through the grinder twice for good texture. You can also cut it into chunks to make stews, marinate it and use it for shish kebab, or bone and stuff it. You may want to cook the thighs whole or you can cook them in combination with other turkey parts. Turkey thighs can be used in place of beef in many recipes, and you may elect to proceed along these lines in adapting some of your own favorite beef recipes. The dishes that follow have a wide range of flavors, textures, and ethnic origins. I'm sure you'll enjoy them.

DOVER PLAINS TURKEY BURGERS WITH MUSHROOM SAUCE

1 egg
2 tablespoons grated onion
2 tablespoons tomato paste
¼ cup wheat germ
1¼ teaspoons plus a pinch of salt
Freshly ground pepper to taste
1 pound raw ground turkey thigh
   meat (ground twice)
1 tablespoon vegetable oil

2 tablespoons margarine or butter
¼ pound mushrooms, sliced
1 tablespoon flour
1 cup half and half (milk and cream
   dairy product) or milk
Pinch of thyme
2 tablespoons chopped parsley
1 tablespoon sherry

Beat the egg lightly and add the onion, tomato paste, wheat germ, 1¼ teaspoons salt, and the pepper and mix well. Add the ground turkey meat and mix again. Form into 4 patties or burgers.

In a skillet over medium heat brown the burgers well on one side in the vegetable oil and 1 tablespoon margarine or butter. Turn over and sauté a minute. Reduce heat to low, cover skillet, and cook 5 minutes or until burgers are no longer pink in the center. Remove burgers from the skillet and keep them warm. To the skillet add the remaining 1 tablespoon margarine or butter. Sauté the mushrooms over high heat until they brown slightly. Reduce heat to low and sprinkle in the flour, stirring. Add the half and half or milk and cook, stirring constantly, until thickened. Add thyme, pinch of salt, pinch of pepper, parsley and sherry and cook several minutes, stirring. Serve the burgers on a heated serving platter with the sauce spooned over them.

Makes 4 servings. Recipe can be doubled.

TURKLETTES A L'ORANGE

Serve Turklettes à l'Orange when you want an elegant yet inexpensive dish. The turklettes look like individual birds and have a lovely orange flavor.

6 small turkey thighs
¼ pound turkey sausage (mild)
1 cup coarse dry bread crumbs
2 teaspoons grated onions
1 tablespoon grated orange zest
½ teaspoon grated lemon zest

¼ teaspoon salt
Freshly ground pepper to taste
Generous pinch of rosemary
1 tablespoon chopped parsley
2 tablespoons orange juice
Melted margarine or butter

Bone the turkey thighs without cutting through the back skin. There is only one straight bone to remove.

Preheat oven at 325°F. (163°C.). Break up the sausage into a bowl. Add all the remaining ingredients except the melted margarine or butter and combine well. Spread the mixture on the cut sides of the turkey thighs, dividing equally, and fold over the meat to enclose the filling. Sew the edges together using a needle and white kitchen thread, so the filling does not show.

Arrange the turklettes in a single layer in a greased shallow baking dish. Brush with melted margarine or butter. Cover with aluminum foil. Bake about 1½ hours, or until tender when pierced with a sharp-tined fork. Turn every half hour during baking, and baste with melted margarine or butter. Remove the foil before final 30 minutes of baking. Snip threads and remove before serving on a heated platter.

Makes 6 servings.

CONNOISSEUR'S
STUFFED CABBAGE

2 slices bacon
2 tablespoons margarine or butter
1 cup chopped onions
1 garlic clove, finely minced
½ pound mushrooms, sliced
1 tablespoon chopped parsley
½ teaspoon thyme
¼ teaspoon nutmeg
1 teaspoon salt
Freshly ground pepper to taste
2 eggs
2 slices firm slightly dry bread
   (preferably whole wheat)
1 pound raw ground turkey thigh
   meat (ground twice)
1 large cabbage

2 small or 1 large carrot, sliced
1 small onion, sliced
1 celery rib with leaves, sliced
1 1-pound can Italian tomatoes
1 10½-ounce can turkey gravy, or 1
   generous cup homemade turkey
   gravy (if not available use equal
   amount of beef gravy)
2 cups turkey stock or chicken
   broth
1 cup dry white wine
1 bay leaf
2 whole cloves
1 tablespoon cornstarch mixed with
   2 tablespoons cold water

In a skillet sauté the bacon slices until crisp. Remove and drain on paper towels. To the fat remaining in the skillet add 1 tablespoon margarine or butter and sauté the onions until soft and lightly browned. Add the garlic and sauté another minute. Remove onions and garlic with a slotted spoon and place in a bowl. Crumble the bacon and add to the onions. To the skillet add the remaining 1 tablespoon margarine or butter and sauté the mushrooms a few minutes, turning all the time, until they begin to exude their moisture. Remove from heat and add to the onion mixture. Add the parsley, thyme, nutmeg, salt, and pepper and mix well.

In a small bowl beat the eggs. Crumble the bread into the eggs and mix well. Add to the onion mixture. Add the ground turkey and mix, preferably with your hands, until well combined.

Cut out and remove as much of the core from the cabbage as possible. Plunge the cabbage into a large pot of boiling water. As outside leaves loosen and become pliable in a minute or two, remove them, one at a time, and drain in colander. Continue cooking the cabbage until all the leaves have been removed and drained. It will probably be necessary to use a small sharp knife to separate the leaves after the first few have been removed.

Beginning with the largest leaves stuff the cabbage leaves one at a time as follows. With a sharp knife cut off the rib from the back of the cabbage leaf so that the leaf is pliable. Put about ¼ cup of the turkey mixture on the leaf, about 1½ inches from the bottom. (Larger leaves will require up to ⅓ cup, and smaller leaves will require only 3 tablespoons.) With fingers shape the turkey filling into a cylindrical mound, crosswise on the leaf. Turn up the bottom of the leaf to cover the filling. Turn in the two sides of the leaf over the filling. Roll the cabbage leaf up and place the filled leaf, seamside down, on a plate. Continue until there is no more filling left.

Line the bottom and part way up the sides of a large pot with some of the unused cabbage leaves. (Reserve the balance, if any, for another use.) Scatter the carrots, onions, and celery over the cabbage leaves in the pot. Break up the tomatoes with a fork, or put briefly through a food processor fitted with a steel blade along with the liquid from the can. Turn the tomatoes and tomato liquid into a bowl. Add the turkey gravy, turkey stock or chicken broth, and wine to the tomatoes, and mix.

Arrange the cabbage rolls in the pot over the carrots, onion, and celery in neat rows, seam sides down. Pour the tomato mixture over them. Add bay leaf and cloves. Cover the pot, place over heat, and bring to boil. Lower heat and simmer, covered, 1½ to 2 hours, altering the position of the cabbage rolls part way through cooking so all cook evenly. Remove the cabbage rolls and keep them warm.

Strain the sauce into a saucepan and boil down to 2 cups. Add the cornstarch mixture and cook, stirring constantly, until thickened slightly. Arrange the stuffed cabbage rolls on a heated platter and pour the sauce over them.

Makes 14 or more rolls, depending on the size of the cabbage leaves used. Allow 2 per serving.

TURKEY CHILI WITH BEANS

Here's a chili you can really get your teeth into, because the meat is diced, rather than being ground up. It's satisfying to eat and has a good chili flavor.

3 cups coarsely chopped onions
⅓ cup chopped green pepper
2 tablespoons or more vegetable oil
2 pounds raw turkey thigh meat,
    diced (If you wish you can
    include some diced breast
    meat.)
1 27- or 28-ounce can crushed
    Italian tomatoes
2 15-ounce cans kidney beans
¼ cup chopped parsley

1 garlic clove, minced
1 bay leaf
3 tablespoons chili powder, or to
    taste
1 tablespoon paprika
2 teaspoons cumin
2 teaspoons salt
Cayenne pepper to taste
1 tablespoon vinegar
2 tablespoons masa harina *
¼ cup cold water

In a top-of-stove casserole sauté the onions and green pepper in 2 tablespoons vegetable oil until the onions are soft. Remove the onions and green peppers with a slotted spoon. Add the diced turkey meat to the casserole and cook, stirring, until it loses its red color, adding more vegetable oil if necessary. Return the onions and green peppers to the casserole. Add the tomatoes, kidney beans, parsley, garlic, bay leaf, chili powder, paprika, cumin, salt, cayenne, and vinegar and bring to simmer. Cover and simmer 2 hours, stirring often. Mix the masa harina with the water and add to the casserole, stirring constantly for a minute or two. Cook for 1 hour longer, covered.

Makes 10 or more servings.

* Masa harina is a finely ground corn meal product that is excellent for thickening chili. If not available, substitute flour.

TURKEY THIGHS ALPILLES

3¼ to 4 pounds turkey thighs
Flour
4 or more tablespoons vegetable oil
    (preferably olive oil)
Salt to taste
Freshly ground pepper to taste
½ cup turkey stock or chicken broth
1 teaspoon rosemary
2 tablespoons finely chopped
    onions

1 garlic clove, minced
4 cups fresh peeled tomatoes cut in
    1-inch cubes
⅓ cup coarsely cut up pitted black
    olives (preferably Calamata or
    Nicoise olives)
⅓ cup coarsely cut up pitted green
    olives (preferably cracked green
    olives)

Dust the turkey thighs with flour and brown them in a large skillet in 2 tablespoons vegetable oil, adding more oil if necessary. Drain off the oil from the skillet when the thighs are brown and sprinkle the thighs with salt and pepper. Add the turkey stock or chicken broth to the skillet. Sprinkle ½ teaspoon rosemary over the thighs. Cover skillet and simmer 1½ hours, or until tender when pierced with a sharp-tined fork, turning once during cooking.

Sauté the onions and garlic in remaining 2 tablespoons vegetable oil until onion is softened. Add the tomatoes, pepper, and remaining ½ teaspoon rosemary. Cook about 5 minutes, but do not allow tomatoes to become mushy. Add the black and green olives and heat through.

Meanwhile, slice the meat from the turkey thighs, discarding bones. Return the meat to the skillet and toss gently to heat through. Spoon the tomato-olive mixture onto a large heated platter and arrange the turkey slices in the center.

Makes 8 servings.

TURKEY THIGHS COLUMBIA

3 cups red wine
¼ cup olive oil
¾ cup finely chopped onions
1 garlic clove, minced
1 bay leaf
6 juniper berries
5 or 6 peppercorns
4 to 4½ pounds turkey thighs
16 pitted prunes
¼ cup Port wine

2 tablespoons vegetable oil
Salt to taste
Freshly ground pepper to taste
1½ cups peeled diced carrots
⅔ cup peeled shallots
¼ cup brandy
1¾ cups beef broth
3½ cups peeled, diced white turnips
3 tablespoons cornstarch
¼ cup cold water

Combine the wine, olive oil, onions, garlic, bay leaf, juniper berries, and peppercorns in a large glass or ceramic bowl or baking dish. Arrange the turkey thighs in the bowl or baking dish and spoon the marinade over them. Cover and allow to marinate in the refrigerator 24 hours, turning several times.

Soak the prunes in hot water to cover 20 to 30 minutes. Drain. Add the Port to the prunes and set aside.

Meanwhile remove the turkey thighs from the marinade and pat them dry. Reserve the marinade. Brown the thighs in the vegetable oil in a large skillet.

Preheat the over at 325°F. (163°C.). Transfer the thighs to a casserole and sprinkle them with salt and pepper. Sauté the carrots and shallots in the oil remaining in the skillet and add them to the casserole along with the brandy. Add the beef broth to the skillet and bring to boil, stirring to loosen brown particles adhering to the skillet. Add to the casserole. Pour the marinade into the skillet and bring to boil. Strain into the casserole. Cover and bake 1 hour, turning the thighs over after 30 minutes. After the thighs have baked 1 hour add the prunes and Port and the diced turnips. Cover and bake 30 minutes longer or until thighs are tender when pierced with a sharp-tined fork, and turnips are done. Remove thighs from the casserole. Combine the cornstarch and water and add to the casserole. Cook, stirring constantly, over medium heat until thickened. Taste and adjust seasoning if necessary.

Slice the meat from the thighs, discarding the bones. Arrange the slices on a heated serving platter. Spoon some of the sauce over the meat and serve the balance of the sauce in a heated sauce boat.

Makes 8 servings.

LEMON-MARINATED TURKEY THIGHS

3½ pounds turkey thighs	5 peppercorns
1 cup lemon juice	2 cups turkey stock or chicken
½ cup olive oil	broth
2 tablespoons oregano	3 tablespoons flour
2 garlic cloves, smashed	

Combine the lemon juice, olive oil, oregano, garlic, and peppercorns. Pour over the turkey thighs arranged in a single layer in a glass or ceramic baking dish. Cover and refrigerate 24 hours, turning several times.

Preheat oven at 325°F. (163°C.). Remove turkey thighs from marinade and arrange in a single layer in a shallow top-of-stove baking dish, skin side down. Bake 30 minutes. Turn skin side up, baste with marinade, and continue baking, basting every 20 minutes to interior temperature of 185°F. (85°C.), or until tender when pierced with a sharp-tined fork. Arrange thighs on heated serving platter. Drain fat from baking dish. Place over heat and stir in flour. Cook for a minute, stirring. Add turkey stock or chicken broth gradually and continue to heat, stirring constantly, until thickened. Taste and adjust seasoning if necessary. Pour over thighs.

Makes 6 servings.

RAGGEDY TURKEY ROLLS

3½ to 4 pounds turkey thighs
2 eggs
2 large potatoes
6 carrots, scraped and coarsely
  shredded
1 cup chopped onions
½ cup chopped green pepper

1 garlic clove, minced
2 tablespoons lemon juice
½ teaspoon thyme
2 teaspoons salt
Freshly ground pepper to taste
Vegetable oil

    Remove and discard skin from turkey thighs, remove meat from bones, cut into chunks, and grind twice. Place in a bowl. Add eggs and mix well.

    Preheat oven at 400°F. (204°C.). Peel the potatoes and shred them coarsely. Add to the ground turkey mixture. Add the carrots, onions, green pepper, garlic, lemon juice, thyme, salt, and pepper and mix well. You will need to use your hands to get the ingredients well combined. Form into cylinders about 4 inches long and 2 inches in diameter. Arrange in a greased baking dish and bake about 45 minutes, brushing the tops of the turkey rolls with vegetable oil halfway through the baking.

Makes 18 to 20 rolls.

CARAWAY TURKEY RAGOUT

1½ to 2 pounds turkey thighs,
  boned and cut into 1-inch cubes
3 tablespoons vegetable oil
1 cup chopped onions
1½ cups beef broth
1 tablespoon caraway seeds
1 bay leaf
1 teaspoon salt

Freshly ground pepper to taste
1 teaspoon ginger
1 teaspoon sugar
¼ cup vinegar
½ medium size red cabbage cut in
  1-inch cubes
1½ tablespoons flour mixed with ¼
  cup cold water

    In a top-of-stove casserole or Dutch oven brown the turkey cubes in 2 tablespoons vegetable oil. Remove the turkey cubes with a slotted spoon. Brown the onions in the casserole, adding a tablespoon of vegetable oil. Return the turkey cubes to the casserole and add the beef broth, caraway seeds, bay leaf, salt and pepper. Bring to boil, reduce heat, cover, and simmer about 30 minutes. Stir in the ginger, sugar, vinegar and cabbage cubes. Cover and simmer 30 minutes longer or until the cabbage is tender. With a slotted spoon transfer the turkey and cabbage to a heated serving platter. Add the flour mixture to the casserole and bring to boil, stirring constantly, until thickened. Simmer a minute, stirring. Pour over turkey and cabbage.

Makes 4 servings.

TURKEY BARLEY SKILLET

1 cup chopped onions	1 tablespoon dehydrated sweet
1 tablespoon margarine or butter	pepper flakes
4 tablespoons vegetable oil	1 tablespoon paprika
¾ cup barley	1 teaspoon Worcestershire sauce
1¾ cups beef broth	1 tablespoon sesame seeds
1 turkey thigh weighing 1¼ to 1½	Salt to taste
pounds	Freshly ground pepper to taste
1 cup thinly sliced celery	1 to 2 cups boiling water
	1 cup fresh or frozen green peas

Sauté the onions in a large skillet in margarine or butter and 1 tablespoon vegetable oil until slightly softened. Add the barley and sauté a few minutes longer. Add the beef broth, bring to boil, cover, lower heat, and simmer 15 minutes over low heat.

Meanwhile remove and discard skin from the turkey thigh, remove the meat from the bone, cut in chunks, and put through meat grinder. In another skillet sauté the ground turkey meat in 2 tablespoons vegetable oil, breaking up with a spatula or pancake turner until meat loses its red color. Remove the meat from the skillet with a slotted spoon. Add 1 tablespoon oil to the skillet and sauté the celery until lightly browned.

When barley has cooked 15 minutes add the sautéed turkey meat and the celery to it, along with the sweet pepper flakes, paprika, Worcestershire sauce, seasame seeds, salt, and pepper, and enough boiling water so the mixture is quite loose. Combine well, cover, and simmer 30 minutes or until barley is tender, stirring once or twice. Add the peas, cover and cook about 3 to 5 minutes or until the peas are just tender. Serve on heated platter.

Makes 4 servings.

TURKEY STRIPS
IN FRAGRANT PESTO SAUCE

You can't go wrong serving thin spagetti or linguine with this dish, and if you like you can serve the turkey strips and the pesto sauce over spaghetti on a platter.

2½ pounds turkey thighs
1 tablespoon vegetable oil
1 tablespoon margarine or butter
2 garlic cloves
2 to 2½ cups loosely packed fresh
    basil leaves
½ teaspoon salt

1 tablespoon pine nuts (pignolias)
3 tablespoons freshly grated
    Parmesan, Romano or Sardo
    cheese
2 tablespoons olive oil
¾ cup chicken broth

In top-of-stove casserole or Dutch oven brown the turkey thighs in vegetable oil and margarine or butter. Meanwhile in a food processor fitted with steel blade or an electric blender process the garlic. Add basil leaves gradually and process until pulverized. Add the salt, pine nuts, and grated cheese and process until the mixture becomes a smooth paste. Add the olive oil gradually with machine turned on.

Add the chicken broth to the browned turkey thighs, along with the pesto (basil mixture). Bring to simmer, lower heat, cover, and simmer 1½ hours or until tender when pierced with a sharp-tined fork, turning over after 45 minutes.

Slice meat from thighs and arrange on heated serving platter. Pour the pesto sauce over the meat.

Makes 4 servings.

Part 4—Winging It

If the only turkey wing you've ever eaten has been part of a roast turkey, you're in for a wonderful surprise. You can buy fresh or frozen turkey wings by the packageful and cook them in many tempting ways. The meat is light, juicy, and flavorful.

There are three sections to a wing. Since there's not much meat on the wing tip it's a good idea to remove it and add it to whatever turkey bones or pieces you might be saving in the freezer for making turkey stock or soup. Cut the remainder of the wing into two parts at the joint and you have two tender moist white meat turkey parts to cook into a lovely dish. There's more meat on these pieces than you might expect. A "young turkey wing" averages 1¼ pounds, and two of them make enough for three or even four servings. The largest of the three wing sections is often cut off and sold separately, and a package of them is sometimes labelled "drumettes". These cuts have all the flavor of a drumstick, but are a lighter, moister meat, and have none of the tendons to contend with that you find in a drumstick.

Unless you're buying turkey wings for making stock or a similar purpose, read the label and examine the package carefully before you buy, because the "drumettes" are sometimes removed, leaving "turkey wing sections" that consist only of the wing tip and the second joint. These "turkey wing sections" are often on sale, but it's worth paying a few cents extra to get the entire wing, which includes the "drumette", since all turkey wings are usually reasonably priced anyway.

ROSEMARY BAKED TURKEY WINGS

4 pounds turkey wings, separated at joints
6 tablespoons margarine or butter
1½ teaspoons powdered rosemary (or a scant tablespoon of
rosemary pounded in a mortar and pestle until pulverized)
1 teaspoon salt
Freshly ground pepper to taste

Preheat oven at 350°F. (177°C.). Arrange wing sections in greased shallow baking dish in which they will fit in a single layer, reserving wing tips for another use if desired. Melt margarine or butter in a small saucepan. Remove from heat. Add powdered rosemary, salt, and pepper, and stir with a basting brush to combine. Brush the mixture all over both sides of the turkey wing sections. Bake 30 minutes. Turn and baste again, making sure rosemary mixture is well combined. Reduce oven temperature to 325°F. (163°C.), and bake another 30 minutes or until tender when pierced with a sharp-tined fork.

Serve hot, or cool, wrap tightly and chill. These wings are delicious eaten cold and make great picnic fare.

Makes 4 servings.

TURKEY WINGS MADAGASCAR

⅓ cup whole wheat flour
1 teaspoon salt
Freshly ground pepper to taste
1 teaspoon paprika
3-3½ pounds turkey wings,
  separated at joints
2 tablespoons margarine or butter
2 tablespoons vegetable oil
2 cups chopped onions
1 garlic clove, minced

2 cups turkey stock or chicken
  broth
¼ teaspoon thyme
1 bay leaf
1 tablespoon green peppercorns, or
  more to taste, crushed
½ pound curly noodles (sometimes
  called klops, southern style
  dumplings, noodle loops, etc.)
1 tablespoon cornstarch combined
  with 2 tablespoons water

Combine flour, salt, pepper, and paprika. If desired reserve turkey wing tips for another use. Dust turkey wing sections well with the flour mixture. Melt 1 tablespoon margarine or butter in large heavy skillet or top-of-stove casserole. Add 1 tablespoon vegetable oil and brown the turkey wing sections, adding more butter or margarine and vegetable oil as necessary. Remove turkey wing sections from skillet. Add onions and sauté until lightly browned. Add the garlic, turkey stock or chicken broth, thyme, bay leaf, and green peppercorns and heat to boiling. Reduce the heat, arrange the turkey wing sections in the skillet, cover, and simmer 1 hour, or until tender when pierced with a sharp-tined fork, turning the wing sections over after 30 minutes.

Meanwhile cook noodles in boiling salted water according to package directions. Remove turkey wing sections from skillet and keep them warm. Add cornstarch mixture to skillet and cook, stirring, until thickened. Simmer a few minutes. Drain noodles and arrange them on a heated serving platter. Arrange the turkey wing sections over the noodles and pour the sauce over all.

Makes 4 servings.

TURKEY WINGS WITH WHEATY SPRING ONION DUMPLINGS

3¼ to 4 pounds turkey wings, separated at joints
1¼ cups flour
1 or more tablespoons margarine or butter
3 or more tablespoons vegetable oil
3 cups or more turkey stock or chicken broth
1 bay leaf
¼ teaspoon thyme
¼ teaspoon rosemary
Freshly ground pepper to taste

1 egg
¼ cup wheat germ
½ cup milk
¼ cup chopped scallions, including some of green part
1½ teaspoons baking powder
½ teaspoon salt
¼ teaspoon powdered rosemary (or pulverize enough rosemary in a mortar and pestle to measure ¼ teaspoon)

Dust the turkey wing sections with about ¼ cup flour, reserving wing tips for another use if desired. Brown in 1 tablespoon margarine or butter and 1 tablespoon vegetable oil in a top-of-stove casserole or Dutch oven, adding more margarine or butter and vegetable oil if necessary. Add the turkey stock or chicken broth, bay leaf, thyme, rosemary, and pepper, and bring to boil. Lower heat, cover, and simmer 1 hour or more or until tender when pierced with a sharp-tined fork. Preheat oven at 225°F. (107°C.).

Beat the egg lightly in a bowl. Add the milk and stir. Add 1 cup flour, the wheat germ, chopped scallions, 2 tablespoons vegetable oil, the baking powder, salt, and powdered rosemary and mix well.

Transfer turkey wing sections to an ovenproof platter. Cover with aluminum foil and set in oven.

Measure liquid in casserole and add enough turkey stock, chicken broth, or water to measure 3 cups. Pour into casserole and bring to simmer. Dividing into 8 equal parts, spoon the dumpling dough into the casserole. Allow to cook in the simmering liquid for 10 minutes, or until the dumplings rise to the top. Arrange the dumplings on the platter with the turkey wing sections. Pour the sauce over all, or spoon some of the sauce over the turkey and dumplings and serve the balance in a heated sauce boat.

Makes 4 servings.

CHOW-CHOW TURKEY WINGS

3½ to 4 pounds turkey wings,
   separated at joints
Flour (preferably whole wheat
   flour)
2 tablespoons or more margarine or
   butter

1 tablespoon or more vegetable oil
2 tablespoons minced onion
1 cup turkey stock or chicken broth
Salt to taste
Freshly ground pepper to taste
½ cup chow-chow (mustard pickles)

Dust the turkey wing sections with flour, reserving the wing tips for another use if desired. Sauté in 1 tablespoon margarine or butter and 1 tablespoon vegetable oil until brown on all sides, adding more margarine or butter and vegetable oil if necessary. Remove the wing sections. Add 1 tablespoon margarine or butter to the pan and sauté the minced onion for a minute or two. Add turkey stock or chicken broth, salt, and pepper, and heat to boiling. Return the wing sections to the pan, lower heat, cover and simmer one hour or until tender when pierced with a sharp-tined fork, turning once during cooking.

Meanwhile cut the pickles into small pieces. When the wing sections are done arrange on heated serving platter. Add the mustard and cut-up pickles to the pan and heat for a few minutes, stirring. Spoon over the wing sections.

Makes 4 servings.

WINGING IT OVER SEASHELLS

3 pounds turkey wings, separated at
   joints
Flour
2 tablespoons or more margarine or
   butter
1 tablespoon or more vegetable oil
⅔ cup finely diced ham
1 cup finely chopped onions
1 celery rib, finely chopped
1 carrot, finely chopped

1 1-pound can Italian tomatoes
2 tablespoons chopped parsley
2 teaspoons paprika
¼ teaspoon red pepper flakes, or to
   taste
1 cup turkey broth or chicken stock
½ pound small seashell pasta,
   preferably whole wheat pasta
¼ cup freshly grated Parmesan,
   Romano, or Sardo cheese

Dust turkey wing sections with flour, reserving the wing tips for another use if desired. In a large skillet brown the turkey wing sections in 1 tablespoon margarine or butter and 1 tablespoon vegetable oil, adding more margarine or butter and vegetable oil if necessary. Remove turkey wing sections from skillet. Add 1 tablespoon margarine or butter to skillet along with the ham and sauté a minute, stirring. Add onions and celery and sauté a few minutes more, stirring. Add carrots, tomatoes with their liquid, parsley, paprika, red pepper flakes, pepper, and turkey stock or chicken broth, and bring to boil, stirring. Return turkey wing sections to skillet, cover, lower heat, and simmer 1 hour or until tender when pierced with a sharp-tined fork, turning occasionally and basting with the sauce.

Meanwhile cook the seashell pasta in boiling salted water according to package directions *al dente*. Drain in colander. Arrange on heated serving platter. Arrange the wing sections over the seashells. Spoon the sauce over top and sprinkle with the grated cheese.

Makes 6 servings.

BUTTERMILK WINGS

2½ to 3¼ pounds turkey wings,
  separated at joints
1 cup buttermilk
1 cup flour
1 teaspoon salt
Freshly ground pepper to taste

⅓ cup freshly grated Parmesan,
  Romano, or Sardo cheese
1 teaspoon paprika
1 teaspoon savory
½ cup melted margarine or butter

Preheat oven at 325°F. (163°C.). Dip turkey wing sections in the buttermilk which has been poured into a flat soup plate, reserving the wing tips for another use if desired. Combine flour, salt, pepper, cheese, paprika, and savory in another flat soup plate. Roll the turkey wing sections in the mixture. Brush them with the melted margarine or butter and arrange in a shallow greased baking dish into which they will fit in a single layer. Bake 1½ hours or until tender when pierced with a fork. Arrange on heated platter and serve.

Makes 3 to 5 servings.

NIPPY CHIPPY WINGS

2½ to 3¼ pounds turkey wings,
  separated at joints
Whole wheat flour
1 egg
2 tablespoons milk

1 4½ ounce bag barbecue-style
  potato chips, crushed
1½ teaspoons chili powder, or to
  taste
Cayenne pepper to taste

Preheat oven at 325°F. (163°C.). Rub flour well into turkey wing sections, reserving the wing tips for another use if desired. Beat the egg with the milk in a flat soup plate. Put the crushed potato chips into another flat soup plate. Dip each turkey wing section first into the egg and then into the crushed chips. Arrange the wing sections in a greased shallow baking dish into which they will fit in a single layer. Bake 45 minutes. Sprinkle with the chili powder and cayenne. Bake an additional 45 minutes or until tender when pierced with a sharp-tined fork. Serve on heated platter.

Makes 3 to 5 servings.

MUSHROOM TURKEY WINGS WITH SWEET RED PEPPERS

2½ to 3 pounds turkey wings, separated at joints (reserve wing tips for another use)
1 tablespoon or more margarine or butter
1 tablespoon or more vegetable oil
1 medium onions, sliced
½ pound mushrooms, sliced
1 cup turkey stock or chicken broth

1 cup sweet red pepper strips in vinegar and brine, drained (This product, displayed in the pickle sections of food markets, comes in a quart jar and is usually called sweet California wonder peppers. The peppers are whole or are in large pieces.)
2 tablespoons chopped parsley
½ teaspoon salt, or to taste
Freshly ground pepper to taste

In a large skillet sauté the turkey wing sections in 1 tablespoon margarine or butter and 1 tablespoon vegetable oil until brown on all sides. Remove turkey wing sections from skillet. Sauté the onions in the skillet, adding a little more oil if necessary, until brown. Remove the onions from the skillet. Add a little more margarine or butter to the skillet and sauté the mushrooms until lightly browned. Remove the mushrooms from the skillet. Return the turkey wing sections to the skillet and spoon the onions and mushrooms over them. Add the turkey stock or chicken broth, the sweet red pepper strips, parsley, salt and pepper. Simmer, covered, about 1½ hours, or until tender when pierced with a sharp-tined fork, turning once after 45 minutes. If necessary add a small amount of boiling water to the skillet so that the wing sections stay moist. Serve on heated platter.

Makes 4 servings.

TURKEY WINGS
IN MEXICAN GREEN SAUCE

¼ cup pumpkin seeds
¼ cup sliced or slivered almonds
¼ cup walnuts
1 or 2 chilies serrano, seeded and
   chopped
1 cup chopped green (bell) peppers
1 cup chopped onions
1 teaspoon salt
2 tablespoons chopped coriander
   leaves, cilantro, or flat leaf
   parsley

1 garlic clove, cut up
1 13-ounce can Mexican green
   tomatoes (tomatillo entero *)
1 cup turkey stock or chicken broth
4 pounds turkey wings, separated at
   joints (reserve wing tips for
   another use if desired)
2 tablespoons vegetable oil

Place pumpkin seeds, almonds, walnuts, chopped chilies, green pepper, onions, salt, coriander leaves, and garlic into a food processor fitted with steel blade, or into an electric blender, and blend until fine. Add the Mexican green tomatoes with their liquid and the turkey stock or chicken broth and blend until the tomatoes are pulverized. If using an electric blender you may need to prepare this mixture in several small batches.

Brown the turkey wing sections in a top-of-stove casserole or Dutch oven in the vegetable oil. Add the green sauce mixture and bring to simmer. Cover, lower heat, and simmer 2 hours or until wings are very tender when pierced with a sharp-tined fork, and the sauce thickens. If necessary remove turkey wings when they are tender and boil down the sauce a little. Serve on heated platter.

Makes 6 servings.

* Mexican green tomatoes are not the same as unripe red tomatoes. They are a different vegetable altogether, so do not make substitutions. If bought fresh, Mexican green tomatoes have a thin dry membrane on the outside that is easily removed, and has the texture and appearance of an onion skin. The tomatoes can be bought in cans where Mexican foods are sold or in specialty food stores.

FINE NOODLES AND WINGS WITH MUSTARD HORSERADISH SAUCE

3½ pounds turkey wings, separated at joints (reserve tips for another use if desired)
3 or 4 scallions, including some of green part, chopped
1 cup chopped onions
2 medium carrots, chopped
1 rib celery, chopped
3 sprigs parsley
1 bay leaf

Salt to taste
Freshly ground pepper to taste
2 cups turkey stock or chicken broth
2 tablespoons prepared mustard (preferably Dijon)
1 tablespoon horseradish
1 tablespoon cornstarch combined with 1 tablespoon water
¼ pound fine egg noodles

Place turkey wing sections into a large heavy saucepan or top-of-stove casserole. Add scallions, onions, carrots, celery, parsley, bay leaf, salt and pepper. Pour turkey stock or chicken broth over wing sections. Bring to boil, reduce heat, cover, and cook 1½ hours or until tender when pierced with a sharp-tined fork, turning once or twice during cooking. Remove wing sections from saucepan and keep them warm.

Skim any excess fat from the liquid, and strain the liquid into a measuring cup. You should have 1½ cups liquid. Pour into a clean saucepan and bring to boil. If necessary boil down until you have 1½ cups remaining. Add the mustard, horseradish and cornstarch mixture and cook, stirring, until the mixture thickens.

Meanwhile cook and drain the noodles.

Arrange the noodles on a heated serving platter. Arrange the wing sections on the noodles, and pour the sauce over all.

Makes 4 servings.

Part 5—The Neck and the Tail

Although you can't find packages of turkey necks all the time, it's worth keeping your eye out for them, because they make positively delectable cassoulets and stews. The necks come packaged with the skin removed, and there's lots of meat on them. Buy several packages when you see them and keep extras in the freezer so you'll have them when you want them. Try one of the recipes in this section and I'm sure that if you aren't familiar with turkey neck dishes you'll be won over.

If you're a turkey tail devotee, and it seems there are many, you'll also find some dishes here that are different and appealing. Chances are you've only eaten the roasted tail of a whole bird, but you can buy this part by the package too and try it as a separately cooked dish.

CASSOULET FOR TURKEY LOVERS

1 pound Great Northern beans, or
    other dried white beans
½ onion stuck with 1 whole clove
2 to 2½ pound turkey necks without
    skin (6 pieces)
2 tablespoons or more vegetable oil
1 pound kielbasa (Polish sausage)
2 cups finely chopped onions
2 garlic cloves, minced
1 bay leaf
¼ teaspoon thyme

¼ teaspoon rosemary
1 teaspoon salt, or to taste
Freshly ground pepper to taste
1¾ cups beef broth
1 tablespoon tomato paste
5 or 6 strips bacon
1 cup (approximately) fine dry
    breadcrumbs
3 tablespoons melted margarine or
    butter

Place beans in a large pot and cover them with cold water to a level about 4 inches above the beans. Place the clove-stuck onion in the pot with the beans. Bring to boil and allow to boil 1 or 2 minutes. Turn off heat and allow beans to sit in the hot water 1 hour. (If you prefer you may soak the beans in cold water overnight in place of this step. In that case add the clove-stuck onion in the following step.)

Cover beans, bring to boil, lower heat, and simmer 1½ hours or until beans are just tender. Check the water level occasionally and if necessary add boiling water to the beans. Remove from heat, but do not drain.

Meanwhile in a top-of-stove casserole or Dutch oven brown the turkey necks in 1½ tablespoons vegetable oil. Remove the turkey necks.

Add ½ tablespoon more vegetable oil and brown the kielbasa. Return the turkey necks to the casserole and add the chopped onions, garlic, bay leaf, thyme, rosemary, salt, pepper, beef broth, and tomato paste. Bring to simmer, reduce heat, cover, and simmer 1 hour, turning pieces of meat over after 30 minutes. Remove from heat.

Preheat over at 400°F. (204°C.). Cut the kielbasa into 2-inch lengths. Lay the bacon strips in the bottom of a large earthenware beanpot or similar casserole. Drain the beans, reserving the liquid, and spoon half the beans on top of the bacon. Arrange the turkey necks and pieces of kielbasa over the beans. Spoon the remaining beans on top. Pour the remaining ingredients from the casserole over the beans. The liquid should just barely cover the top layer of beans. If it does not, add some of the bean cooking liquid to the proper level. Sprinkle enough bread-crumbs over the top to make a thick layer. Sprinkle the breadcrumbs with the melted margarine or butter. Bake 1½ hours, reducing the oven temperature to 350°F. (177°C.) after the first 20 minutes.

Check several times during baking to make sure the beans do not become too dry. If they do, add a little of the bean cooking liquid.

Makes 6 generous servings.

POPE'S NOSE SPECIAL

1¾ to 2 pounds turkey tails (6 tails)
1 garlic clove, minced
1 8-ounce can tomato sauce
2 tablespoons vinegar
1 teaspoon Worcestershire sauce

2 tablespoons India relish or pickle relish
½ teaspoon oregano
Freshly ground pepper to taste

Preheat oven at 325°F. (163°C.). Arrange turkey tails in baking dish into which they just fit comfortably. Combine remaining ingredients and pour evenly over the turkey tails. Bake 1½ to 2 hours, or until tender when pierced with a sharp-tined fork, basting and turning every 20 minutes. Arrange on heated platter.

Makes 2 or 3 servings. Recipe can be doubled.

TURKEY NECK FRICASSEE
WITH CORN AND GREEN PEPPERS

1½ pounds skinless turkey necks cut
   into 3 or 4 inch lengths
1¾ cups beef broth
2 cups water
1 cup chopped green pepper
½ teaspoon celery seeds
½ teaspoon thyme

1 garlic clove, minced
1 bay leaf
Salt to taste
Freshly ground pepper to taste
2 cups corn kernels
2 tablespoons cornstarch mixed
   with ¼ cup cold water

Place turkey necks into large heavy saucepan with beef broth and water. Bring to boil, skimming off particles as they rise to the surface. When no more particles rise to the surface add the green pepper, celery seed, thyme, garlic, bay leaf, salt, and pepper. Lower heat, cover, and simmer 1 hour. Add the corn kernels and cook 3 minutes. Remove the turkey necks. Add the cornstarch mixture and cook, stirring constantly, until slightly thickened. Arrange the turkey necks in a large deep serving bowl or soup tureen, and pour the corn mixture over them. Serve in soup plates.

Makes 4 to 5 servings.

RAGOUT ROBERT

2 pounds skinless turkey necks, cut
   into pieces not longer than 4
   inches
2 tablespoons margarine or butter
2 tablespoons vegetable oil
1½ cups chopped onions
1 garlic clove, chopped
5 medium carrots, scraped and cut
   into 3-inch lengths
2 tablespoons chopped parsley

1 bay leaf
½ teaspoon thyme
1 teaspoon salt
Freshly ground pepper to taste
1¾ cups beef broth
1 tablespoon Sauce Robert (bottled
   sauce available in supermarkets
   and specialty food stores)
1 cup lentils

In a top-of-stove casserole or Dutch oven, brown the turkey necks lightly in 1 tablespoon margarine or butter and 1 tablespoon vegetable oil. Remove necks. Add the remaining 1 tablespoon margarine or butter and 1 tablespoon vegetable oil to the casserole and sauté the onions and garlic until lightly browned. Return the turkey necks to the casserole. Add the carrots, parsley, bay leaf, thyme, salt, pepper, beef broth, and Sauce Robert. Bring to boil, reduce heat, cover, and simmer 30 minutes. Add the lentils and turn over the turkey necks. Make certain that all the lentils are immersed in the liquid. Cover and simmer another 30 minutes or until turkey necks and lentils are tender, adding a little boiling water if necessary during cooking. Spoon into a heated serving dish.

Makes 4 or 5 servings.

HOISIN TAILS WITH RICE

1¾ to 2 pounds turkey tails (6 tails)   **½ cup rice**
¼ cup hoisin sauce

Brush turkey tails all over with hoisin sauce and allow to stand at room temperature for 30 minutes.

Preheat oven at 375°F. (191°C.). Arrange the turkey tails on a baking sheet or in a shallow baking pan, spacing well apart. Bake 45 minutes or longer until tender when pierced with a sharp-tined fork, turning twice during baking.

About 20 minutes before the turkey tails have finished baking place the rice in a saucepan and cover with boiling water to a level 1 inch above the rice. Bring to boil, lower heat, cover, and simmer 20 minutes or until tender. Serve with the turkey tails on heated platter.

Makes 2 or 3 servings. Recipe can be doubled.

PEANUT-ROASTED TURKEY TAILS

1 egg	½ teaspoon salt
2 tablespoons milk	Freshly ground pepper to taste
Dash of Tabasco sauce	¾ cup roasted salted peanuts, very
¼ cup flour	finely chopped
1 tablespoon paprika	1¾ to 2 pounds turkey tails (6 tails)

Preheat oven at 375°F. (191°C.). Break the egg into a shallow soup plate and beat lightly with the milk and Tabasco sauce. Combine the flour, paprika, salt, and pepper in another flat soup plate. Place chopped peanuts into another flat soup plate. Dip each turkey tail in egg mixture, then in flour mixture, again in the egg mixture, and finally in the chopped peanuts. Arrange in greased shallow baking pan or on greased baking sheet, spacing well apart. Bake 45 minutes or longer until tender when pierced with a sharp-tined fork, turning twice during baking. Arrange on heated platter and serve.

Makes 2 or 3 servings. Recipe can be doubled.

Part 6—Boneless Turkey Breast

It seems that Americans have always had a weakness for the breast meat of turkey. Back in the early 1800s Texans could buy large wild turkeys from the Indians, and often ate only the breast meat. The balance, fortunately, didn't go to waste, but was given to their Mexican servants, who knew a thing or two about cooking turkey parts. Before the wild turkey became scarce in Missouri, the breast was often the only part of the bird that was used.

American turkey processors today, who know how to use every part of the bird, supply us not only with tender bone-in turkey breasts, but also extra-easy-to-handle boneless turkey breast. The one that is a staple in any frozen turkey case is the boneless white meat turkey roast weighing between 1½ and 2 pounds. For most of the recipes in this section such roasts should be completely thawed (overnight in the refrigerator will do it) before using, and the accompanying gravy packet either discarded or reserved for another use. These roasts also come with half dark meat and half light meat, but to my mind these two-tone roasts have an unnatural look. This is a matter of personal preference, however, and if you like the half-and-half roast, by all means use it in place of the white.

As discussed in Chapter 2, you can also make your own boneless white meat turkey roast, which is an economical thing to do. There is also a standard-weight four pound breast and thigh boneless turkey roast which is excellent for cooking "as is" or even better when stuffed and roasted. The best way to get a large boneless turkey breast, since they are not always available, is to buy a bone-in turkey breast and bone it out yourself. Recipes for these various types of turkey breast roasts follow.

When slicing a boneless turkey roast use a sharp straight-edged slicing knife, preferably one of a good quality stainless steel, or a ham and roast beef knife to get smooth slices without tearing.

MAPLE-BAKED BONELESS TURKEY ROAST

1 1½ to 2 pound boneless white meat turkey roast, frozen

½ cup (approximately) maple syrup

Preheat oven at 400°F. (204°C.). Remove roast from aluminum container in which it is packed (if any). Place in greased heavy shallow baking dish, as near to size of the roast as possible. Brush the roast all over with maple syrup. Cover with aluminum foil and bake 30 minutes undisturbed. Brush with more maple syrup and drippings from bottom of baking dish. Bake, covered, 30 minutes longer. Lower oven temperature to 325°F. (163°C.). Brush the roast with pan drippings and pour about ¼ cup maple syrup over it. Continue roasting about 30 minutes longer, or until meat thermometer inserted in center of roast registers 170°F. (77°C.), or until tender when pierced with a sharp-tined fork, brushing the roast every 10 minutes with the pan drippings. Remove from roasting pan and set on wooden carving board. Allow to stand 15 minutes, and slice into ¼-inch thick slices. Or cool, refrigerate, and slice thinly, serving the meat cold on a chilled platter.

Makes 6 or more servings.

SUPREME OF TURKEY WITH HAM FILLING

The filling of Supreme of Turkey with Ham Filling has a subtle pleasing flavor, the meat is tender, and the dish itself is very elegant. You can serve it hot with its accompanying sauce, or thinly sliced after chilling without the sauce. The latter way is excellent as a summer dish, and looks very attractive when served.

1 7½-pound (approximately) bone-in turkey breast with ribs, portion of wing meat and portion of back and neck skin attached
1½ cups chopped onions
¾ cup or more butter or margarine
1 garlic clove, finely minced
¼ pound mushrooms, chopped
1¾ cups very finely diced French or Italian bread
¼ cup dry white wine
½ pound finely diced ham
⅛ teaspoon cinnamon
Freshly ground pepper to taste
Dash of cloves
2 tablespoons flour
1½ cups turkey stock or chicken broth

If using a fresh turkey breast have the butcher bone it for you, leaving it in one piece. Do not have it cut into two parts and make sure he does not cut the skin. If using frozen turkey breast allow to thaw completely and bone, making certain not to cut through turkey skin which holds the breast meat together (see Index, How to bone a turkey breast leaving the skin intact).

Sauté onions in 2 tablespoons butter or margarine in a skillet over low heat until soft. Add 2 more tablespoons butter or margarine. Raise heat and add garlic and mushrooms. Sauté a minute or two. Remove skillet from heat. Add 2 more tablespoons butter or margarine and stir until melted. Sprinkle the diced bread with the wine and toss. Add to the onion-mushroom mixture and toss well. Add the ham and toss well. Add cinnamon, pepper, and cloves and toss again.

Lay the boned turkey breast on a wooden board or work table, skin side down. Open out the turkey breast to lie as flat as possible. Spoon the filling onto the turkey breast, towards the center and one side. Spread to within one inch of the edge on the side where the filling is. Fold the other side of the turkey breast over the filling so that the edges meet at the sides. Skewer together around the edges where possible, and sew the remaining edges together with a large needle and white kitchen thread. Skewer any loose pieces of turkey onto the breast. The filling should be sealed in quite well. Place the breast in a greased 2-inch deep roasting pan a little larger than the breast. (If desired, the turkey breast may now be covered and refrigerated for 1 or 2 hours before roasting, but not longer.)

Preheat oven at 325°F. (163°C.). Melt about half a stick of butter or margarine and brush over the turkey breast. Roast 30 minutes. Brush with melted butter or margarine and roast 30 minutes longer. Brush again with melted butter or margarine and turn the turkey breast over, using a pancake turner to loosen the breast from the pan and turn it. Do not spear it with a fork. Brush with melted butter or margarine and continue to roast, basting or brushing frequently, for a total roasting time of 2½ hours, or until meat thermometer inserted into thickest part of turkey breast (not filling) registers 175°F. (79°C.), or until tender when pierced with a sharp-tined fork.

Place turkey breast on wooden carving board. Remove all skewers. Snip kitchen thread and pull out. Allow turkey breast to stand about 25 minutes before slicing.

Meanwhile, drain all but about 2 tablespoons fat from the roasting pan. Place over low heat. Sprinkle in the flour and stir for a few minutes. Add the turkey stock or chicken broth and bring to boil, stirring to loosen the brown particles in the pan bottom. Reduce heat. Taste and correct seasoning if necessary and allow the sauce to simmer until ready to slice the turkey, stirring occasionally.

Cut the turkey breast into slices ½-inch thick, and arrange on heated platter. Serve the sauce in a heated sauce boat.

Makes 10 to 12 servings.

TURKEY TONNATO

1 large onion, sliced
1 cup (approximately) vegetable oil,
    preferably olive oil
2 celery ribs, cut up
2 medium carrots, scraped and
    sliced
2 bay leaves
2 whole cloves
Generous pinch of thyme
3 or 4 parsley sprigs
1 teaspoon salt
1 garlic clove, smashed

6 peppercorns
3 cups dry white wine
1½ to 2 pound boneless white meat
    turkey roast (if frozen
    completely thawed)
2½ cups turkey stock or chicken
    broth
1 6½ ounce can tuna, drained
6 anchovy fillets
¼ cup lemon juice
2 tablespoons or more capers

Sauté onions in 3 tablespoons oil until golden. Add the celery, carrots, bay leaves, cloves, thyme, parsley, salt, garlic, peppercorns, and wine. Bring to boil, lower heat, and simmer 7 minutes.

Place turkey roast into an enameled pan or a glass or ceramic bowl and pour the wine mixture over it. Allow to cool. Cover and refrigerate 24 hours, turning several times.

Remove turkey roast from bowl. Pour the wine mixture into a cocotte, top-of-stove casserole, or Dutch oven. Add the turkey stock or chicken broth and bring to boil, skimming off any particles that rise to the surface. Place the turkey roast into the casserole. Lower heat, cover, and simmer 1 hour, or until meat thermometer inserted in center of roast registers 170°F. (77°C.) or until tender when pierced with a sharp-tined fork, turning the turkey roast over after 30 minutes. Remove the turkey roast from the casserole and allow to cool. Strain the cooking liquid and reserve it for another use.

When the turkey roast is cool remove the skin from the visible part of the turkey roast, and discard it.

In a food processor fitted with steel blade or in an electric blender combine the tuna, anchovy fillets and lemon juice until puréed. Gradually add ½ cup oil in a steady stream with the machine turned on. Place the turkey roast into an enameled pan or glass or ceramic bowl just large enough to fit comfortably. Sprinkle 2 tablespoons capers over the turkey roast. Pour the tuna sauce over the turkey roast. Cover tightly and refrigerate 24 hours, turning several times.

To serve, slice thinly, arrange on chilled platter, and spoon some sauce over the slices. Sprinkle with a few capers. Serve the remaining sauce in a chilled sauce boat.

Makes 6 or more servings.

TURKEY BREAST, CIAMBOTTA STYLE

1 3½ pound boneless turkey roast, if frozen, thawed completely (a small size roast may be used if desired)
1 tablespoon margarine or butter
2 tablespoons or more olive oil
1 cup chopped onions
2 large tomatoes, unpeeled, chopped

2 medium zucchini, sliced
1 medium eggplant, unpeeled, cut into ½ to ¾-inch cubes
1 green pepper, chopped
½ teaspoon oregano
1 teaspoon salt
Freshly ground pepper to taste
¼ cup red wine
1 teaspoon sugar

Brown the turkey roast in a top-of-stove casserole in the margarine or butter and 1 tablespoon olive oil, adding more olive oil if necessary. Remove the turkey roast from the casserole. Lower the heat, add the onions to the casserole, and sauté until lightly browned, adding more olive oil if necessary. Raise heat. Add 1 tablespoon olive oil and the tomatoes and cook for a minute, stirring. Add the zucchini, eggplant, and green pepper, and cook, stirring and tossing the vegetables, for 8 to 10 minutes.

Arrange the turkey roast in the casserole with the vegetables.

Lower heat, cover, and simmer, stirring the vegetables every 15 minutes and spooning the liquid over the turkey roast, for 45 minutes. Add the wine and sugar, cover, and continue to cook, stirring and basting every 15 minutes, an additional 45 minutes, or until meat thermometer inserted in center of turkey roast registers 170° to 175°F. (77° to 79°C.), or until tender when pierced with a sharp-tined fork. Remove turkey roast and allow to stand on wooden carving board 15 minutes. Meanwhile allow vegetables to continue simmering, uncovered.

Remove strings from turkey roast. Slice and serve on heated platter with the vegetables.

Makes 8 servings.

CINNAMON TURKEY WITH CRISP POTATOES

For the turkey:
1 or more tablespoons margarine or butter
1 or more tablespoons vegetable oil
1 1½ to 2 pound boneless white meat turkey roast (if frozen, completely thawed)
¾ cup finely chopped onions
2 medium carrots, finely chopped
1 cup dry white wine
½ cup turkey stock or chicken broth

2 teaspoons cinnamon
½ teaspoon salt
Freshly ground pepper to taste
½ cup sour cream
1 egg yolk
1 teaspoon lemon juice

For the potatoes:
6 medium size potatoes
1 tablespoon or more salt
¼ cup melted lard or bacon fat

For the turkey: Pat the turkey roast completely dry with paper towels. Brown it in a top-of-stove casserole in 1 tablespoon margarine or butter and 1 tablespoon vegetable oil. Remove the turkey roast and sauté the onions and carrots in the casserole until lightly browned, adding more margarine or butter and vegetable oil if necessary. Return the turkey roast to the casserole. Add the wine and turkey stock or chicken broth. Sprinkle the cinnamon, salt, and pepper over the turkey. Bring to boil, reduce heat, cover, and simmer 30 minutes. Turn the turkey over and cook 30 minutes longer, or until thermometer inserted in center registers 170°F. (77°C.), or until tender when pierced with a sharp-tined fork. Remove turkey from casserole and set on a wooden carving board for about 15 minutes.

Meanwhile prepare the sauce. Transfer the remaining casserole ingredients to a food processor fitted with steel blade or an electric blender and process until the vegetables are completely pulverized. Return the mixture to the casserole. Mix a little of the casserole liquid with the sour cream. Then stir the sour cream into the casserole. Place over gentle heat. Add a little of the casserole liquid to the beaten egg yolk and add to the casserole, stirring constantly. Add the lemon juice and heat until quite warm, but do not allow to boil.

For the potatoes: While the turkey is simmering prepare the potatoes. Preheat the oven at 400°F. (204°C.). Peel the potatoes and cut into thirds. Place in a saucepan with 1 tablespoon salt and cold water to cover amply. Bring to boil. Remove from heat and drain. Scratch surfaces of the potatoes lightly with a fork. Place the potatoes in a baking pan large enough to fit in one layer without crowding. Pour the melted lard or bacon fat over the potatoes and toss to coat all sides well. Bake 45 minutes, or until tender when pierced with a fork, turning over after 25 minutes.

To serve: Slice turkey thinly and arrange the slices on a heated long narrow or oval platter. Spoon some of the sauce down the center of the slices. Serve the balance of the sauce in a heated sauce boat. Arrange the potatoes in a heated serving dish and sprinkle lightly with salt.

Makes 8 servings.

SAVORY MUSHROOM-STUFFED BONELESS TURKEY BREAST

1 4-pound breast and thigh boneless turkey roast (if frozen, completely thawed)
2 tablespoons margarine or butter
1½ to 2 cups finely chopped mushrooms
1 cup finely chopped onions
½ teaspoon marjoram
½ teaspoon salt
Freshly ground pepper to taste
6 tablespoons Port wine
½ cup finely chopped carrot
3 cups turkey stock or chicken broth
2 tablespoons chopped parsley
2 tablespoons cornstarch

Cut about ¾ pound of the thigh meat off the turkey roast. Cut it up and put it though a meat grinder or a food processor fitted with a steel blade. Sauté the mushrooms and ½ cup of the chopped onions in the margarine or butter for about 5 minutes. Remove from heat. Add the ground thigh meat along with the marjoram, salt, pepper, and 2 tablespoons Port wine, and mix well. Open the turkey breast, slitting it if necessary to make it lie flat. Pat it dry with paper towels. Spoon on the mushroom filling, banking it toward the center and spreading it to within one inch of the side. Fold the turkey over the filling sandwich fashion. Tie up the turkey with kitchen string in 5 places, 4 around the turkey crosswise, and 1 lengthwise.

Preheat the oven at 450°F. (232°C.). Place the turkey, skin side down, into a shallow roasting pan or baking pan just a little larger than the turkey. Bake 15 minutes. Add the chopped carrot, remaining ½ cup chopped onion, and 1 cup of the turkey stock or chicken broth which has been heated. Reduce oven temperature to 350°F. (177°C.) and bake 15 minutes longer. Stir ingredients in bottom of pan and baste the turkey every 15 minutes with the pan liquid until thermometer inserted in thickest part of turkey breast registers 175°F. (79°C.), or until tender when pierced with a sharp-tined fork, about 1½ hours.

Set turkey roast on a wooden carving board and allow to sit 15 minutes before slicing. Meanwhile add the remaining 2 cups turkey stock or chicken broth to the roasting pan. Place on stove and bring to boil, stirring. Add the chopped parsley and the cornstarch which has been mixed with the remaining 4 tablespoons Port. Simmer, stirring constantly, until all particles on pan bottom have loosened and the sauce thickens. Taste and correct seasoning if necessary. Strain the sauce. Put the strained vegetables through a food processor fitted with steel blade or through a blender or food mill and add back to the sauce.

Slice turkey and spoon the sauce over the slices or serve in heated sauce boat.

Makes 12 or more servings.

Part 7—Turkey Cutlets

If anything could be better than turkey breast, it's turkey breast cut into beautiful cutlets. They can be sautéed with a few other ingredients and be ready in a matter of minutes, or they can be rolled up with interesting fillings, or treated in other taste-tempting ways, as you'll see in the following recipes.

Turkey cutlets can be bought prepackaged, or you can cut your own from a turkey breast as discussed in Chapter 2. If you cut your own it will be more economical. One way to treat a whole turkey breast is to pull back the skin from one side and slice off the meat into cutlets. Then you can stuff that side of the breast, cover with the skin, pin it down, and cook the entire breast which you've converted into a half meat and half stuffing dish.

Turkey cutlets that are prepackaged are one of the more expensive turkey cuts, but, compared to meat prices in general, not high. A little goes a long way with turkey cutlets, too, and, compared with veal prices, they're inexpensive. Turkey cutlets can be treated like veal cutlets in almost any recipe, so if you've had a favorite veal cutlet recipe in mothballs waiting for lower veal prices, try it instead with turkey cutlets. They're extremely tender, cook very quickly and have a lovely mild flavor that goes well with subtle flavorings as well as with more robust ones.

If you want to flatten turkey cutlets before cooking them place them between two sheets of waxed paper or plastic wrap and pound them with the flat side of a broad cleaver or the flat side of a meat mallet. Whether the recipe calls for them to be flattened or not, always pat them dry with paper towels before sautéeing, to prevent them from simmering.

DUSSELDORF TURKEY CUTLETS

4 or more turkey cutlets ¼- to ⅜-
  inch thick (about ¾ pound)
Flour
1 tablespoon or more margarine or
  butter
1 tablespoon or more vegetable oil
2 tablespoons minced shallots

¼ cup dry white wine
⅓ cup cream
½ teaspoon salt
Freshly ground pepper to taste
1 tablespoon Düsseldorf mustard (if
  not available use a mild Dijon)

Pound the cutlets between two sheets of waxed paper or plastic wrap
to flatten as much as possible. Pat dry with paper towels. Dust with flour.
Sauté in 1 tablespoon margarine or butter and 1 tablespoon vegetable oil
until lightly browned, 2 minutes or less on each side. Remove to heated
serving platter. Add the shallots to the sauté pan, adding more margarine
or butter and vegetable oil if necessary, and cook for a minute, stirring.
Add the wine and cook, stirring, until the wine is almost evaporated.
Add the cream, salt, and pepper, and cook, stirring until the mixture
bubbles. Remove from heat and stir in the mustard. Pour over the turkey
cutlets. Serve immediately.

Makes 4 servings.

TURKEBABS

¼ cup lemon juice
¼ cup soy sauce (preferably tamari
  soy sauce)
1 teaspoon coriander
¼ teaspoon cardamom
¼ teaspoon cumin
1 garlic clove, minced

2 tablespoons minced onion
Generous pinch of red pepper
  flakes
1 pound turkey cutlets ½-inch thick,
  cut into bite-size pieces about 1
  inch square
Vegetable oil

Combine lemon juice, soy sauce, coriander, cardamom, cumin, garlic, onion, and red pepper flakes in a bowl. Add turkey pieces and combine well. Cover and refrigerate 2 or 3 hours, turning once or twice. Drain, reserving the marinade. Do not pat the turkey pieces dry. Thread them onto 8 7-inch or 8-inch wooden skewers, dividing equally.

Heat about ¼ inch of vegetable oil in a large skillet and brown the skewered turkey, 4 skewers at a time, for 4 to 5 minutes over medium to low heat, turning often. Do not allow the turkey to become at all dry. When all the skewers have been browned place them on a heated serving platter. Pour off the oil and add the reserved marinade to the skillet. Heat, stirring to loosen all browned particles from skillet. Pour over the turkey skewers, or put in a small heated sauce boat.

Makes 4 servings.

TURKEY PARMESAN CUTLETS

8 turkey cutlets ½ inch thick,
   weighing about 1 pound
¼ cup whole wheat flour
1 teaspoon salt
Freshly ground pepper to taste
1 teaspoon oregano
2 egg whites

2 tablespoons cold water
½ cup wheat germ
½ cup freshly grated Parmesan,
   Romano, or Sardo cheese
1 tablespoon or more margarine or
   butter
1 tablespoon or more vegetable oil

Pat the turkey cutlets dry with paper towels. In a flat soup plate combine flour, salt, pepper, and oregano. In another flat soup plate beat the egg whites just until foamy. Add the cold water and combine. In another flat soup plate combine the wheat germ and grated cheese. Dip the cutlets, one at a time, in the flour mixture, coating evenly, then in the egg white mixture, and finally in the wheat germ-cheese mixture, coating thickly.

In a skillet melt 1 tablespoon margarine or butter with 1 tablespoon vegetable oil. Heat until just bubbly. Sauté the cutlets, a few at a time, over low heat for 5 minutes on each side, adding more margarine and oil as necessary. Do not crowd the cutlets while sautéeing. Serve immediately, arranged on heated serving platter.

Makes 4 servings.

TURKEY TAPINADE

8 turkey cutlets ¼ inch thick
(generous 1¼ pounds)
Juice of half a lemon
½ teaspoon oregano
2 teaspoons plus 1 tablespoon olive
oil
4 anchovy fillets, patted dry with
paper towels
1½ teaspoons capers

1 cup cut-up pitted black olives
(preferably Calamata or Nicoise)
1 teaspoon brandy
Salt to taste
Freshly ground pepper to taste
1 or 2 eggs
⅓ cup fine dry bread crumbs
⅓ cup wheat germ
Vegetable oil for frying (preferably
olive oil)

Arrange the turkey cutlets on a plate. Sprinkle them with the lemon juice, oregano, and 2 tablespoons olive oil. Set aside for 30 minutes, turning several times.

Meanwhile put anchovy fillets and capers through a food processor fitted with steel blade or through an electric blender. Add the olives and blend. Add the brandy and 1 tablespoon olive oil and blend. This mixture may also be made in a mortar and pestle.

Pat turkey cutlets thoroughly dry with paper towels. Sprinkle them with salt and pepper. Spread the anchovy mixture on one side of each cutlet, dividing equally. Arrange the cutlets on a plate, anchovy side up. Cover and chill 1 hour in the refrigerator or 20 minutes in the freezer.

Beat an egg in a flat soup plate. Combine bread crumbs and wheat germ in another flat soup plate. Place a turkey cutlet into the beaten egg, spread side up. Spoon some egg over the top. Lift the cutlet and set it in the breadcrumb mixture. Sprinkle some crumbs over the top and pat them to make them adhere. Set the cutlet on a plate. Continue until all cutlets have been coated, beating a second egg if required. Allow the cutlets to set for 15 minutes.

Heat ¼ inch vegetable oil in a skillet. Brown the cutlets slowly on both sides over low heat, about 4 minutes on each side. Turn them carefully. Drain on paper towels, spread side up. Serve on a heated platter, spread side up.

Makes 8 servings.

POMMERY TURKEY ROULADES

8 turkey cutlets ¼- to ⅜-inch thick, as long and as wide as possible
1½ cups very finely chopped onions
¼ teaspoon thyme
1 small crumbled bay leaf
¼ teaspoon rosemary
4 tablespoons or more vegetable oil
1 tablespoon margarine or butter
1 cup very finely chopped green pepper
3 large slices rye bread (not thin-sliced)

3 tablespoons Pommery mustard (if not available, use Dijon)
1 garlic clove, minced
1 egg, beaten
Salt to taste
Freshly ground pepper to taste
½ cup red wine
1 cup beef broth
1 tablespoon cornstarch mixed with 2 tablespoons cold water

Place turkey cutlets between waxed paper or plastic wrap and flatten slightly with the side of a cleaver or meat mallet. Sauté the onions with the thyme, bay leaf, and rosemary in 1 tablespoon vegetable oil and the margarine or butter for 5 minutes, until lightly browned. Add 1 tablespoon vegetable oil and the green pepper and cook, stirring, 4 or 5 minutes. Transfer to bowl.

Spread the rye bread slices with mustard on both sides, and brown them lightly in a skillet in 1 tablespoon vegetable oil, adding more oil as necessary. Cut the fried bread into tiny squares and add them to the bowl, along with the garlic, egg, salt, and pepper.

Preheat oven at 325°F. (163°C.). Spread the turkey cutlets with the filling mixture, dividing equally. Roll up the cutlets, starting at the narrow end. Secure as much as possible with toothpicks. Brown the turkey rolls in 1 tablespoon vegetable oil on all unopened sides, adding more vegetable oil if necessary. Arrange the turkey rolls in a baking dish fairly close together. Pour the wine and beef broth in the skillet and bring to boil, stirring and scraping bottom of skillet to remove all browned particles. Pour over the turkey rolls. Cover the baking dish with aluminum foil. Bake 45 minutes or until tender when pierced with a sharp-tined fork.

If serving hot, arrange turkey rolls on heated serving platter. Place the baking dish over medium heat and add the cornstarch mixture, stirring constantly, until mixture thickens and all brown particles from baking pan have been loosened. Pour over turkey rolls and serve. If serving cold, omit making the sauce. Cool the turkey rolls, wrap, and chill. Slice to serve.

Makes 8 servings.

TURKEY PICCATA

1 pound turkey cutlets, ¼ inch thick	Salt to taste
2 tablespoons margarine or butter	Freshly ground pepper to taste
¼ cup lemon juice	2 tablespoons chopped parsley

Flatten turkey cutlets by placing them between waxed paper or plastic wrap and pounding with flat side of a cleaver or meat mallet. Pat the cutlets dry with paper towels. Melt the margarine or butter in a skillet until bubbly. Sauté the cutlets, 2 or 3 minutes on each side, over medium to low heat. Remove to a heated serving platter. Add the lemon juice, salt, and pepper to the skillet and bring to boil, scraping up all brown particles from the bottom of the skillet. Pour over the cutlets. Sprinkle with parsley and serve immediately on heated platter.

Makes 4 servings.

TURKEY CUTLETS WITH GREEN PEPPERCORNS

4 turkey cutlets about ¼-inch thick (¾ pound or more)	1 teaspoon crushed green peppercorns
Flour	¼ cup dry white wine
1 tablespoon margarine or butter	2 tablespoons brandy
1 tablespoon vegetable oil	½ teaspoon salt
1 tablespoon grated onion	Freshly ground pepper to taste

Pound the turkey cutlets between 2 pieces of waxed paper or plastic wrap to flatten a little. Dry with paper towels. Dust with flour. Sauté in skillet in the margarine or butter and vegetable oil until lightly browned, about 3 minutes on each side. Remove cutlets and keep warm.

Add the onion and crushed green peppercorns to the skillet and cook a minute or two, stirring. Add the wine, brandy, salt, and pepper, and cook another minute. Add 1 tablespoon flour and blend in. Cook another minute. Spoon evenly over the cutlets and serve immediately on a heated platter.

Makes 4 servings.

TURKEY MARSALA WITH TWO KINDS OF MUSHROOMS

¼ cup thinly sliced dried mushrooms
½ cup hot water
½ pound fresh mushrooms, sliced
2 tablespoons or more margarine or butter
2 tablespoons or more vegetable oil
Flour

4 or more turkey cutlets ¼- to ⅜-inch thick (about ¾ pound)
¼ cup Marsala wine
Freshly ground pepper to taste
½ cup turkey gravy (homemade or canned)
3 tablespoons chopped flatleaf parsley
Salt (optional)

Preheat oven at 200°F. (93°C.). Soak the dried mushrooms in hot water for 30 minutes. Meanwhile in a skillet sauté the fresh mushrooms in two batches over medium high heat in 1 tablespoon margarine or butter and 1 tablespoon vegetable oil, adding more margarine or butter and vegetable oil if necessary. Place the sautéed mushrooms on an ovenproof platter and set in the oven to keep warm.

Dry the turkey cutlets with paper towels. Dust well with flour and shake off the excess. In the same skillet in which the mushrooms were sautéed, sauté the cutlets for a minute or two on each side in 1 tablespoon margarine or butter and 1 tablespoon vegetable oil, adding more margarine or butter and vegetable oil if necessary. Set the cutlets on the platter with the sautéed mushrooms to keep them warm.

To the skillet add the dried mushrooms and the liquid in which they were soaked, adding the liquid slowly to prevent any grit which may have settled to the bottom from being transferred to the skillet. Add the Marsala, pepper, and turkey gravy, and heat, stirring, until mixture simmers. Reduce heat, cover, and simmer 15 minutes. Return sautéed mushrooms to the skillet. Add the parsley and simmer a minute. Taste for seasoning and add salt or pepper if necessary. Pour mushroom mixture over cutlets and serve on a heated platter.

Makes 4 to 5 servings.

4

Half a Turkey Is Better Than None

(INCLUDES CUT-UP TURKEY AND MIXED PARTS)

Half angel and half bird.
—ROBERT BROWNING, *Rabbi Ben Ezra*

There are lots of ways you can cut up with a turkey that may never have occurred to you. First of all, consider half a turkey. Some butchers and supermarkets will sell you half a turkey, but if they won't, they'll be happy to cut a whole frozen turkey in half with their powerful meat saw and wrap up both halves for you. Then you can treat one as a turkey half and the other as parts, cutlets, basis for stock, and so on. Or you may want to cut off all the thighs, drumsticks, wings and tail from both halves, and have two breast sections to use. Next, you can have a turkey cut into quarters and cook the quarters separately. Sometimes you'll find packaged hindquarters for sale, and you can cook them as you would cook half a turkey. The possibilities are endless.

This chapter offers some good ideas for cooking these various cuts. A recipe for a superb Half Turkey on Golden Sauerkraut Bed, for example, is bound to convince you there's more than one way to roast a bird. Incidentally, if the turkey your butcher has cut in half is fitted with metal trussing wire rather than a skin strip for tucking in the legs, the butcher will not cut through the wire, since it would ruin his saw. For this reason you may have to remove the wire yourself with a pair of pliers.

There are any number of ways to cook a cut-up turkey, and if your butcher doesn't cut it up for you (and he can't very well if it's solidly frozen), thaw it and cut it up yourself. It's not difficult to do and complete directions are given in Chapter 2, "How to cut up a whole turkey in order to use the various parts." Turkeys of up to about seven pounds are generally most satisfactory for preparing the recipes presented in this chapter. Larger turkeys give you pieces that are too bulky. If you prefer, for many of these recipes, you can use various prepackaged turkey parts and cut them into smaller parts. For example, use wings and thighs, cutting the wings apart at the joints, and cutting the thighs, if necessary, into two or three pieces according to the recipe you're using. Or you might want to cut up a small breast and combine it with wings, thighs, or drumsticks. You'll find all the recipes made with cut-up turkey or mixed parts hearty and satisfying.

TURKEY CUMBERLAND

Turkey half weighing about 6 pounds	2 tablespoons lemon juice
	2 tablespoons cider vingear
Salt	Cayenne pepper to taste
¼ cup margarine or butter	1 tablespoon cornstarch combined
½ cup red or black currant jelly	with 2 tablespoons cold water
¼ cup Port wine	Turkey stock or chicken broth
2 teaspoons prepared mustard	(optional)

Wash and pat turkey half thoroughly dry with paper towels. Rub cut side of turkey half with salt. Place cut side down, in shallow roasting pan just large enough to fit comfortably. Preheat oven at 325°F. (163°C.).

Melt the margarine or butter in a small saucepan with the currant jelly. Heat, stirring, until the jelly has melted. Remove from heat and stir in the Port, mustard, lemon juice, vinegar, 1 teaspoon salt, and a dash of cayenne, or to taste. Brush the turkey all over with the currant jelly mixture.

Roast until meat thermometer inserted in center of inside thigh muscle adjoining the body registers 180 to 185°F. (82 to 85°C.), or until tender when pierced with a sharp-tined fork, brushing with the currant jelly mixture every 20 minutes. If the wing starts to brown too much wrap it in aluminum foil. Set turkey half on a wooden carving board and allow to stand 15-20 minutes before carving. Meanwhile, spoon off excess fat from roasting pan. Add the remaining currant jelly mixture along with the cornstarch mixture. Heat to boiling, stirring constantly. Lower heat and simmer a few minutes. If the sauce is too thick add a little turkey stock or chicken broth and heat thoroughly. Serve in a heated sauce boat.

Makes 6 to 8 servings.

TURKEY IN ONION AND TOMATO SAUCE PROVENÇAL

2 cups sliced onions
3 tablespoons vegetable oil
1 28-ounce can ground peeled
   Italian tomatoes
1 cup dry white wine
2 garlic cloves, finely minced
1 bay leaf
½ teaspoon thyme
¼ teaspoon fennel seed
1 generous pinch of saffron
1 2- to 3-inch piece dried orange
   peel *

Pinch of freshly ground pepper
Dash of cayenne
1 4-pound turkey cut into serving
   pieces, or equal amounts of
   turkey parts (wing sections and
   combination of drumsticks,
   thighs, or breast pieces)
1 teaspoon salt
1 cup (approximately) turkey stock
   or chicken broth

In top-of-stove casserole sauté onions in vegetable oil 10 minutes over low heat, covered, stirring occasionally. The onions should be soft but not brown. Add the tomatoes, wine, and garlic, and bring to boil. Add the bay leaf, thyme, fennel seed, saffron, orange peel, pepper, and cayenne, and stir to combine. Sprinkle the turkey pieces with salt and add them to the casserole, spooning the tomato-onion mixture over them. Add enough turkey stock or chicken broth to almost cover the turkey pieces. Bring to simmer, cover, lower heat, and simmer 45 minutes. Turn turkey pieces over and continue cooking another 30 minutes or until the thickest turkey part is tender when pierced with a sharp-tined fork.

Remove turkey pieces and keep them warm. Discard bay leaf and orange peel. Boil down the sauce until it has thickened. Arrange the turkey pieces on a heated serving platter and spoon some of the sauce over them. Serve the balance of the sauce in a heated sauce boat.

Makes 6 to 8 servings.

* For dried orange peel wash and dry an orange. With a sharp knife peel the orange part of the rind off in one piece, if possible, peeling round and round the orange from top to bottom. Hang the peel up in a dry airy place until dry. Store in an airtight jar at room temperature for use when needed. A piece of dried orange peel is a nice addition to stews.

TURKEY VERDE DOBLE

3 pounds cut-up turkey or turkey
  parts
Turkey stock or chicken broth
1 onion slice
Salt to taste
4 peppercorns
1 medium carrot, scraped and cut
  up
1 pound fresh spinach or 1 10-
  ounce package frozen leaf
  spinach

2 tablespoons margarine or butter
Freshly ground pepper to taste
Dash of nutmeg
8 ounces green (spinach) noodles
1 tablespoon flour
½ cup milk
1 egg
¼ cup freshly grated cheese (any
  kind)

Place turkey parts into a large saucepan and add enough turkey stock or chicken broth to just cover. Bring to boil, skimming until no more particles rise to the surface. Add the onion slice, salt, peppercorns, and carrot, and bring to boil. Lower heat, cover, and simmer until tender when pierced with a sharp-tined fork. Remove turkey pieces from saucepan and remove the meat from the bones. Discard bones and skin and cut the turkey meat into dice. Boil down the liquid in the saucepan to measure 1 cup and set aside.

Wash the spinach and simmer in a saucepan in its own water, covered, until it wilts. Or cook frozen spinach according to package directions until spinach is separated. Drain. Toss the spinach with 1 tablespoon margarine or butter, salt and pepper to taste, and a dash of nutmeg.

Cook the noodles according to package directions until nearly tender. Drain.

Preheat oven at 350°F. (177°C.). In a saucepan melt the remaining 1 tablespoon margarine or butter. Add the flour and blend well. Add the reserved 1 cup of turkey stock and the milk, and cook, stirring constantly, until thickened. Remove from heat.

In a greased 2-quart casserole arrange half the noodles. Arrange the spinach mixture over the noodles. Arrange the diced turkey over the spinach. Arrange the remaining noodles over the turkey. Beat the egg well and add it to the slightly cooled turkey stock mixture, beating briskly with a wire whisk. Pour over the noodles in the casserole. Sprinkle with the cheese and bake until bubbly, about 20 minutes. If necessary run under the broiler a minute or two to brown the top.

Makes 4 or more servings.

TIPSY TURKEY

3½ to 4 pounds turkey drumsticks
  and thighs
3 cups sherry (preferably medium to
  sweet)
1 or more tablespoons vegetable oil
4 or more tablespoons margarine or
  butter
1 teaspoon salt

Freshly ground pepper to taste
1 bay leaf
¾ pound tiny white onions, peeled
1 28-ounce can concentrated
  crushed tomatoes
½ cup cut-up pitted green olives
  (preferably cracked green olives)

Cut turkey thighs into two or three pieces, depending on size of the thighs. Arrange all the turkey pieces in a glass or ceramic bowl and pour the sherry over them. Cover and refrigerate 8 hours, turning several times.

Remove turkey pieces from sherry and pat dry with paper towels. Reserve the sherry. In a large skillet or top-of-stove casserole brown the turkey pieces, a few at a time, in 1 tablespoon vegetable oil and 1 tablespoon margarine or butter, adding more margarine or butter and vegetable oil as necessary. Return all the browned turkey pieces to the skillet and add 3 tablespoons margarine or butter, the salt, pepper, bay leaf, onions, and tomatoes, along with the reserved sherry. Bring to boil, spooning the mixture over the turkey pieces. Lower heat, cover, and simmer 30 minutes. Uncover and simmer another 30 minutes. Add the olives and simmer another 15 minutes or until the thickest turkey part is tender when pierced with a sharp-tined fork. Serve on heated platter.

Makes 6 servings.

PEPPERY RED ONION TURKEY

12 garlic cloves
4 teaspoons salt
2 teaspoons plus a pinch of oregano
½ teaspoons cumin
4 allspice berries
5 whole cloves
1¼ teaspoons peppercorns

4 teaspoons plus ¾ cup white
  vinegar
1 5-pound turkey, cut into serving
  pieces
9½ cups water
4 cups thinly sliced red onions
2 long thin hot green peppers
Vegetable oil

Peel and slice 6 of the garlic cloves and place in a mortar, preferably one made of stone or china. Add 2 teaspoons salt, ½ teaspoon oregano, and the cumin, and crush into a paste with a pestle. In an electric blender whirl the allspice berries, whole cloves, and 1 teaspoon peppercorns until reduced to a powder. Add the spice mixture to the mortar and mix well. Add 4 teaspoons vinegar and mix again.

Using about one-third of the spice paste, rub each piece of turkey all over lightly. Arrange the pieces in a large saucepan, cover, and leave at room temperature about 45 minutes. Meanwhile heat a cast iron griddle or frying pan over medium heat. Put 3 garlic cloves on the griddle and allow them to toast, turning, until browned all over and skins loosen. Remove from stove and remove skins from the garlic.

Add enough water to the saucepan containing the turkey pieces to just cover the turkey pieces, about 8 cups. Bring to simmer, skimming off particles that rise to the surface. Add the toasted garlic cloves, a pinch of oregano, and 1 teaspoon salt, and place lid on saucepan, slightly ajar. Continue to simmer until turkey pieces are just tender, about 30 to 40 minutes, rearranging them once during cooking.

While the turkey is cooking place the sliced red onions in a bowl with ¼ teaspoon peppercorns, ½ teaspoon oregano, the remaining 3 garlic cloves, peeled and sliced, 1 teaspoon salt, ¾ cup white vinegar, and 1½ cups water. Toss well, cover, and set aside.

Spear the hot green peppers one at a time with a long fork and hold them over a flame or electric stove burner until seared and blistered on all sides. Place the peppers in a plastic bag for 20 to 30 minutes to help loosen their skins. Peel off skins. Cut off tops of the peppers, slit down the side and remove seeds and membranes. Set aside the peppers. (Do not rub your eyes while handling the peppers, and wash hands afterwards.)

When the turkey pieces have finished cooking remove them from the liquid and set aside to cool slightly. Meanwhile boil down the liquid until it measures 3 cups or a little less. Strain the broth and pour into a clean saucepan.

Preheat the broiler. Rub turkey pieces all over with the remaining spice paste. Arrange them on a baking sheet. Brush with vegetable oil and broil until nicely browned on one side. Turn, brush the other side with vegetable oil, and broil until nicely browned. Arrange on a heated serving platter.

Remove the red onion slices from the vinegar mixture with a slotted spoon and add them, along with the peeled peppers, to the broth in the saucepan. Bring to boil, lower heat, and simmer about 2 minutes. Pour over the turkey pieces.

Makes 6 to 8 servings.

SPRINGTIME TURKEY CASSEROLE

4 to 4½ pounds turkey parts (wing sections, drumsticks, thighs and breast meat, or any combination of them)
2 or more tablespoons vegetable oil
3 or more tablespoons margarine or butter
1½ cups chopped onions
2½ cups diced celery
½ pound mushrooms, sliced
1 10-ounce package frozen peas or 2⅓ cups shelled fresh peas

1 10-ounce package frozen cauliflower
1 cup boiling water
1 tablespoon flour
1 cup turkey stock or chicken broth
Salt to taste
Freshly ground pepper to taste
1 teaspoon oregano
¼ cup sherry
¼ cup chopped parsley

In a large skillet brown the turkey parts in 2 tablespoons vegetable oil, adding more oil if necessary. Set turkey parts aside. Preheat oven at 325°F. (163°C.). To the oil in the skillet add 1 tablespoon margarine or butter. Sauté the onions and celery until the onions are transparent. Remove with a slotted spoon and place in a bowl. Add 2 more table-spoons margarine or butter to the skillet and sauté the mushrooms 2 or 3 minutes. Remove them with a slotted spoon and add to the bowl.

Place the peas and cauliflower in a saucepan and pour the boiling water over them. Cover and bring to boil. Remove from heat and drain immediately. Add the peas and cauliflower to the bowl.

To the skillet add the flour and cook a minute, stirring. Add the turkey stock or chicken broth gradually, stirring constantly, and cook until thickened, scraping up browned particles from bottom of skillet. Add the salt, pepper, oregano, sherry, and parsley. Remove from heat.

Toss the vegetables in the·bowl together gently. Arrange them in a casserole with the browned turkey parts. Pour the sauce over all. Bake until the thickest turkey part is tender when pierced with a sharp-tined fork, about 1½ to 2 hours. Serve on heated platter.

Makes 4 to 6 servings.

GINGERSNAP TURKEY

1 tablespoon coarsely chopped
   fresh ginger root or canned
   green ginger
2 tablespoons capers
3 tablespoons red wine vinegar
1 teaspoon tarragon
½ cup crushed gingersnaps
2 cups beef broth
1 4-to-5 pound turkey, cut into
   serving pieces

1 tablespoon or more margarine or
   butter
1 tablespoon or more vegetable oil
2 cups chopped onions
1 garlic clove, minced
1 bay leaf
¼ teaspoon thyme
3 tablespoons chopped parsley

Put ginger and capers through food processor or electric blender. Add the vinegar and tarragon and blend again. Add the gingersnaps and blend again. Add 1 cup beef broth gradually.

Preheat oven at 325°F. (163°C.). In a skillet brown the turkey pieces in 1 tablespoon margarine or butter and 1 tablespoon vegetable oil, and transfer them to a top-of-stove casserole. In the same skillet brown the onions, adding more margarine or butter and vegetable oil if necessary. Add the garlic and toss for a minute. Add the onions and garlic to the casserole. Add the remaining 1 cup beef broth to the skillet and bring to boil, stirring to loosen brown particles on bottom of skillet. Pour into the casserole. Add the bay leaf, thyme and parsley to the casserole. Pour the gingersnap mixture over all. Place the casserole over heat and bring to simmer. Cover and place in the oven. Bake 1½ hours or until the thickest turkey part is tender when pierced with a sharp-tined fork, turning the turkey pieces after 45 minutes.

Makes 6 servings.

WATERZOOI OF TURKEY

4 tablespoons margarine or butter

3 medium size leeks, cut in julienne strips 2 to 3 inches long

3 medium size onions, cut in julienne strips 2 to 3 inches long

3 medium size carrots, cut in julienne strips 2 to 3 inches long

3 ribs celery, cut in julienne strips 2 to 3 inches long

1 4 to 4¾ pound turkey, cut into serving pieces and washed, but not dried

Salt

2 cups dry white wine

3 to 4 cups (approximately) chicken broth

½ teaspoon tarragon

6 egg yolks

1 cup heavy cream

Melt the margarine or butter over a low flame in a large heavy top-of-stove casserole. Add the leeks, onions, carrots, and celery, and cook, covered, 15 minutes, stirring and turning occasionally. Remove the vegetables from the casserole with a slotted spoon and set aside.

Preheat the oven at 325°F. (163°C.). Sprinkle turkey pieces lightly with salt and arrange in casserole. Cover and place over medium heat for 5 minutes. Turn the pieces over and arrange the reserved vegetables over them. Cover and place over heat again for 5 minutes. Neither the turkey pieces nor the vegetables should be allowed to brown. Pour in the wine and enough chicken broth to almost cover the turkey and vegetables. Add the tarragon and bring to simmer, covered.

Transfer the casserole to the oven and bake, covered, about 1¼ hours, or until the turkey pieces are tender when pierced with a sharp-tined fork, turning and rearranging the turkey pieces once during cooking. Remove casserole from oven and place over low heat.

Beat the egg yolks and stir in the cream. Add a cup of the hot broth from the casserole to the egg-cream mixture, a little at a time, stirring constantly. Then swirl the egg-cream mixture into the casserole. Taste and correct seasoning if necessary. Cook 4 or 5 minutes until slightly thickened, but do not allow to simmer.

Serve in soup bowls with knives, forks and soup spoons.

Makes 6 servings.

HALF TURKEY ON GOLDEN SAUERKRAUT BED

5 pounds sauerkraut or 3 1-pound-
11-ounce cans
3 cups chopped onions
1 cup (approximately) vegetable oil
½ cup chopped parsley
2 garlic cloves, minced
1 dried red chili, seeds removed,
chopped or crumbled

1 tablespoon paprika
½ cup margarine or butter
1 teaspoon salt
Freshly ground pepper to taste
1 cup or more turkey stock or
chicken broth
Half turkey weighing 5½ to 6
pounds

Place the sauerkraut in a colander and rinse under cold running water. Squeeze dry and set aside.

Preheat oven at 325°F. (163°C.). In a skillet sauté the onions in ½ cup vegetable oil until soft but not brown. Add the parsley, garlic, chili, paprika, and margarine or butter and stir until the margarine or butter is melted. Add the sauerkraut to the skillet, a handful at a time, stirring until well combined each time. Add the remaining oil, a few tablespoons at a time as necessary, and sauté until the sauerkraut is golden. Add the salt, pepper, and 1 cup turkey stock or chicken broth. Transfer the sauerkraut and liquid to a roasting pan just large enough to hold the turkey half comfortably. Set the turkey half on the sauerkraut, cut side down.

Bake 2 hours or until meat thermometer inserted in center of inside thigh muscle adjoining the body registers 180 to 185°F. (82 to 85°C.), or until tender when pierced with a sharp-tined fork, basting every 30 minutes with pan juices and adding more hot turkey stock or chicken broth, or boiling water, if necessary, to provide liquid for basting and prevent drying of the sauerkraut.

Arrange the sauerkraut on a heated serving platter. Set the turkey half on the bed of sauerkraut, cut side down. To serve, carve the turkey and serve some sliced turkey over a serving of sauerkraut on each plate.

Makes 10 or more servings.

MARMALADE-BAKED TURKEY HALF

Turkey half weighing about 6
  pounds
Salt
¼ cup melted margarine or butter
½ cup orange marmalade (bitter or
  sweet)

1 tablespoon cider vinegar
1 teaspoon chicken broth
  concentrate (if not available use
  a gravy seasoning such as Maggi)
Freshly ground pepper to taste

Preheat oven at 325°F. (163°C.). Wash and pat turkey half thoroughly dry with paper towels. Rub the cut side lightly with salt. Place the turkey half in a roasting pan, cut side down. Brush with melted margarine or butter. Roast 1 hour, brushing every 20 minutes with the melted margarine or butter.

Meanwhile melt the marmalade in a saucepan, stirring. Remove from heat and add the chicken broth concentrate, ½ teaspoon salt, and pepper. After the turkey half has roasted 1 hour and 20 minutes brush it with the marmalade mixture and pour half of the remaining marmalade mixture over the turkey half. Continue roasting, basting every 20 minutes with more of the marmalade mixture, adding the remaining marmalade mixture at the time of the final basting. When meat thermometer inserted in center of inside thigh muscle adjoining the body registers 180°F. (82°C.) or when tender when pierced with a sharp-tined fork, remove from oven and place on a wooden carving board. Allow to stand 15 to 20 minutes before carving.

Makes 6 to 8 servings.

TURKEY NORMANDY

1 6- to 7-pound turkey, cut into serving pieces
2 or more tablespoons vegetable oil
2 or more tablespoons margarine or butter
5 tart red apples
¼ cup chopped dried apricots
¼ cup chopped onions

1 teaspoon salt, or to taste
Freshly ground pepper to taste
Generous pinch of nutmeg
⅛ teaspoon cinnamon
1 cup turkey stock or chicken broth
¼ cup apricot brandy
½ cup heavy cream

Preheat oven at 325°F. (163°C.). Brown turkey pieces, a few at a time, in a large skillet in 1 tablespoon vegetable oil and 1 tablespoon margarine or butter, adding more vegetable oil or margarine or butter as necessary, and transferring the pieces, as browned, to a large casserole. Wash and core the apples and cut into eighths. Scatter them among the turkey pieces in the casserole. Sprinkle the chopped apricots and onions, salt, pepper, nutmeg, and cinnamon over the turkey and apples. Add the turkey stock or chicken broth and the apricot brandy to the skillet in which the turkey pieces were browned. Cook, stirring until mixture boils and all browned particles are loosened from skillet bottom. Pour over the turkey and cover the casserole.

Bake 1½ hours, or until the thickest turkey part is tender when pierced with a sharp-tined fork, basting every 30 minutes with the liquid in the casserole, and turning the turkey and apple pieces so that those on the top are transferred to the bottom during cooking. Remove the casserole from the oven and add the cream. Bring almost to simmer on low heat. Serve from casserole.

Makes 8 to 10 servings.

CHAMPAGNE TURKEY

3 pounds turkey thighs and drumsticks (if turkey legs are whole, cut them at the joint)
1¾ cup turkey stock or chicken broth
2 cups water
1 large slice of onion
1 teaspoon chervil
¼ teaspoon thyme
8 peppercorns
1 teaspoon salt, or to taste

¾ pound mushrooms, sliced
2 or more tablespoons butter or margarine
1 split of champagne
Freshly ground pepper to taste
1 cup half and half (milk and cream dairy product), scalded
¼ cup finely chopped parsley
2 tablespoons cornstarch combined with 2 tablespoons water

Place turkey pieces in a large saucepan, top-of-stove casserole, or Dutch oven. Add the turkey stock or chicken broth and water and bring slowly to boil, skimming until particles no longer rise to the surface. Add the onion slice, chervil, thyme, peppercorns, and ½ teaspoon salt if desired. Lower heat, cover, and simmer 1½ hours or until tender when pierced with a sharp-tined fork, turning pieces over after 45 minutes.

Remove turkey pieces from casserole. Pull off skin, remove turkey meat from bones, and remove tendons from drumsticks, discarding skin, bones and tendons. Cut the turkey meat into slices ¼ to ½-inch thick. Cut the slices into pieces about 1 inch square, or as close to 1 inch as possible. Set aside. Strain the broth from the casserole into a saucepan and boil down until it measures 1 cup.

In a skillet sauté the mushrooms in 2 tablespoons butter or margarine until lightly browned, adding more butter or margarine if necessary. Remove the mushrooms from the skillet with a slotted spoon. Add the boiled-down broth and the champagne to the skillet and bring to a simmer, scraping up brown particles from skillet bottom. Add ½ teaspoon salt, pepper, the half and half, and 2 tablespoons parsley, and again bring to simmer. Add the turkey pieces and the mushrooms and heat a minute or two. Add the cornstarch mixture and bring to simmer, stirring constantly, until thickened. Cook several minutes more, stirring, until well heated through. Taste and adjust seasoning if necessary. Turn into a shallow heated serving dish or into a chafing dish set over hot water. Sprinkle with the remaining 2 tablespoons parsley. Serve in heated serving dish, or if in chafing dish keep over hot water until ready to be served.

Makes 8 servings.

GARLIC-MARINATED BROILED TURKEY

If you tend the cooking carefully you can broil small turkey parts or a cut-up small turkey with good results. Constant basting and careful checking of internal temperature of the turkey pieces will give you juicy meat. Marinating gives an excellent flavor to broiled turkey and helps it to prebaste itself. Use either a small cut-up turkey from about four to seven pounds for broiling, or a selection of small turkey parts. While you can use any marinade you wish, or simply baste the turkey with vegetable oil while broiling, I think you'll find the following marinade (which was mentioned in Chapter 2 to be used for whole roasted unstuffed turkey) hard to beat.

¾ cup vegetable oil
⅓ cup lemon juice
1 tablespoon minced garlic
2 teaspoons salt
⅛ teaspoon freshly ground pepper

1 tablespoon paprika
1 teaspoon celery seed
4 or more pounds small turkey parts
   or a whole turkey cut into
   serving pieces

Combine all ingredients except the turkey in a small bowl. Pour the marinade over the turkey parts in a glass or ceramic bowl or shallow baking dish. Cover and refrigerate 24 to 32 hours, turning several times.

Set the broiler rack in the oven so that the tops of the turkey parts will be 3 inches from the heat when placed in the broiler. Preheat the broiler. Shake the excess marinade from the turkey piece. Crack the wings at the joints so they will not stick up into the heat source. Arrange the turkey pieces on the broiler rack. Broil, turning each piece and brushing it with the excess marinade every 5 minutes. Begin checking for doneness after about 25 minutes. Small wings or thin breast pieces may be done in this short a time. Wrap in aluminum foil to keep warm while the other pieces continue to broil. Some pieces may take as long as 40 to 45 minutes. To test for doneness insert an instant-reading thermometer into the thickest part of a turkey piece. Light meat should register 170 to 175°F. (77 to 79°C.) when done, and dark meat 180 to 185°F. (82 to 85°C.). If you don't have an instant-reading thermometer test with a sharp-tined fork and broil until tender. Be certain to turn every piece and brush it with marinade every 5 minutes. If you run out of marinade, which is unlikely, brush with plain vegetable oil.

Makes 6 or more servings.

WHITE WINE AND HERB-MARINATED TURKEY BREAST HALF OR HINDQUARTER

This is one of my favorite simple ways to roast turkey. You can use the versatile marinade as suggested in this recipe, or when roasting a whole unstuffed turkey. For the latter, see White Wine and Herb Marinade and Basting in the index for the method to follow.

½ cup vegetable oil
1 cup dry white wine
1 tablespoon thyme
1 tablespoon oregano
1 teaspoon fennel seeds
1 tablespoon salt

Freshly ground pepper to taste
1 2½ to 3 pound turkey breast half
   or turkey hindquarter
1 large onion, cut into eighths pie-
   fashion

Combine the vegetable oil, ½ cup wine, thyme, oregano, fennel seeds, salt, and pepper. Pour over the turkey breast half or hindquarter in a glass or ceramic baking dish or casserole. Cover and refrigerate 24 to 48 hours, turning several times and spooning the marinade over the turkey. Remove from the refrigerator 30 minutes before ready to cook.

Preheat oven at 325°F. (163°C.). Remove the turkey from the marinade and place it, skin side up, in a shallow roasting pan just large enough to fit. Roast for 20 minutes. Meanwhile add the remaining ½ cup wine to the marinade. Baste the turkey with the marinade. Roast another 20 minutes. Scatter the onions in the roasting pan around the turkey. Pour the remaining marinade over the turkey and the onions. Continue to roast, basting every 20 minutes, for total roasting time of 1½ hours, or until meat thermometer inserted in thickest part of turkey breast half registers 170 to 175°F. (77 to 79°C.), or until meat thermometer inserted in center of inside thigh muscle adjoining the body (if roasting a hindquarter) registers 180°F. (82°C.), or until tender when pierced with a sharp-tined fork.

Place the turkey on a wooden carving board and allow to stand 10 to 15 minutes. Meanwhile keep the onions in the roasting pan warm. To serve, slice the turkey and arrange the slices on a heated serving platter. Spoon the onions with a little of the pan juices over the slices.

Makes 6 or more servings.

5

Whole Turkey, Roast Turkey, and Splendid Stuffings

As for the turkey, which was our only roast, it was charming to look at, flattering to the sense of smell, and delicious to the taste. And as the last morsel of it disappeared, there arose from the whole table the words: "Very good! Exceedingly good! Oh! Dear sir, what a glorious bit!"
—JEAN ANTHELME BRILLAT-SAVARIN,
The Physiology of Taste

Americans love roast turkey, not just at holiday times but all year round, and have been known to become quite unhappy when deprived of it. This was as true two hundred years ago as it is today. According to a February 1771 entry in the diary of a young woman living on Long Island, her father wouldn't let her have a turkey roast for a supper to which she had invited her friends. She felt so bad about it she thought she'd never get over it.

Mexicans (who are also Americans) love roast turkey too and don't deprive themselves of it if they can help it. They're also the world's most inventive cooks at preparing turkey dishes of all kinds, as well they might be, since they've been at it for hundreds of years. Turkey is considered a dietary staple in many areas of Mexico as well as a holiday meat all over the nation. It's not unusual in residential areas of modern Mexico City to see a few turkeys walking around a yard, and just before Christmas it's a common sight to see tethered turkeys everywhere waiting to become part of festive dinners.

In spite of tradition, all whole turkeys don't have to be roasted in the oven. Neither do they have to be stuffed. They don't even have to be served hot. There are other ways to cook them that include steaming, spit roasting, braising, and outdoor kettle cooking, and all these methods are covered in this chapter. But, since roast turkey is such an all-time favorite, we'll start first with directions for all the steps in stuffing, trussing, timing, carving, and serving the beautiful bird. Then we'll proceed to the recipes that include other cooking methods.

You can buy whole turkeys three ways—frozen, fresh (sometimes referred to as fresh-chilled), and fresh killed (live poultry that's killed and cleaned on the spot). Please read Chapter 2 which discussed each type, and also gives information on what to look for when you buy a turkey, how to store it, and how to thaw it if it's a frozen bird. Cooking directions are the same for all turkeys once the frozen ones have thawed or the fresh killed ones have come out of rigor (twelve or more hours after killing).

Roast Turkey

What Size Turkey To Buy

There are so many variables to consider that you can't predetermine the ideal size turkey to buy for a given number of people. This is true for a number of reasons; the first is how many real portions you need compared to the number of guests. Some people eat a small portion, while others eat a large one and come back for seconds or thirds. The majority of people at a particular dinner may like light meat, or they may prefer dark meat, so that you may run out of one before the other with a bird that you thought was just the right size. You may also want to be sure to have lots of leftovers for making other dishes, or you may want to freeze some for future eating, in which case you'd want to buy a really generous size turkey.

All things considered, it's fairly safe to say that, on the average, ¾ pound of turkey per serving is a good rule of thumb. If the turkey is under 12 pounds, you should increase the figure to nearer 1 pound per serving, and if it's over 12 pounds, figure a little less than ¾ pound per serving because the amount of meat in relation to bone increases with the size of the turkey. Remember too that cooking your turkey properly, so that it doesn't dry out and shrink, will increase the number of servings, as will the proper carving of the bird. The drumsticks and thighs, for instance, should be cut into serving slices, as discussed later on in this chapter, rather than being distributed as single servings. Slicing drumsticks and thighs also makes for a fairer distribution of dark meat. With these thoughts in mind you can use the following as a general guide for numbers of servings (not numbers of persons), keeping in mind that this doesn't allow for any leftovers.

Number of Servings	Weight of Ready-to-cook Turkey
6 to 10	6 to 8 lbs.
10 to 15	8 to 10 lbs.
15 to 20	10 to 12 lbs.
20 to 26	12 to 14 lbs.
26 to 32	14 to 16 lbs.
32 to 40	16 to 20 lbs.
40 to 50	20 to 24 lbs.

How to Prepare the Turkey for Roasting

Having purchased the turkey and thawed it if frozen, or after waiting the necessary twelve hours or more if it's fresh-killed, you're now ready to proceed with the roasting. Remove the giblets and the neck from the neck cavity and the body cavity. Wash them under cold running water, dry them, set them on a plate, cover, and refrigerate until you're ready to use them. Although they're pretty scarce on the turkeys you buy these days, you may see a stray pinfeather or two on the bird, which you'll want to remove. Use a strawberry huller or pinfeather picker, or a pair of tweezers for the operation.

Wash the body cavity, neck cavity, and outside of the turkey under cold running water. Put a raised wire rack in the sink to rest the turkey on so that you don't have to hold the weight of the turkey while rinsing it out, and to keep the bird out of direct contact with the sink. Drain out the water and pat the turkey thoroughly dry, inside and out, with paper towels. Rub salt lightly in the body and neck openings. The bird is now ready to stuff. If you plan to roast the bird unstuffed you can put a few pieces of onion and celery, or apple halves or peeled orange in the neck and body cavities. Or you may wish to marinate the turkey. Recipes for this are included in this chapter. If you're roasting the turkey unstuffed skip the following paragraphs up to "How To Truss the Turkey."

How Much Stuffing to Allow for a Roast Turkey

A good rule of thumb in figuring the amount of stuffing that will go into the neck and body cavities of a turkey is a generous half cup per pound of bird. While you repeatedly see articles and cookbooks that instruct you to use 1 cup of stuffing per pound of bird, you'll find it's impossible to get that much into the creature. Twelve cups of stuffing, for instance, can't be put into a twelve pound turkey unless you drive it in with a mallet.

After a turkey reaches the weight of approximately 12 pounds, as it grows larger its body cavity does not get proportionally larger, so you will not have twice as large a body cavity in a 24 pound turkey as in a 12 pound one. This is because the breast and thighs get larger and larger, but the bone structure changes only a little.

For this reason you will find that a 21-pound bird, for example, will not take the expected 10½ cups of stuffing, but closer to eight cups.

The word to keep in mind when filling a turkey with stuffing is "loose." Don't pack tightly at all. You want to end up with a just moist or even slightly dry flavorful stuffing, not a sodden mass.

Actually there isn't any need to worry about how much stuffing to prepare, and in most cases it's really nice to make more than you need for the turkey itself. After the bird is stuffed, see how much is left over, select a nice covered casserole of the proper size (even if it's just one cup), grease it well, and put the extra stuffing in it. Bake it, covered, from about 45 minutes to an hour, toward the end of the turkey roasting time. But take a look at it after the first 30 minutes and then every 15 minutes and only bake it until you like the way it looks. Stuffing baked in a casserole is a little drier than the same stuffing cooked in the bird, and is crunchy on top. Many people prefer it to the stuffing cooked in the bird. So you may choose to put all the "stuffing" in a large casserole and bake it separately rather than put any of it in the turkey.

Another way to use extra stuffing is to fill hollowed-out tomatoes or green peppers with it and bake them along with the turkey. You'll need to make sure, of course, that the stuffing flavor doesn't clash with the flavor of the vegetable.

If you can't decide on which stuffing to make for the turkey you can give everyone an extra treat by making two different kinds. One can go inside the bird and the other into a casserole.

Please note that all the stuffing recipes in this book make enough for any size bird up to about 22 pounds. As already mentioned, since there are not tremendous differences in the sizes of the body cavities of turkeys, make any stuffing recipe for any size bird, stuff the bird loosely, and bake the remaining stuffing, if any, in a greased covered casserole.

How to Stuff the Turkey

Just before you're ready to put the turkey into the oven is the time to stuff it. Don't do it the night before, and never stuff a turkey and then freeze it. If you know that you'll be pressed for time when it comes to getting the turkey into the oven, you can speed things along by having all the stuffing ingredients fixed ahead of time. For instance, if you'll be needing a cup of chopped onions and a cup of chopped celery, chop them and store them in covered glass jars in the refrigerator overnight so they're ready to work with when you need them.

Spoon some stuffing loosely into the neck cavity. Pull the neck skin to the back of the turkey, turn it under neatly if there is sufficient skin to do so, and secure the skin of the back with a poultry pin or small skewer.

For ease in stuffing the body cavity, place the turkey, neck end down, in a large bowl. Spoon in the stuffing loosely and shake the turkey by the drumsticks once or twice during the operation.

How to Truss the Turkey

The purpose of trussing a turkey is to make the bird as compact as possible so that it will roast evenly throughout and not dry out. There are two methods for doing this, one with a trussing needle and string, and the other without.

Method 1—No Strings. If you wish, trim the pointed ends off the wingtips with a sharp knife or cleaver. Twist the wing tips behind the shoulder joints so that the turkey rests with wings akimbo and will not rock around when you put it into the roating pan. If the turkey is equipped with a metal trussing wire in the body cavity opening, slip the ends of the legs, one at a time, under the wire. If this is difficult to do, push the drumstick straight back toward the neck so that the leg bends at the joint, and then slip the leg under the wire. If the turkey has a band of skin at the body cavity opening, tuck the ends of the legs, one at a time, under the band. Leave the tail loose.

Method 2—With Trussing Needle (See illustrations). Thread a trussing needle (a 12-inch one is ideal) with a long piece of soft strong twine and make a knot at the eye. Trim the pointed ends off the wingtips with a sharp knife or cleaver if desired. Twist the wing tips behind the shoulder joints. Keep the turkey on its back. Lift a drumstick and push the needle through at the joint of the thigh and drumstick. Continue to push the needle straight through the body and through the leg on the opposite side at the same point as the first leg. Turn the turkey over on its breast. Push the needle through the flesh of the second joint of the wing on the same side of the turkey. Remove poultry pin or skewer holding the neck

HOW TO TRUSS A TURKEY WITH A TRUSSING NEEDLE

Pushing the needle through at the joint of the thigh and drumstick, through the body, and through the leg on the opposite side at the same point as the first leg

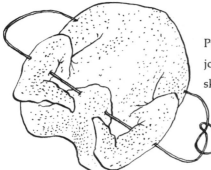

Pushing the needle through the second joint of the wing, neck skin and back skin, and second joint of the other wing

Needle pushed through lower back near tail and skin at tip of breast, before tightening string

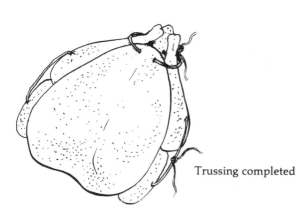

Trussing completed

skin, and run the trussing needle through the neck skin and the back skin, then through the flesh of the second joint of the other wing. Pull the string up tightly and tie a double knot. Trim off the ends of the string.

Now push the needle straight across through the lower back near the tail. Push the needle through the skin at the tip of the breast. Pull the string up tightly, enclosing the ends of the drumsticks. Tie tightly with a double knot. Trim off the ends of the string. Leave the tail loose.

Regardless of which trussing method you've used, place the turkey, breast side up, into a roasting pan. If you wish you may place the bird on a rack in the roasting pan, but I have found no advantage in roasting a turkey on a rack. If you use a rack, the back of the turkey does not brown. Replace any stuffing that may have fallen from the body cavity during trussing. Brush the turkey all over with melted margarine or butter or other basting liquid, or according to recipe directions. Place in preheated 325°F. (163°C.) oven.

Roasting Methods

The most satisfactory method of roasting a turkey is in an uncovered roasting pan, with or without a rack, according to preference. The turkey should be roasted without a lid, which makes for a nice crisp skin. If the turkey is covered with a lid it is, essentially, being braised rather than roasted. This is a good method for cooking turkey, particularly a wild turkey, which does not have the fat that a domestic turkey has. But it is not a roast turkey, and any recipe using this method is treated as braised turkey in this book.

I haven't included any instructions for roasting turkey in a brown paper bag. Brown paper bags were not designed to be used as cooking vessels, and no paper bag manufacturer lists the materials used to make the bag nor do they suggest the use of bags in cooking. Since there is no way to know if any harmful substance that may be in the paper may permeate the turkey or its juices during cooking, I choose not to experiment with the method. If you want to roast a turkey in paper, I suggest that as an alternative to a brown paper bag you use white parchment paper that's made for kitchen use. (See recipe for Parchment-Roasted Turkey in this chapter.)

Wrapping a turkey completely in aluminum foil in order to roast it produces a bird that is more braised or stewed than roasted, and the skin and flesh tend to split on the breast and thighs. However, aluminum foil is very useful and, in fact, almost indispensable in roasting in an open pan. After the turkey has browned sufficiently it's advisable to construct a loose aluminum foil tent, shiny side out, to place over the bird. Remove it when basting, and replace. This keeps the breast, which is generally cooked well ahead of the thighs, from becoming too brown or from drying out. You can also wrap the ends of the drumsticks in foil to keep them from browning too much.

While it wouldn't occur to many people to roast a turkey in the plastic wrapping in which it comes, it has been done. But the result is a turkey which is more boiled or stewed in its own juice than roasted, so this method certainly isn't recommended. However, the turkey industry is working on film overwraps in which turkeys can be roasted, and one such wrapping will dissolve during the roasting and completely disappear by the time the turkey is done. Turkeys in this kind of wrapping will have to be cooked from the frozen state. Whether or not this is an invention to be welcomed by good cooks remains to be seen.

If you have a very large clay baker, you can roast a small turkey in it. It will produce a tender turkey, but it will not be brown. Follow the recipe for Clay Baker Turkey Breast with Veggies (see index), omitting the green beans, tomatoes, and mushrooms if you wish.

About Thermometers and Testing for Doneness

There are two types of thermometers you can use for roasting turkey or any other meat. One is the tiny Instant-Reading Thermometer. This is by far the nicest thermometer one can have for roasting and many other cooking purposes. Its stem is very thin and when inserted in the turkey gives an accurate reading in a few seconds. When using a gas or electric oven this thermomenter is left neither in the turkey, nor in the oven. It's used only to take a reading and then taken out again. This thermometer is sometimes called a Microwave Thermometer, and when used in a microwave oven can be left in the turkey. The advantages of this thermometer with the thin stem are that it does not leave a large hole in the meat and does not conduct heat to the inside of the meat. Readings can also be taken in more than one spot if you wish.

The other type of thermometer to use in testing how well done a roasting turkey is, is the standard meat thermometer. It has a wider, thicker stem than the instant-reading type. The thermometer is inserted in the turkey and left in the oven throughout the roasting. While its thick stem may account for a slight loss of juice from the turkey, this instrument will give you the information you want.

The best place to insert a thermometer in a turkey is the inner part of the thigh, in its center, but without touching the bone. This is the last part of the turkey to cook through, so you can be sure when it's done, the rest of the turkey is too. When the thermometer inserted in this part of the thigh registers 180° to 185°F. (82 to 85°C.), remove the turkey from the oven immediately.

Some turkeys have small built-in meat thermometers inserted in them. These little gadgets are designed to pop up when the internal temperature of the turkey is 180 to 185°F. (82 to 85°C.). Due to the fact that the thermometer is inserted in the breast and that the breast meat roasts faster than the thigh, it's advisable to test the thigh, too.

If you don't own a meat thermometer (although everyone will find it worthwhile to invest in an instant-reading instrument), test the turkey with a sharp-tined fork on the inner part of the thigh. The turkey should be done when this spot feels fork-tender to you. Some people roast their turkeys until the legs move freely, but it's more likely that if you roast them that long they'll be dry and overdone.

The time chart for roasting turkey shown below gives a general idea of the length of time it will take to roast stuffed turkeys. Unstuffed birds take a little less time, up to about 30 minutes less, to roast. Whether you use this chart or not, do use a meat thermometer if you have one, or test with a fork as described above. No chart can tell you exactly when your turkey will be done. Most charts printed on turkey wrappers and in newspaper articles give excessive roasting times, so they're best ignored. A 12-pound turkey, for example, which is one of the most popular sizes, is often shown to require 4½ or more hours, at which point it would be dried out and certainly not at its best. Here are more realistic times for turkeys:

Weight of Ready-to-Cook Turkey	Roasting Time at 325°F. (163°C.) for Stuffed Turkey
6 to 8 lbs.	1¾ to 2 hrs.
8 to 12 lbs.	2 to 2½ hrs.
12 to 14 lbs.	2½ to 3 hrs.
14 to 16 lbs.	3 to 3½ hrs.
16 to 20 lbs.	3½ to 4 hrs.
over 20 lbs.	4 or more hrs.

Basting During Cooking

The turkey should be basted during roasting every 20 minutes, either with one of the following basting liquids or whatever an individual recipe may call for.

BASTING LIQUIDS FOR ROAST TURKEY

FOR STUFFED TURKEYS:

Margarine or Butter—¼ to ½ cup, melted. Amount needed will depend on the size of the turkey.

Salt Water Basting—This is an old fashioned basting method that gives the turkey skin a mildly salty taste and an unusual texture.

5 teaspoons salt	**Flour**
1 cup hot water	**2 tablespoons melted butter or margarine**

Combine the salt and hot water. When the turkey is ready to go into the oven, brush it all over with the salt water. Roast 1 hour and 20 minutes, brushing every 20 minutes with the salt water. At the time of the last brushing, dust the turkey all over lightly with flour. This is done most easily by putting the flour in a shaker or a small fine strainer and shaking it over the turkey. Then brush all over with the melted butter or margarine and roast 20 minutes longer. Brush again and baste with pan drippings. Continue basting with pan drippings every 20 minutes until turkey has finished roasting.

Lemon Butter—½ cup melted margarine or butter combined with ⅓ cup lemon juice. For a small bird use ¼ cup melted margarine or butter and 2½ tablespoons lemon juice.

Vegetable Oil—Brush turkey with vegetable oil for three bastings, and thereafter baste with pan drippings.

FOR UNSTUFFED TURKEYS:

Any of the above bastings may be used, or one of the following:

GARLIC MARINADE AND BASTING

¾ cup vegetable oil	**⅛ teaspoon freshly ground pepper**
⅓ cup lemon juice	**1 tablespoon paprika**
1 tablespoon minced garlic	**1 teaspoon celery seed**
2 teaspoons salt	

Combine all ingredients and brush all over exterior of turkey and generously inside the neck opening and body cavity. Place remaining marinade in a glass jar, seal tightly, and refrigerate. Cover the turkey with aluminum foil or plastic wrap, set on a plate, and refrigerate 24 to 32 hours, turning several times. Roast, following general roasting directions, and brush with remaining marinade, using all marinade by the third basting.

MARMALADE BASTING

Follow directions for Marmalade Baked Turkey Half (see index), rubbing salt inside the turkey neck opening and body cavity rather than on the cut side of the turkey half.

WHITE WINE AND HERB MARINADE AND BASTING

½ cup vegetable oil
1 cup dry white wine
1 tablespoon of thyme
1 tablespoon oregano

1 teaspoon fennel seeds
1 tablespoon salt
Freshly ground pepper to taste
1 onion, cut in quarters

Combine the vegetable oil, ½ cup wine, thyme, oregano, fennel seeds, salt, and pepper. Brush all over the outside of the turkey and inside the neck opening and body cavity. Cover turkey with aluminum foil or plastic wrap, set on a plate, and refrigerate 24 hours. Roast, following general roasting directions, with one onion piece inserted in the neck opening and the remaining onion pieces inside the body cavity. Add the remaining wine to the roasting pan after the second basting.

CUMBERLAND BASTING

Baste turkey with melted margarine or butter until last 40 minutes of roasting. Then baste at 20 minute intervals with purchased Cumberland Sauce or with the basting in the recipe for Kettle Cooker Cumberland Basted Turkey (see index).

For even browning use a brush to apply the basting ingredients to the turkey for the first two or three bastings. After that there will be enough pan juices, and the turkey will have enough of an even coating to use a bulb baster for the remainder of the roasting time.

If you wish, you can place a clean white cloth or a double thickness of cheesecloth, dipped into the basting liquid, over the turkey, and then baste directly over the cloth during the roasting. With this method you won't find it necessary to use an aluminum foil tent. The cloth should be removed toward the end of the roasting for a final browning. Either the cloth or the aluminum foil tent will prevent overbrowning and drying of the breast.

While the Turkey is Roasting

While the turkey's in the oven, cook the giblets (unless you want them for another use) so that you can cut them up and have them ready to use in Classic Giblet Gravy or in Giblet Stuffing Balls, (see recipes in this chapter). Of course, you may prefer to include the giblets in the stuffing ingredients of the turkey, whether the stuffing recipe calls for them or not, in which case you'd have to cook and chop them before the turkey is put into the oven. For directions on how to cook the giblets see the recipe for Classic Giblet Gravy.

When the Turkey is Done

After you have removed the roasted bird from the oven, take it from the pan and place it on a wooden carving board to cool for 15 to 20 minutes before carving. This will make the meat juicier and the carving easier.

While the turkey is standing, make pan gravy or giblet gravy (see recipes that follow), or, if you prefer, simply keep the pan juices warm and spoon them over the turkey slices after you've carved the bird. Spoon off any excess fat in the juices before serving.

Carving the Turkey

It's great fun to know how to carve a turkey properly, and if you don't know how to do it, you'll find it a very satisfying thing to learn. Everyone admires a good carver, and it does seem to lend a certain gracious atmosphere to a gathering when a good carver is performing. If you're a woman don't wait for a man to do the carving, but learn to do it yourself just as you've probably learned how to select wines, once both inviolable male rights. People often shy from carving or regard it as an onerous task simply because they don't know how to go about it properly. The way to start is with good tools and a general knowledge of a turkey's anatomy.

TOOLS OF THE TRADE

Carving Knife. A good knife is the key to proper turkey carving. You need a knife with a semi-flexible straight (not serrated) 8- to 10-inch blade, ending in a V shape. The knife should be thin and have a good quality blade that will take a good edge. A fine stainless steel knife is ideal. Carbon steel knives are fine, but they tend to discolor the meat and must be wiped clean during the carving.

Steel or Knife Sharpeners. Always make sure the knife is sharp before starting to carve. It can be sharpened with a steel, an electric sharpener, or a sharpener that consists of a series of hard steel discs through which the knife is drawn. The latter two methods are quite satisfactory but do wear the blade down a little. The terms sometimes used for making the knife edge sharp with a steel are "resetting" or "trueing" the blade, since the steel doesn't actualy "sharpen" a knife. In any case, to use a steel hold it in your left hand (assuming you're right handed; if not, do the reverse) horizontally slanted away from you, with your thumb on top. Hold the knife in your right hand with the point up. Place the heel of the blade (part near the handle) underneath the tip of the steel at about a 20° angle. Draw the blade from the heel to the point, drawing it toward you across the steel, using light pressure. Then place the heel of the blade on top of the tip of the steel, and use the same motion in drawing the blade along the steel. Repeat for a total of about five times on each side. Do this every time before you use the knife. Just a quick word about knife care; don't put the knife into water. To preserve the quality of the blade wash the knife under hot running water with soap, rinse, and dry as soon after using the knife as possible.

Other Utensils. The other equipment you'll need to work with are a two-tined fork (preferably with long tines and a guard) for holding the

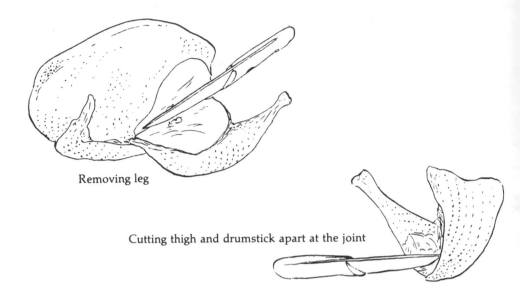

Removing leg

Cutting thigh and drumstick apart at the joint

turkey, a wooden carving board on which to do the carving, and a warm platter on which to lay the slices of meat you carve. Don't try to carve on the platter because you'll hurt the knife edge if you hit it against the platter and probably scratch the surface of the platter as well. You'll find yourself cramped for space, too, if you try to carve the bird while it's on the platter.

CARVING

You can use either the Standard Style of carving, with the turkey on its back, or the Side Method, with the bird on its side.

Standard Style. (See illustrations) Place the carving board in front of you with the turkey resting on its back and its legs pointing to your right. Carve only on one side of the turkey at a time. Begin by removing the leg nearest you. Insert the fork into the leg, or place it astride the keel bone (breast bone), whichever feels more comfortable to you. Make a cut in front of the thigh downward to the joint that holds it to the backbone. Then make another cut in back of the thigh downward to the joint. Cut between the leg and the thigh and remove the leg. Put down the fork and grasp the end of the leg with a napkin and bend it toward you and down to remove it. If necessary use the fork to help pry the leg loose at the joint. Lay the leg down, brown side down, and cut the thigh and drum-

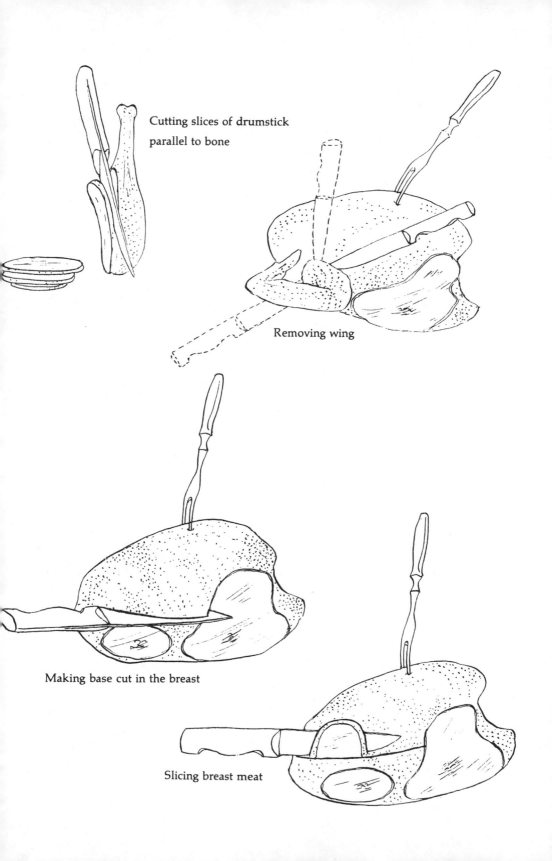

Cutting slices of drumstick
parallel to bone

Removing wing

Making base cut in the breast

Slicing breast meat

stick apart at the joint, cutting at an angle. Insert the fork in the thigh and cut slices of thigh meat parallel to the bone. Arrange the slices on a heated platter. Insert the fork in the drumstick and cut slices parallel to the bone, arranging them on the platter with the thigh slices. Don't be concerned about getting all the meat off the bones. It can be salvaged later in the kitchen.

Next remove the wing. The wing joint is more firmly attached to the body than the leg joint. Insert the fork in the keel bone and make a small cut in front of the wing or shoulder joint. Make another cut in back of the shoulder joint to meet the first cut at the joint. Make a third cut under the wing to the joint, turning the knife inward toward the front of the shoulder. Insert the fork at the joint and push out to remove the wing. Place the wing, brown side down, on the carving board. Cut it apart at the joints, setting aside the wing tip, and arrange the remaining wing sections on the platter. If the turkey is very large you may want to divide the meat from the larger of the two wing sections.

Now slice off the breast meat. Hold the fork astride the keel bone. Holding the knife parallel to the carving board near the bottom of the breast, make a straight cut all the way through to the ribs. This is the base cut, and most of the breast slices you cut will stop at this cut. Starting at the front end of the turkey, slice the breast meat downward in long thin slices, ending at the base cut. Slice a little higher with each succeeding slice until there is no more breast at the front end. Then slice the back portion of the breast. Arrange the slices on the platter with the dark meat as you cut them.

If you are serving the turkey yourself, place one or two slices of breast meat, depending on the size of the slices, and one slice of dark meat onto each heated plate. If more turkey is needed repeat the entire carving proceedure on the opposite side of the turkey.

Don't forget that the best part of the turkey is still on the carcass—the "oysters," the meaty little circular morsels on either side of the backbone near the thighs. If anyone asks for them, find an excuse not to remove them. Savor them later in the kitchen. They're your reward for carving the turkey so beautifully.

Side Method. (See illustrations) If you're nervous about knives this method may not be for you, since some of the carving is done toward you. But if you're sure of yourself and have a good sharp knife, you may prefer this method. It's easier to carve the leg meat this way, and with practice, you can carve the breast quickly by this method.

Place the turkey on its side, with the breast away from you, onto the carving board. Using a napkin, hold the wing that's near you with the left hand and cut the wing at the second joint. Place on the carving board and cut off the wing tip and set aside. Put the other wing section on a heated serving platter.

SIDE METHOD OF CARVING

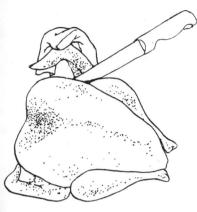

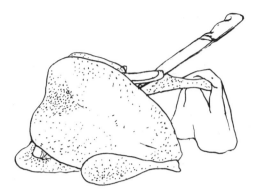

Cutting the wing at the second joint

Slicing meat off the drumstick and thigh

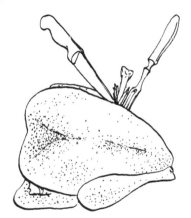

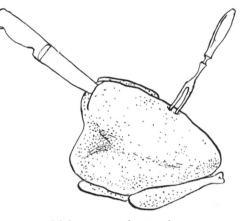

Drumstick lifted to be cut
off at thigh joint

Making vertical cut in breast
in front of the wing joint
(the base cut)

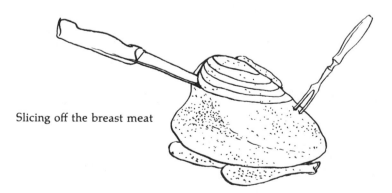

Slicing off the breast meat

HOW TO CARVE A TURKEY
AND PUT IT BACK TOGETHER AGAIN

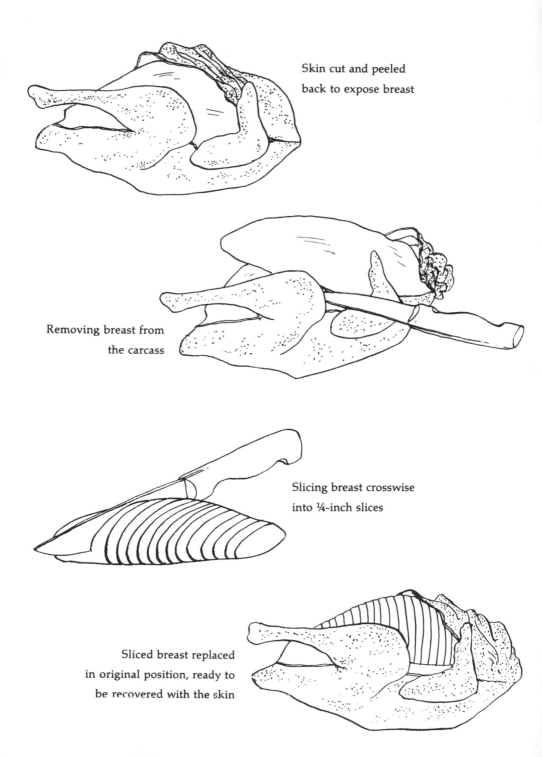

Skin cut and peeled
back to expose breast

Removing breast from
the carcass

Slicing breast crosswise
into ¼-inch slices

Sliced breast replaced
in original position, ready to
be recovered with the skin

Next, holding the drumstick with the napkin, slice the meat off the drumstick and thigh until the thigh bone is exposed. Arrange the slices on the platter with the wing section. Lift the drumstick and cut it off at the thigh joint. Cut the remaining meat off the drumstick and arrange on the platter. Using the long-tined fork instead of the napkin, insert the fork into the turkey to steady the bird and run the knife point completely around the thigh bone to loosen it. Pry up with the fork and pull the thigh bone out. Slice the thigh meat that remains on the turkey and arrange it on the platter. When all thigh meat has been cut away you will have worked down to the "oyster" at the side of the backbone. Lift it out.

Now slice off the breast meat. Holding the turkey steady with the fork, make a deep vertical cut in the breast just in front of the wing joint, as far as you can cut. This is the base cut, and most of the breast slices you cut will stop at this cut. Starting from the center of the breast cutting toward you, cut large thin slices toward the base cut. Arrange the slices on the platter with the dark meat.

If you are serving the turkey yourself, place one or two slices of breast meat, depending on the size of the slices, and one slice of dark meat, onto each heated plate. If more turkey is needed, turn the bird over on its other side and repeat the entire carving procedure. Finally, remove the remaining wing sections and any remaining breast meat.

OTHER CARVING METHODS FOR DIFFERENT PURPOSES

Kitchen carving. If you've cooked a whole turkey and want to carve it to use the meat for various purposes, or if you simply prefer to do your cutting up in the kitchen, the following method, which is often used in commercial kitchens, will help you to utilize each part of the bird to best advantage.

You'll use a boning knife, rather than a carving knife, for the major part of this carving. Place the turkey on its side on a wooden carving board. Holding the wing with your left hand make a circular cut around the wing joint to open up the bone socket. Cut closely around the shoulder joint to leave the most white meat possible remaining on the breast. Twist the wing in the socket, cut the tendons at the joint, and remove the entire wing. Set aside.

Next remove the leg. Holding the end of the drumstick with your left hand cut the skin between the body and the thigh, and pull the leg outward and downward to free the hip joint. Using the tip of the knife loosen the thigh meat, including the "oyster" in back of the thigh next to the backbone. Cut the skin along the back and separate the drumstick and thigh. Remove the thigh bone.

Next remove the entire breast sections, one at a time. Slide the knife down along one side of the keel bone from one end to the other, working toward the breastbone area. Continue cutting to the shoulder joint following the curve of the wishbone. Then continue cutting over the ribs from the underside of the wing socket joint, back to the beginning. Put your fingers down into the cut along the keel bone and gently ease the breast outward, lifting away from the bone in one piece, using the knife to loosen any meat that sticks to the bone. Repeat the entire procedure on the other side of the turkey. Slice or use each part of the meat as desired.

Carving a turkey and putting it back together again. (See illustrations) You might want to serve a turkey this way for a buffet or for a special presentation at the table. It arrives looking uncarved, when in fact, the breast meat is completely sliced, covered by the skin, and put back on the turkey ready to serve. There are two drawbacks you should be aware of before deciding on this method. The first is that the legs and wings don't get carved at all, unless you want to carve them after presenting the roast. The second is that the turkey has to be cold before you carve it in order to keep the skin from shrinking. Therefore, you'll be serving cold turkey. Unless you serve it right away after cooling and carving, you'll have to refrigerate it until serving time to prevent the possibility of food spoilage.

Here's how to do the carving. Using a sharp boning knife, cut through the skin only, starting at the base of the wishbone and cutting across to the wing, going around the wing, across the bottom, and up over the top of the hip joint where the thigh joins the body, and to the rear, Loosen the skin at the rear of the bird and peel it back carefully until the entire breast is exposed, but do not detach the skin. The next step is to separate the breast meat from the carcass. Do this by cutting along the top of the keel bone toward the breast bone, and continue to cut out the breast meat following the contour of the body. Cut across horizontally near the bottom of the breast and remove the breast in one piece. This should leave a little ledge of meat against which to brace the slices when you put them back on the carcass.

Next slice the breast meat crosswise into slices ¼ inch thick, keeping the slices in order.

Repeat the entire operation with the other side of the breast. Reassemble the slices and place them back on the carcass in the original positions on each side of the breast bone. Pull the skin back carefully over the carved breast meat. If necessary, secure with a toothpick or two. If desired, decorate the turkey with parsley sprigs. You may also wish to use spiced crabapples or similar edible decorations for winter holiday occasions.

CLASSIC GIBLET GRAVY

You can use this recipe not only for making giblet gravy, but also for cooking giblets that you want to use for other purposes. If you aren't making gravy, omit the cornstarch and Port wine, and follow the directions in the first two paragraphs only.

Giblets and neck from 1 turkey	1 rib celery with leaves, cut into
6 to 8 cups cold water	several pieces
2 teaspoons salt	1 carrot, scraped and cut in half
4 or 5 peppercorns	Half an onion
1 bay leaf	3 or 4 tablespoons cornstarch
¼ teaspoon thyme	½ cup Port wine
½ teaspoon rosemary	

Wash giblets and neck under cold running water. Place in a saucepan with enough water to cover well. Bring to a boil, skimming off particles as they rise to the surface. When particles no longer rise to the surface add salt, peppercorns, bay leaf, thyme, rosemary, celery, carrot, and the onion. Lower heat, cover, and simmer 1½ hours with lid slightly ajar, removing the liver from the saucepan after 15 minutes. Cool and cut the liver into small pieces. Cover and refrigerate while continuing to simmer the remaining giblets.

After 1½ hours remove the giblets from the broth. Strain the broth and discard the vegetables. Cut the heart and gizzard into small pieces, discarding any membrane or gristle. If the giblets are too hot to handle, hold them with a fork while cutting them up. Pull the meat from the turkey neck and shred it. Add the meat and the giblets to the strained broth, along with the cut-up liver.

Cool and refrigerate the broth unless the turkey is going to be removed from the oven within about half an hour. (Bacteria builds up quickly in broth left standing at room temperature.) When the turkey has been removed from the roasting pan, skim off as much fat as possible from the drippings and discard. Add the turkey broth with the giblets to the roasting pan. Set over medium heat and cook, stirring to loosen all brown particles from the pan bottom, until mixture comes to a simmer. Add 3 tablespoons cornstarch combined with the Port wine and cook, stirring constantly, until thickened slightly. If a thicker gravy is desired, mix another tablespoon of cornstarch with a tablespoon or two of cold water and add to the gravy, continuing to stir until thickened further. Taste the gravy and adjust the seasoning if necessary. Simmer a few minutes, or until the turkey is ready to be carved, stirring often. Serve in a heated sauce boat.

Makes about 6 cups.

TURKEY PAN GRAVY

This is a flavorful alternative to Classic Giblet Gravy, if you choose to keep the giblets for some other use.

Roast turkey pan containing
  drippings
4 cups turkey stock or chicken
  broth
1 teaspoon celery salt, or to taste
Freshly ground pepper to taste

Generous pinch of thyme
¼ teaspoon marjoram
1 tablespoon snipped chives
3 tablespoons cornstarch combined
  with ¼ cup Port or Madeira wine

Remove any excess fat from the roasting pan. Add the turkey stock or chicken broth to the roasting pan, along with the celery salt, pepper, thyme, marjoram, and chives and bring to boil, stirring to loosen all browned particles on pan bottom. Add the cornstarch mixture and cook, stirring constantly, until thickened. If not thick enough add another tablespoon of cornstarch mixed with a tablespoon of cold water or stock and cook, stirring, until thickened. Taste and adjust seasoning if necessary. Reduce heat and allow to simmer, stirring often, 10 to 15 minutes. Serve in heated sauce boat.

GIBLET STUFFING BALLS

Giblets and neck from 1 turkey
4 cups cold water
1 teaspoon salt
6 peppercorns
1 rib celery, cut up
1 carrot, scraped and cut in half
Half an onion
½ teaspoon plus ⅛ teaspoon thyme
1 bay leaf
½ teaspoon rosemary

⅛ teaspoon nutmeg
3 tablespoons chopped parsley
1 teaspoon grated lemon zest
Freshly ground pepper to taste
⅛ teaspoon marjoram
2 eggs, lightly beaten
4 cups moist breadcrumbs
2 tablespoons or more margarine or
  butter

Place neck and giblets in a saucepan with the cold water. Bring to boil, skimming, until particles no longer rise to the surface. Add the salt, peppercorns, celery, carrot, onion, ½ teaspoon thyme, bay leaf, and rosemary. Cover and simmer 1½ hours with lid slightly ajar, removing the liver after 15 minutes and refrigerating it, covered.

Remove neck and giblets after 1½ hours. Strain the broth and discard the vegetables. Cut the liver, heart, and gizzard up finely. Remove the meat from the neck and shred it.

Combine the giblets and neck meat with the nutmeg, parsley, lemon zest, pepper, remaining ⅛ teaspoon thyme, marjoram, and eggs. Add the breadcrumbs and mix well. Add some of the broth, 2 tablespoons at a time, until the mixture holds together. Divide into 16 equal parts, and form each into a ball in the palms of your hands.

Sauté the stuffing balls slowly in a skillet in the margarine or butter until nicely browned all over, adding more margarine or butter as necessary. Reserve remaining broth for another use.

Makes 16 balls.

OLD FASHIONED BREAD STUFFING

½ cup plus 2 tablespoons margarine
  or butter
¼ to ½ pound mushrooms, sliced
1½ cups chopped onions
¼ cup chopped parsley and celery
  leaves combined
½ teaspoon sage

1 teaspoon thyme
⅛ teaspoon mace
1 teaspoon salt
Freshly ground pepper to taste
10 cups crumbled white bread
  crumbs made from firm type
  bread

Sauté the mushrooms in 2 tablespoons margarine or butter until lightly browned. Set aside.

In a large skillet melt the ½ cup margarine or butter. Add the onions and sauté until soft. Add the parsley and celery leaves, sage, thyme, mace, salt, and pepper, and sauté another minute. Transfer mixture to a bowl. Add the mushrooms and any melted margarine or butter in the pan with them. Add the bread crumbs and toss gently but thoroughly until well combined. Stuff turkey immediately.

APPLE-SWEET SAUSAGE STUFFING

1½ pounds Italian sweet sausage	1 teaspoon basil
2 cups chopped onions	1 teaspoon salt
1½ cups diced celery	Freshly ground pepper to taste
2 cups peeled, diced, tart apples	8 cups whole grain bread cubes,
2 eggs	toasted in moderate oven until
⅛ teaspoon sage	dry and lightly toasted
1 teaspoon marjoram	¼ cup freshly grated Parmesan,
½ teaspoon thyme	Romano, or Sardo cheese

Slit sausage and remove casing. Break up sausage and sauté in a skillet, turning and continuing to break up until lightly browned. Remove the sausage with a slotted spoon and place it in a bowl. To the fat remaining in the skillet add the onions and celery and sauté until the onions are soft. Add the apples and sauté a few minutes longer. Add the mixture to the sausage meat in the bowl.

Beat the eggs lightly and add the sage, marjoram, thyme, basil, salt, and pepper. Add to the sausage mixture. Add the toasted bread cubes and the cheese and mix well. Stuff turkey immediately.

TWICE-WILD STUFFING

Wild rice and dried wild mushrooms combine to make this excellent and very special stuffing. While dried mushroom packages are not always labeled "wild" you can buy them anyway, because these mushrooms often are the wild varieties and have the kind of flavor you want for the stuffing. The exceptions to this are champignons de Paris, *which like the fresh American mushrooms don't have a sufficiently pungent flavor, and Chinese mushrooms, which have a flavor that's not appropriate in this recipe.*

½ cup dried European wild mushrooms, such as *cèpes, chanterelles, pfifferlinge,* or Polish mushrooms	1 cup finely chopped celery
	4 tablespoons margarine or butter
	Freshly ground pepper to taste
	Generous pinch of thyme
⅔ cup wild rice	Generous pinch of oregano
1 teaspoon salt	Generous pinch of marjoram
2 cups chopped onions	¼ cup sherry

Place dried mushrooms in a small bowl and cover with warm water. Allow to stand 30 minutes or longer. Remove from water and chop. Meanwhile rinse the wild rice in cold water if package directions so indicate. Bring 3 cups of water to a boil in a saucepan. Add the salt and the wild rice and boil 25 minutes, stirring occasionally. Remove from heat and drain well in a sieve or colander.

Sauté the onions and celery in the margarine or butter until slightly softened, about 5 to 10 minutes. Remove from the heat. Add the pepper, thyme, oregano, and marjoram and mix. Add the mushrooms, wild rice and sherry and toss well. Stuff the turkey immediately.

PORK AND PISTACHIO STUFFING

½ cup finely chopped onions
½ cup margarine or butter
1 pound ground pork
¼ pound finely chopped chicken
  livers
1 teaspoon salt
Freshly ground pepper to taste

½ teaspoon nutmeg
1 cup shelled pistachio nuts
¼ cup sherry
5 cups crumbled bread crumbs
  made from Italian bread with
  sesame seeds

In a skillet sauté the onions in 2 tablespoons margarine or butter until soft. Add the ground pork, raise the heat and cook, breaking up the meat with a fork or pancake turner until it loses its pink color. Bank the pork to the side of the skillet. Add the chicken livers to the skillet and cook, turning, until they lose their pink color. Remove skillet from heat. Add the salt, pepper, nutmeg, and pistachio nuts, and mix well. Add the sherry and mix. Transfer the mixture to a bowl.

Melt the remaining margarine or butter in the skillet. Add the bread crumbs and toss. Add the bread crumbs to the bowl and combine gently but thoroughly. Stuff the turkey immediately.

WALNUT-PRUNE-GINGER STUFFING

12 ounces pitted prunes
½ cup Port or Madeira wine
1 cup finely chopped onions
½ cup margarine or butter
2 cups chopped peeled apples
2 cups coarsely chopped walnuts
3 tablespoons drained chopped
   preserved ginger in syrup

2 teaspoons finely chopped zest of
   lemon rind
1 teaspoon salt
Freshly ground pepper to taste
¼ teaspoon allspice
⅛ teaspoon nutmeg
4 cups crumbled whole wheat
   bread crumbs

Chop the prunes and combine them with the Port or Madeira in a small bowl. Allow to stand for 30 minutes or longer. Meanwhile sauté the onions in margarine or butter until soft. Transfer to a bowl. Add the apples, walnuts, ginger, lemon zest, salt, pepper, allspice, and nutmeg, and toss well. Add the bread crumbs, a cup at a time, tossing gently but thoroughly each time. Add the prunes and their liquid and toss again. Stuff the turkey immediately.

CORNBREAD-TURKEY SAUSAGE STUFFING

For the cornbread: *
2 eggs
1 cup milk
¼ cup margarine or butter, melted
1½ cups corn meal (preferably stone
   ground corn meal)
3 teaspoons baking powder
¾ teaspoon salt
2 tablespoons brown sugar

For the balance of the stuffing:
1 12-ounce package mild turkey
   sausage

¼ cup chopped parsley
¼ cup margarine or butter
2 cups chopped onions
¼ cup chopped green pepper
2 cups diced celery
½ teaspoon sage
½ teaspoon thyme
½ teaspoon savory
1 teaspoon salt
Freshly ground pepper to taste
½ cup turkey stock or chicken broth

For the cornbread: Preheat oven at 375°F. (191°C.). Beat the eggs and add the milk and melted margarine or butter. Place a well-greased 8-inch square baking pan in the oven. Combine the cornmeal, baking powder, salt, and brown sugar and add to the egg-milk mixture, stirring quickly. Remove the hot baking pan from the oven and turn the corn meal mixture into it, scraping out the bowl quickly with a rubber spatula. Place the baking pan in the oven immediately and bake about 25 minutes or until a cake tester inserted into the center comes out clean. Cut into squares, remove from baking pan, and cool on wire rack until cool enough to handle.

For the stuffing: Crumble the cornbread into a bowl. Break up the turkey sausage into small pieces and sauté it in a skillet until lightly browned and crumbly. Add it to the cornbread, along with the parsley, mixing lightly. Melt the margarine or butter in the skillet. Add the onions, green pepper, and celery, and sauté until the onion is slightly soft. Add the sage, thyme, savory, salt, pepper, and turkey stock or chicken broth, and toss lightly. Remove from heat. Add to the cornbread mixture in the bowl and toss lightly. Stuff the turkey immediately.

* Use this recipe or any cornbread recipe that makes an 8-inch square loaf.

BRANDIED CHESTNUT STUFFING

1 generous cup chopped onions
1 cup thinly sliced celery
½ cup margarine or butter
Cooked chopped giblets and neck
  meat from 1 turkey (see Classic
  Giblet Gravy for cooking
  directions)
¼ cup chopped parsley
½ teaspoon thyme
1 teaspoon marjoram

¼ teaspoon sage
¼ teaspoon nutmeg
1 teaspoon salt
Freshly ground pepper to taste
2 15½ ounce cans whole chestnuts
  packed in water, drained
6 cups ⅜-inch French or Italian
  bread cubes, dried out for 30
  minutes in 250°F. (121°C.) oven
½ cup brandy

Sauté the onions and celery in a skillet in the margarine or butter until onions are transparant. Remove from the heat. Transfer to a bowl. Add the chopped giblets and neck meat, parsley, thyme, marjoram, sage, nutmeg, salt, and pepper, to the bowl. Break up the chestnuts into small pieces and add them to the bowl. Add the bread cubes and toss well. Sprinkle with the brandy and toss again. Stuff the turkey immediately.

APRICOT-BROWN RICE STUFFING

1 6-ounce package dried apricots
½ cup raisins
Pinch of allspice
2½ cups turkey stock or chicken broth
1 pound bulk pork sausage
½ pound chicken livers, cut into small pieces
½ cup shallots, minced
¼ teaspoon thyme

Freshly ground pepper to taste
1 teaspoon salt
2 tablespoons margarine or butter
1 cup brown rice
1 garlic clove, minced
½ cup dry white wine
1 bay leaf
Generous pinch of saffron
¼ teaspoon oregano

Simmer the apricots, raisins, and allspice in 1 cup of the turkey stock or chicken broth for 10 minutes. Cut the apricots into small pieces and turn the mixture into a bowl. Sauté the sausage in a skillet over medium heat, breaking it up with a fork, until the sausage has lost its pink color and is crumbly. Remove the sausage with a slotted spoon and add it to the apricot mixture.

To the fat remaining in the skillet add the chicken livers, shallots, thyme, pepper, and salt, and sauté over high heat until the chicken livers have lost their pink color. Remove with a slotted spoon and add to the apricot mixture.

Melt the margarine or butter in the skillet and add the brown rice. Cook, stirring, for several minutes until the rice changes color. Add the garlic, wine, bay leaf, saffron, oregano, and the remaining 1½ cups turkey stock or chicken broth. Lower heat, cover and cook 40 minutes or until the rice is almost tender, adding a little more turkey stock, chicken broth, or water if necessary. Add the rice to the apricot mixture and combine well. Stuff the turkey immediately.

POTATO NUGGET-PARSLEY STUFFING

6 cups peeled diced raw potatoes
    (place in a bowl of cold water as
    you peel and dice the potatoes
    to prevent browning)
4 tablespoons butter or margarine
4 tablespoons vegetable oil
1½ cups chopped onions

1 cup thinly sliced celery
2 eggs
⅔ cup chopped parsley
½ teaspoon thyme
2 teaspoons salt
Freshly ground pepper to taste
4 cups bread crumbs

Drain diced potatoes and pat dry on paper towels. Sauté, half at a time, in a large skillet in 2 tablespoons butter or margarine and 2 tablespoons vegetable oil, along with half of the onions and celery, until lightly browned all over. Sauté the second half of the potatoes, onions and celery in the remaining margarine or butter and vegetable oil.

In a bowl beat the eggs lightly. Add the parsley, thyme, salt, and pepper and mix well. Add the bread crumbs and toss lightly. Add the potato mixture and toss lightly but thoroughly. Stuff the turkey immediately.

OYSTER-LEMON STUFFING

½ cup margarine or butter
1 cup chopped onions
1 cup finely sliced celery and
    chopped celery leaves combined
½ teaspoon thyme
½ teaspoon rosemary
1 teaspoon salt

Freshly ground pepper to taste
2 tablespoons grated lemon zest
Pinch of mace
6 cups bread crumbs made from
    hard French or Italian bread
1 pint fresh shucked oysters with
    liquid

Melt the margarine or butter in a skillet and sauté the onions and celery until the onion is soft. Remove from heat. Add the thyme, rosemary, salt, pepper, lemon zest, and mace, and mix well. Add the bread crumbs and toss gently but thoroughly. Cut the oysters in two or three pieces each, and add them to the bread mixture, combining well. If the mixture is too dry add a little of the oyster liquid. Stuff the turkey immediately.

TURKEY FINOCCHIO

Fennel, fresh from the garden or the greengrocer, gives this stuffing its exquisite flavor. It's one of my favorite recipes and I rank it as a gourmet dish. It's easy to make, too, which makes it even more appealing.

2 medium or 3 small fennel bulbs
½ cup margarine or butter
1 garlic clove, minced
Freshly ground pepper to taste
1 teaspoon salt
1 teaspoon oregano

3 tablespoons freshly grated
   Parmesan, Romano, or Sardo
   cheese
4 cups crumbled bread crumbs,
   preferably whole wheat

Cut off and discard any stems of the fennel bulbs that are blemished or tough, retaining those that are tender and unblemished. Trim the base of the fennel bulbs. Discard any outside leaves that are tough or discolored. Cut the fennel bulbs in quarters lengthwise. Then slice them ¼-inch thick. If any of the pieces are more than 1 inch long, cut them in half. You should have about 10 cups of fennel slices, but the measurement does not need to be exact.

Melt the margarine or butter in a large skillet over low to medium heat. Sauté the fennel pieces about 15 minutes, turning often. Add the garlic and sauté another minute. Remove from heat. Transfer the fennel to a bowl. Add the pepper, salt, oregano, grated cheese and toss well. Then add the bread crumbs and toss well. Stuff the turkey immediately.

PINEAPPLE-PLUM STUFFED TURKEY

½ cup margarine or butter
1 cup sliced celery
1 cup chopped onions
1 uncooked turkey liver
5 firm or underripe red or purple
  plums (¾ pound or so)
1 tart green apple, peeled, cored
  and diced
5 slices pineapple (fresh or
  unsweetened canned), cut into
  eighths

¼ cup chopped flat leaf parsley
2 teaspoons salt
Freshly ground pepper to taste
¼ teaspoon sage
½ teaspoon allspice
2 tablespoons cider vinegar
6 cups crumbled bread crumbs,
  preferably a mixture of white
  and whole wheat

Melt the margarine or butter in a skillet and sauté the celery and onions over low heat for about 5 minutes. Remove the celery and onions with a slotted spoon and place in a bowl. Chop the turkey liver and sauté it briefly in the margarine or butter remaining in the skillet. Transfer to the bowl.

Cut the plums into eighths, remove and discard pits, and cut the plum sections crosswise into several pieces each. Add them to the bowl. Add the apple, pineapple, parsley, salt, pepper, sage, allspice, and vinegar, and mix well. Add the bread crumbs and toss gently but thoroughly. Stuff the turkey immediately.

Basting instructions:
¼ cup margarine or butter, melted
1½ cups pineapple juice or pineapple-grapefruit juice

Brush turkey with melted margarine or butter and roast 20 minutes. Pour the pineapple juice over the turkey, brush again with the melted margarine or butter and roast 20 minutes longer. Continue roasting, basting every 20 minutes with the balance of the margarine or butter and the pan juices.

CRACKED WHEAT-GROUND VEAL STUFFING

4 tablespoons margarine or butter
1 cup chopped onions
1 small garlic clove, minced
1 pound ground veal
¼ cup pine nuts (pignolias)
½ cup currants
1 teaspoon cinnamon

¼ teaspoon ground ginger
Generous pinch of saffron
1 teaspoon salt
Freshly ground pepper to taste
1 cup bulgur wheat (cracked wheat)
½ cup dry white wine

Melt margarine or butter in a skillet. Add the onions and garlic and cook over low heat until soft. Remove from the skillet with a slotted spoon and transfer to a bowl. Add the ground veal to the skillet and cook over high heat, breaking up with a fork, until it loses its pink color. Add the veal to the bowl. Add the pine nuts, currants, cinnamon, ginger, saffron, salt, and pepper and mix well. Add the bulgur wheat and mix. Add the wine and mix well.

Stuffing and basting instructions: Rub a little salt and lemon juice in the neck opening and body cavities before stuffing the turkey. Roast the turkey, basting with Lemon Butter *(see index).*

SEVEN-DAY VELVET TURKEY

Although it takes seven days from start to finish, this method of cooking a turkey is practically effortless. Time does all the work for you by curing the bird in salt to produce an unusual velvety-textured turkey that can be sliced paper thin when chilled. The entire cooking operation takes only 45 minutes and the meat is tender and moist. It's a perfect way to cook a bird when you want lots of sliced turkey for a party platter. The whole turkey doesn't look beautiful, so don't think about putting it out for show, but the slices of turkey are perfection itself.

1 5- to 6-pound turkey (not larger)
1 teaspoon Szechuan peppercorns

¼ cup kosher salt

The neck and giblets may be prepared exactly like the turkey, or you may reserve them for another use. Place the peppercorns and salt in a small skillet and set over low heat for 6 minutes, stirring the mixture often with a wooden spoon, and shaking the pan occasionally. Transfer the mixture to a soup plate or bowl to cool.

Wash the turkey and pat dry thoroughly inside and out with paper towels. Wash and dry the giblets if you're using them. Place the turkey on a sheet of waxed paper. Rub the salt and pepper mixture all over the outside and in the neck opening and body cavity of the turkey, and on the neck and giblets. Set the turkey on a large sheet of heavy duty wide aluminum foil with the neck and giblets around it. Rub any of the remaining salt and pepper mixture into the breast and legs of the turkey. Wrap it completely and tightly in the foil. Set it on a platter. Place in the refrigerator for 7 days, turning the package a little each day.

Remove the turkey and giblets from the aluminum foil. Brush off the peppercorns. Dry the turkey and giblets with paper towels. Fold the wings of the turkey under. Set the turkey in a roasting pan just large enough to hold it, and arrange the giblets around the legs. Set the roasting pan on a rack set inside a large preserving kettle or other pot of large diameter. Pour boiling water into the bottom of the kettle to a level of about two inches, making sure not to get any water into the roasting pan with the turkey. Do not cover the roasting pan, but cover the kettle, and set it over high heat. Keep the water at a rolling boil for 45 minutes, adding boiling water whenever necessary. Turn off the heat and allow to stand, covered, for 15 minutes.

Remove the turkey from the pan and allow the body cavity to drain for a few minutes. Place the turkey on a platter. Drain the giblets and put them with the turkey. Pour off the pan juices, cool, and refrigerate or freeze for another use. There will be about 2 cups of rich stock. Allow the turkey to cool for about 30 minutes.

Transfer the turkey and giblets to a large sheet of aluminum foil, wrap tightly, and refrigerate until well chilled. Slice thinly to serve.

Makes 12 or more servings.

PARCHMENT-ROASTED TURKEY

Prepare a turkey for roasting as directed earlier in this chapter. It may be stuffed or unstuffed as you like. Brush it all over with melted margarine or butter. Set the turkey on a sheet of buttered aluminum foil just large enough for it to rest on. Set the turkey and the foil on a large sheet of parchment paper which has been brushed with melted margarine or butter. Wrap the turkey in the parchment. You will probably need to use two overlapping sheets of the parchment paper, which can be sewn together with a needle and kitchen thread. Set the wrapped turkey on a rack in a roasting pan and roast in preheated 325°F. (163°C.) oven. After 1½ hours (if turkey is 8 to 12 pounds) or after 2 hours (if turkey is larger than 12 pounds), remove the parchment paper and pour any juices it may contain into the roasting pan. Set the turkey in the roasting pan without the rack. Continue to roast, basting every 20 minutes, until done.

SPIT-ROASTED
OR ROTISSERIE TURKEY

The continual turning of a spit-roasting turkey, which helps it to do its own basting, results in a good-textured evenly-roasted bird with its juices well sealed in. Many consider this absolutly the best way to roast a turkey, and not without reason. There are many sources of heat and different kinds of equipment that can be used for spit roasting. These include various types and brands of outdoor cookers, electric rotisseries, oven rotisseries, reflector ovens used with open fires in the hearth, and suspension rotisseries used with open fires at campsites or other out-of-door locations. Whichever method of cooker you use, follow the general instructions that come with your particular kind of cooker or rotisserie, along with the directions given below for use with an indoor electric rotisserie. You will also find directions below for constructing a suspension rotisserie for outdoor cooking. With this method you can rotate the turkey without benefit of electricity.

INDOOR SPIT-ROASTING WITH ELECTRIC ROTISSERIE

1 turkey, 8 to 10 pounds, or as
  desired
Melted margarine or butter or a
  combination of:
  ½ cup margarine or butter,
  melted

¼ cup lemon juice
2 tablespoons Worcestershire
  sauce
Stuffing (optional—see index for
  stuffing recipes)

Prepare turkey for roasting, stuffing it if you wish. Spear the spit bar lengthwise through the turkey so that its weight is equally balanced all around in order to have it turn evenly. Next, using strong string, truss the turkey. Tie the wings close to the body with one string. Do not have the wings akimbo. Next tie the legs and tail as close to the body as you can get them. Then either tie the turkey securely to the spit to prevent wiggling and wobbling, or, if your rotisserie comes equipped with holding forks at either end of the spit, push them into the turkey at each end to further secure it. (Depending on the style of the rotisserie, you may need to place one of the holding forks on the spit bar before you spear the spit bar through the turkey.)

Set the spit so that the revolving turkey just clears the coils (or follow manufacturer's instructions.) Set the broiler pan below the bird to catch all the drippings. Brush the turkey every 20 minutes or so with the basting liquid. Spit roast until done. (See "About Thermometers and Testing for Doneness" earlier in this chapter.) Time will vary with the type of spit roaster, size of bird, whether stuffed or not, and so on. Spit roasting takes considerably longer than oven roasting, with an 8 to 9 pound turkey taking around 4 hours to roast.

Remove turkey from spit. Cut and remove all strings. Make Turkey Pan Gravy (see index) with the drippings or serve the turkey with its natural juices. Let turkey stand 20 minutes before carving.

OUTDOOR SPIT-ROASTING WITH SUSPENSION ROTISSERIE

CAMPFIRE ROAST TURKEY

If you love the outdoor life, being in the woods, and cooking over a campfire, this is the turkey roasting method for you. It takes hours of

HOW TO SET UP THE CAMPFIRE AND
CROSSBAR SUSPENSION FOR CAMPFIRE ROAST TURKEY

cooking, many, many armloads of wood, and a constant vigil at the fireside, but the results are more than worth the trouble, because a turkey roasted over a wood fire has a flavor unparalleled by any other roasting technique in my experience. The turkey is actually not roasted *over* the fire, but in front of it. You build a reflector fire, which means that you have some sort of backing to the fire that reflects the heat back toward the turkey which hangs just in front of it.

If you're adept at such engineering, you can suspend the turkey from a dingle stick, but if you're new at this sort of thing you'll probably find it easier to suspend it from a crossbar (see illustration). In either case you'll be able to rotate the turkey as it roasts so that it's done evenly all over.

Step by step here's how to proceed. Set up a fireplace on the ground. Make sure that you brush away any dead leaves and such from directly around the firebed so they don't catch a spark and start the woods blazing. Build a wall with stones around the back and two sides of the fire. Back up the fire with a ready-made reflector, or use a large sheet of heavy duty wide aluminum foil, shiny side toward you. Make sure the foil is well anchored, because once the fire is going you won't be able to get at it very easily to make adjustments. If you can, plan your fire just in front of an embankment. It will be easier to set up the reflector there since you'll then have a natural backing.

Next, lay the fire, but don't light it. Then set up the dingle stick or the crossbar, anchoring it well into the ground and bracing the supports with rocks or stones. Erect either arrangement so that when the turkey hangs it will be just in front of the fire, not over it. And put a drip pan just under where the turkey will hang. Also set it up so that the turkey when suspended will be about 4 inches above the drip pan. Use green wood, not dry wood for all parts of the apparatus, and use an S-hook, stick, and wire or cord as shown in the illustration by which to hang the bird.

The turkey, which can be about any size up to approximately 12 pounds, should be cleaned, dried, and rubbed inside and out with salt, and readied for hanging. Cut off the neck skin. Tie the ends of the legs together tightly. Run a sturdy wooden skewer crosswise through the turkey just below the wing joints, catching in the wing tips to keep them close to the body. Run a second wooden skewer through the turkey crosswise just below the legs. If you don't have any wooden skewers use long thin strong pointed green branches cut from a tree. Don't use dry branches which will catch fire. Now loop some strong cord or light wire around one of the skewers so that the turkey hangs by it. Hang the turkey as illustrated. You will probably need to do some adjusting to get it at the proper height. The weight of the turkey may bend the supporting stick(s) a little, and you'll probably have to shorten the cord or wire.

When the turkey is adjusted and in place over the drip pan just in front of the fire, start the fire going. Brush the turkey all over with vegetable oil, and brush it about every 20 minutes during the roasting. About every 10 or 15 minutes give the turkey a quarter turn. Keep feeding wood onto the fire. You must keep a blazing fire all the time. Red hot coals, which would be fine for grilling a steak, won't do a thing to help roast a turkey. The idea is to have the flames reflect their heat via the aluminum foil or other reflector to do the roasting.

It takes about half an hour per pound of turkey for the roasting, with an eleven pound bird requiring between 5 and 6 hours. Watch the time, and when you feel that the turkey is about half roasted, remove the cord or wire from around the skewer and loop it around the other skewer so that the turkey changes position. If the bird was hanging head down first, now it will be tail down, or vice versa. Continue roasting, turning, and brushing with the oil until the turkey is done.

If you've brought along an instant reading meat thermometer, which clips nicely to your pocket like a pen and is hard to lose, you can use it to determine doneness. Otherwise you'll have to depend on appearances and a prodding or two with a sharp-tined fork to see if the thigh and thickest part of the breast are tender.

If you've been very careful to keep ashes and whatnot out of the drip pan you can use the juices to serve with the turkey, or even make some pan gravy with a little flour, salt, pepper, and water. Actually, the bird will taste so good you won't even be thinking about gravy or juice. You can wait 15 minutes or so before carving if you want to, but you'll probably be so hungry and the turkey will look so delicious that you won't want to wait. Don't. Just dig in and enjoy a marvelous eating experience.

You can, incidentally, roast some foil-wrapped potatoes by propping them against the stones around the edge of the fire about an hour before you judge the turkey will be done. Turn them occasionally. Remove one after half an hour to see how it's doing, and test again in 15 minutes so the potatoes won't overbake. You can also roast ears of corn in the fire by the same method, but these will cook very quickly and can be done almost at the last minute.

OUTDOOR KETTLE COOKER ROAST TURKEY

The outdoor kettle cooker (such as that made by Weber) is ideal for roasting a turkey out of doors in summer or winter in any kind of weather. It produces a tender turkey beautifully browned. Kettle cooker turkeys roast faster than oven-roasted birds, and there is no appreciable difference in the roasting time between stuffed and unstuffed birds.

1 12-pound turkey, or any size you prefer that will fit on the cooker rack comfortably (kettle cookers vary in size)	Melted margarine or butter Stuffing (optional; see index for recipes)

Ready the turkey for roasting as though you were going to roast it in your kitchen oven, stuffing it or not as you wish. Meanwhile build a good charcoal fire, following manufacturer's directions and suggestions, and when the coals are ready, divide them in half and push half to each side of the cooker. Place a drip pan in the center between the coals. Set the rack on the cooker and place the turkey directly on the rack. Brush the turkey all over with the melted margarine or butter. Place the lid on the cooker with all vents open. Brush the turkey with the melted margarine, removing the lid only for this purpose or to add fresh charcoal as needed. Begin to test the inner thigh for doneness after 1½ hours. A 12-pound turkey will be ready after 2 to 2½ hours. In general, allow about 11 minutes per pound for kettle cooker roasting. Remove the turkey from the cooker and allow to stand 20 minutes before carving.

If desired, make gravy using the drippings in the drip pan with excess fat spooned off.

VARIATION

KETTLE COOKER CUMBERLAND-BASTED TURKEY

Prepare the turkey as above, brushing with the following mixture rather than the margarine or butter:

¼ cup margarine or butter	2 tablespoons lemon juice
½ cup red or black currant jelly	2 tablespoons cider vinegar
¼ cup Port wine	1 teaspoon salt
2 teaspoons prepared mustard	Cayenne pepper to taste

Melt the margarine or butter in a small saucepan with the currant jelly, stirring until the jelly has melted. Remove from heat and stir in the remaining ingredients.

The following recipes for roast turkey can be found in other parts of this book. Please consult the index for:

Colonial Roast Wild Turkey

Oven Braised Wild Turkey with Hickory Nut Stuffing

Peanut Stuffed Wild Turkey en Cocotte

Plantation Roast Turkey with Virginia Ham Stuffing and Currant Sauce

Roast Turkey with Prepared Chestnut Stuffing

Roast Wild Turkey with Hunter's Onion Sauce

6

Thanksgiving

Over the river and through the wood,
Now grandfather's cap I spy:
Hurrah for the fun!
Is the pudding done?
Hurrah for the pumpkin pie!
                    —LYDIA MARIA CHILD,
                         Thanksgiving Day

Americans may only have been "talking turkey" since about 1920 when that colloquialism seems first to have appeared in conversation, but their forebears started eating turkey three hundred years earlier in the historic Pilgrim colony of Plymouth, Massachusetts. One feels compelled not only to explore the subject of the first Thanksgiving to try to evoke the authentic picture of the event, but also to speculate how the Pilgrim's first Thanksgiving might have been celebrated if fate had landed them at their original destination far from the New England coast.

What was the first Thanksgiving really like? When was it held, and how long did it last? Who was there? Was it merry? What did they eat? Who did the cooking, and for that matter, the cleaning up? Although one tends to think of the Pilgrims as rather stern and proper people not given to frivolity, theirs was neither a somber festival, nor an especially religious one. True, it was held so that the Pilgrims could give thanks to God for the harvest gathered in, but its main theme was to rejoice in the sharing of plenty. And rejoice they did, for they were grateful that those gathered together had survived an extremely harsh and cruel winter, that food was abundant, that they were at peace with the Indians, and that, for the moment at least, all was right with the world.

An invitation dispatched to the Indians to join the festivities resulted in the somewhat unexpected arrival of 90 guests, all of them male, and presumably with robust appetites. There were in all 140 persons to be fed, and not for just one day, but for three. The Indians were accustomed to harvest and thanksgiving festivals of their own which lasted for several days, and they had no reason to think that the white man's customs would differ in this respect. They stayed on to eat, drink, and revel, but they did think of replenishing some of the food being consumed, and sent out a hunting party which returned with five deer during the course of the celebration. Accounts don't agree as to whether one or all of the deer were eaten then, with the possibility existing that four of them were kept for later use by the Pilgrims. In any case, records show that there were only five mature women in the Pilgrim colony, and they cooked the venison and everything else for the entire feast with some help from younger girls and children.

The time was late September or sometime in October when wild fowl, which constituted the main part of the menu, would have been plentiful in the area. The setting was Plymouth, which then consisted of a common house, three storehouses, and seven thatched-roof houses which the Pilgrims had built during the summer in the style of the English houses they had known at home (no log cabins). Although a small part of the cooking was done in the houses, most was done outdoors over open fires where they spit-roasted venison and the many wild birds they had shot, such as turkeys, which were reported to be "large and fat," geese, ducks, and quail. One account says that the turkeys and geese were stuffed with nuts before roasting. It may have been too late in the season for lobsters, which were everyday fare to them, but they probably tucked oysters or clams into the coals of the fires to roast along with ears of corn. Codfish, eels, and scallops were also on the bill of fare. Iron kettles suspended over the fires held clam chowder and corn-based dishes such as succotash and Indian pudding, all of which the Pilgrims had learned to make from the Patuxet Indian, Squanto, or Tisquantum. Squanto, incidentally, is one of America's most unsung heroes. Having lived with the Pilgrims during their first year and for several years thereafter until the time of his death, he taught them how to farm, fish, and survive in their wilderness home. Without his help they would surely have perished.

In addition to corn, the first year's crop included beans, which would have been used in the Thanksgiving stews or succotash. Corn bread, ash cakes, or hoe cakes would have been baked, and some of the flour from the remaining stores brought over on the Mayflower was used to make biscuits and bread. There were nuts and dried strawberries, gooseberries, plums and cherries. These fruits may have been baked in dough cases somewhat in the style of pies. Grapes grew abundantly around Plymouth and the Pilgrims had both red and white wine, "very sweet and strong," on the first Thanksgiving, along with the "strong waters" that they had brought with them from across the sea.

The food was set out on tables improvised by laying planks on sawhorses. Tree stumps and logs served as chairs for some of the Pilgrims, and the Indians undoubtedly sat on the ground as was their practice. The five busy women were relieved of extensive washing-up duties, since there were practically no pots or pans, only a few knives and wooden cooking spoons, and no forks at all, since these were not yet in general use. Clam shells served as spoons for the diners, some of whom ate from wooden trenchers which were used as plates, and most eating was no doubt managed simply by using the fingers.

The first Thanksgiving was without doubt a time of merrymaking and feasting. The Indians helped to keep the festivities lively, holding bow and arrow marksmanship competitions among themselves. A band of Pilgrim soldiers led by Miles Standish entertained their guests by parading, bugling, and firing volleys of blank ammunition. Everyone except the women, who were more than busy with their culinary chores, joined in games of leaping, jumping, and racing or playing a game called stool ball that resembled croquet somewhat, in that it involved hitting a ball through wickets.

There does not seem to have been a Thanksgiving feast the following year, probably due to the fact that the Pilgrims had depleted their supplies in the previous year's feast, which had led to great deprivation during the winter. The following year, however, the Thanksgiving festival apparently was combined with the wedding feast of William Bradford and was held during the summer. The Pilgrims were not fond of setting calendar dates to be observed, and somehow this seems appropriate for the Thanksgiving date, for even in our own time presidents keep tinkering with Thursdays in November.

Indians invited to the Thanksgiving-wedding feast brought a turkey and three or four bucks and according to an account written by one of the guests, they had "such good cheer that I could wish you some of our share." According to this account the Indians entertained with dancing and a high degree of noise, but there's no way of knowing whether the Pilgrims joined in or not.

It's interesting to speculate how the first Thanksgiving might have been celebrated in terms of food had the Pilgrims not landed at Plymouth. Presumably they had a patent or charter for a tract of land around the mouth of the Hudson River, but they landed 250 miles north of there due to the bad weather and rough waters of the late fall Atlantic crossing.

What would have happened if they had settled somewhere near the mouth of the Hudson River? How would that have affected our celebration of Thanksgiving? It seems likely their feast still would have included turkey, for this great bird had proliferated in its wild state all along the eastern seaboard. But cranberry sauce would probably never have made it to the festive board, for only on Cape Cod does the berry grow in such profusion. Even though cranberries reportedly did not appear at the first Thanksgiving, they were not unknown to the Pilgrims, who called them craneberries since they felt that the blossoms of the plants resembled the heads of cranes. It's said that they eventually learned to make cranberry sauce and tarts, and a jam sweetened with syrup from pumpkin pulp, and we find that cranberry sauce has been on New England Thanksgiving dinner menus since the Seventeenth Century.

There's evidence that the Pilgrims actually wanted to settle in northern Virginia, but either they were unable to obtain a charter for such a settlement and thus had to make arrangements for a more northern home, or they did have a Virginia charter which became worthless once they decided to stay in Massachusetts. If they had settled in Virginia it would have fortified that state's conviction that the first Thanksgiving was really celebrated there.

Virginia's claim is based on the fact that one year before the Pilgrims landed at Plymouth, a group of 39 colonists with a charter from the Virginia Company of London arrived on the shores of the James River where they were assigned a hundred acres not far from the Jamestown Colony. The first item in their charter provided that the day of their landing be kept yearly and perpetually as a day of thanksgiving. So, upon touching ground their first act was to kneel and offer prayers of thanks. It was a brief and simple religious ceremony, but it was observed only for the following two years because the colony was then nearly obliterated by the Indians. In contrast to the Pilgrims' Thanksgiving, there was no food or feasting of any kind involved in the Virginia ceremony, so that presumably no Thanksgiving Day as we know it would have evolved from the Virginia Thanksgiving. Nevertheless, had such a festive day come about, no finer place could have been selected for variety, abundance, and quality of food than Virginia. Wild turkeys were plentiful, as were other birds, deer, other game, and fish, and domesticated animals were soon introduced. Wild fruits and nuts were cultivated, seeds were brought from England, and gardens flourished with vegetables, fruits, and herbs of all kinds. Oranges, spices, and wines were only a few of the foods that were imported to this gourmet's paradise, and more than one housewife was known to remark that she could keep a better table in Virginia than she ever could have in London.

It was more than 200 years before Thanksgiving Day became a feasting day in Virginia. The other southern states, because of the hardships suffered during the Civil War, did not all celebrate the holiday until President Andrew Johnson's Thanksgiving proclamation of 1866.

The observance of Thanksgiving in places other than Plymouth spread to other parts of Massachusetts and New England. For example, after the safe arrival of a fleet of ships in the Massachusetts Bay Colony in 1630, a day of public Thanksgiving was proclaimed. Connecticut soon set an October day for that colony's Thanksgiving day, and eventually it became a custom to celebrate Thanksgiving in all the New England colonies. This tradition gradually spread westward with the pioneers, and southward to other parts of the country. But wherever it was celebrated, Thanksgiving was a regional holiday, with each colony, state, or even county setting its own date, but there was no national consolidation. All these holidays, like the first Thanksgiving, had their roots in old English harvest home festivals which celebrated the successful gathering in of crops. George Washington named several days of Thanksgiving during his term in office, so that one really has to start sorting out what was meant by "a day of Thanksgiving" compared to the real "Thanksgiving Day."

It was ultimately Abraham Lincoln who proclaimed the first annual national Thanksgiving holiday during the Civil War. He probably was influenced in doing so by Sarah Hale, the editor of *Godey's Lady's Book*, who fought a long and vigorous battle through the pages of her magazine for the recognition of Thanksgiving Day as a national holiday. Sarah, who felt that Thanksgiving was equally important in our nation's history as the Fourth of July, wrote on this subject for over twenty years and enlisted many influential people in her cause. *Godey's Lady's Book* may well have been the first magazine not only to campaign for the recognition of Thanksgiving as a national holiday, but also to help its readers by including recipes for making Thanksgiving dishes to accompany the turkey.

The Thanksgiving menus and recipes that follow in this chapter were devised with a number of particular themes in mind. The first is a Pilgrim Father's Thanksgiving Dinner that uses as many of the foods as possible that were eaten at the first Thanksgiving feast. For a taste of the old South, the second menu is a selection of dishes that were served in Colonial Virginia. You'll find a Country Thanksgiving Dinner filled with old-fashioned favorites, and a City Thanksgiving Dinner with an air of sophistication.

For those who love turkey as much as I do, I've designed a Turkey Lover's Thanksgiving Dinner that includes turkey in one of its myriad forms in three of its courses, including dessert (Gobbler Mincemeat Pie). Then there's a Thanksgiving Dinner Elégante for a genuine epicurean feast, as well as a Speedy But Smart Thanksgiving Dinner for the time when you want a beautiful dinner but don't have much time to prepare it.

Now that Thanksgiving has become a national institution, truly the most American of our celebrations, Americans will go to any length when in foreign countries on the fourth Thursday in November to recreate a dinner just like they would enjoy at home. This has led to optimistic foraging in European capitals for cans of American cranberry sauce (usually overpriced), pilgrimages to Army posts in distant places in the hope of purchasing enough canned pumpkin to prepare a pie, buying what appear to be yams in the West Indies, only to find them to be vegetables that blanch to bone color upon cooking, and so on. Throughout these search and seize operations however, one thought is uppermost in the mind, and that is the acquisition of a turkey. For without turkey, what is Thanksgiving Day? Fortunately, turkeys can be bought in many European, Middle Eastern and Far Eastern countries, since the first turkeys were taken to Spain from the Americas in the early 1500s from where they spread to other parts of Europe and points east. Inspired by the idea of Thanksgiving dinner in other countries I've planned three menus with foreign flavors, all centered around turkey, but incorporating the best of native or local foods into the menus. The menus are for a French Thanksgiving Dinner, a Middle Eastern Thanksgiving Dinner, and a Far East Thanksgiving Dinner.

Please note that recipes are included for all menu items marked with an asterisk (*). Other menu items either require no recipe or no cooking, or are for items bought ready made. The menus are planned for eight persons.

Here are some ideas for setting an attractive Thanksgiving table to go along with all the good things you'll be preparing to eat. Brass, pewter, or wooden bowls are good bases for centerpieces, as are baskets, especially those woven by American Indians. Arrange in your centerpiece a selection of autumn fruits and nuts, such as apples, grapes, and walnuts, or cranberries and kumquats. You might prefer to fill your bowl with a selection of colorful winter squashes. Bits of pine, boxwood, or laurel can be tucked among the fruits or vegetables, or you may want to make a complete pine or evergreen arrangement.

Bittersweet or an arrangement of dried flowers or grasses or wheat tied in bundles with autumn colored ribbons are attractive. Consider using two hurricane lamps without candles filled with the fruits or vegetables mentioned, and tie contrasting ribbons around the lamp bases. Little blooming pepper plants from the florist also make bright decorations.

You may want to put a porcelain figure of a turkey in the center of the table, or an old rooster weathervane, or one or two wooden duck decoys. Candlesticks in pewter, copper, or brass are very much in concert with the feeling of the day, or you can cut holes in gourds just large enough for each to hold a candle. If your fruit or vegetable decorations are very bright you may elect to tone them down by decorating with brown and/or wheat-colored ribbon or candles, and use a wheat-colored homespun type tablecloth or napkins. Other good candle colors are dark green, orange, red, or yellow, depending on the other colors in your decor.

PILGRIM FATHERS'
THANKSGIVING DINNER

Oysters on Half Shell

* *Colonial Roast Wild Turkey (see index) with*

* *Classic Giblet Gravy (see index)*

* *Maple Sweet Potatoes*   * *Cape Cod Creamed Onions*

* *Dried Corn Casserole*

* *New England Steamed Brown Bread with Raisins*

* *Cranberry Sauce with Ginger*

* *Dried Fruit Pie*   *Nut Bowl*

New York State Red and White Wines

As mentioned, oysters were probably on the menu at the first Thanksgiving just as they are on this one. The turkey was certainly wild, and could have been roasted either indoors or out. Maple Sweet Potatoes seem appropriate here because we know that the Pilgrims used maple sugar in their cooking. Corn was a dietary staple in Plymouth and was used for many dishes, but to avoid having too many corn-based dishes, in this dinner I've included just one, a chewy Dried Corn Casserole, and instead of corn bread I have substituted steamed brown bread, which became a Massachusetts favorite in later years. Cranberry sauce is on the menu because the Pilgrims eventually learned to use this berry in their cooking.

The wines that the Pilgrims drank were made from local grapes. About the closest to them in our time are New York State grapes. The Benmarl Hudson River Region red wines made from Chancellor or Baco Noir grapes, and the Benmarl Hudson River Region Seyval Blanc (white) would be good choices at your wine shop.

Indians in the area where the Pilgrims made their home were known to have grown popcorn, which they popped in earthenware jars shaken over hot coals. This accomplished, they sometimes poured maple syrup over it and formed it into balls. You might want to consider this as a sticky but grand finale to a Pilgrim Fathers' Thanksgiving Dinner.

OVEN TEMPERATURE AND USE. The turkey and the Dried Corn Casserole share the oven since they both require 350°F. (163°C.) temperatures. When the turkey has been removed from the oven raise the temperature and bake the Maple Sweet Potatoes while the turkey is resting on the carving board before carving. The Dried Fruit Pie can be baked early in the day, or the day before.

* Recipes follow for asterisked items.

MAPLE SWEET POTATOES

3 pounds (approximately) sweet
   potatoes
½ cup maple syrup
½ cup margarine or butter
1 cup apple juice

2 teaspoons grated orange zest
⅛ teaspoon allspice
½ teaspoon salt
Freshly ground pepper or to taste

Scrub the sweet potatoes and place in a saucepan. Cover well with cold water, bring to boil, and boil until tender. Drain and peel.

Preheat the oven at 350°F. (177°C.). Put the sweet potatoes through a ricer or food mill, and place into a bowl. Add the maple syrup, margarine or butter, apple juice, grated orange zest, allspice, salt, and pepper, and combine well. Spoon into a greased 2 or 2½ quart baking dish and smooth the top with a rubber spatula. Cover. (Dish can be made ahead to this point and refrigerated until shortly before serving time. Increase baking time to about 30 minutes if made ahead and refrigerated.) Bake 20 minutes or until heated through.

Makes 8 servings.

CAPE COD CREAMED ONIONS

3 pounds small white onions,
    peeled
¼ cup margarine or butter
3 tablespoons flour
2 teaspoons salt

Generous pinch of cloves
2 cups half and half (milk and
    cream dairy product)
2 tablespoons finely chopped
    parsley

Place onions into a saucepan and cover with boiling water to which 1 teaspoon of the salt has been added. Bring to boil and simmer 20 minutes or just until tender when pierced with a sharp-tined fork. Drain and keep warm.

Melt the margarine or butter in a saucepan. Add the flour, the remaining 1 teaspoon salt, and the cloves and stir with a wire whisk for a minute. Add the half and half and continue stirring with wire whisk until the mixture has thickened. Simmer a few minutes, stirring occasionally.

Place onions in a heated serving dish and pour the sauce over them. Sprinkle with the parsley. Serve immediately.

Makes 8 servings.

DRIED CORN CASSEROLE

If you can find whole kernel dried corn do include this earthy dish in your Pilgrim Fathers' Thanksgiving Dinner, since corn was such a mainstay in the Pilgrim diet. Look in stores that specialize in natural foods or that sell whole grains in bulk. Dried corn requires long cooking, but has a marvelous chewy texture and nutlike flavor.

2 cups whole kernel (not cut) dried corn	2½ cups milk
	½ teaspoon salt
2 tablespoons margarine or butter	Freshly ground pepper to taste
2 tablespoons flour	¼ cup brown sugar, firmly packed

Place corn in a large saucepan or pot and cover with cold water by several inches. Bring to boil and boil 2 minutes. Turn off heat and allow to sit for one hour. Cover and bring to boil again. Reduce heat and simmer 2 hours, checking water level occasionally and adding more boiling water as necessary. At the end of 2 hours some of the corn kernels should have burst open. Drain the corn. Place into a casserole.

Preheat oven at 325°F. (163°C.). In a saucepan melt the margarine or butter. Stir in the flour and cook a minute, stirring. Add 2 cups of milk and cook, stirring continually with a wire whisk, until mixture reaches boiling point. Remove from heat and add the salt, pepper, and brown sugar. Pour over the corn in the casserole. Cover and bake 1 hour. Stir in the remaining ½ cup milk and bake 1 hour longer. If the corn becomes too dry add a little boiling water.

Makes about 8 servings.

NEW ENGLAND STEAMED BROWN BREAD WITH RAISINS

Especially delicious when served warm with butter.

2 cups rye flour
1½ cups corn meal (preferably stone
    ground corn meal)
1 cup whole wheat flour
1½ teaspoons baking soda

½ teaspoon salt
2½ cups buttermilk
1 cup molasses
1 cup raisins

Grease 2 clean coffee cans (12 to 16 ounce size) or similarly shaped cans or molds. Have ready a pot into which both cans will fit comfortably. Set a steamer rack or other metal rack at the bottom of the pot. Have ready enough boiling water to reach halfway up the sides of the cans when they are placed on the rack.

Combine the rye flour, corn meal, whole wheat flour, baking soda, and salt in a bowl. Combine the buttermilk and molasses in another bowl. Add the molasses mixture to the dry ingredients and mix well. Add the raisins and mix in. Spoon into the greased coffee cans, dividing equally. Cover each can with heavy aluminum foil and tie tightly around with string. Place filled cans on the steamer rack in the pot. Place on the stove. Pour in boiling water around the cans so that it reaches a level about halfway up the sides of the cans. Bring to boil with lid on pot. Lower heat and let the water simmer for 2½ hours, checking the water level several times during steaming and add boiling water if necessary.

Lift the cans out of the water carefully. Snip off the strings. Remove the aluminum foil. Turn out the loaves on a wire rack. If possible serve while still warm.

Makes 2 loaves.

CRANBERRY SAUCE WITH GINGER

Crystallized ginger adds a perkiness to cranberry sauce that would have appealed to our Pilgrim fathers, who, having come from England, would have been fond of crystallized ginger. If you want to make this cranberry sauce year 'round, just buy extra bags of cranberries when they're in season and freeze the bags "as is." When you're ready to use them, rinse them in a colander under cold running water without thawing, and use them like fresh cranberries.

1 cup sugar
2 cups water

3 tablespoons slivered sliced
crystallized ginger
1 pound (4 cups) cranberries

In a saucepan combine the sugar and water. Bring to a boil, stirring constantly to dissolve the sugar. When the mixture boils add the crystallized ginger and cranberries and cook, stirring, until most of the cranberries have burst, about 5 minutes. Remove from heat and cool, stirring occasionally. Pour into a bowl, cover, and refrigerate until chilled and slightly firm. (This sauce cannot be molded.) Transfer to a serving dish.

Makes about 8 servings.

DRIED FRUIT PIE

4 ounces dried apples
4 ounces dried pears
3 ounces dried apricots
½ cup raisins
2 tablespoons brown sugar
½ teaspoon cinnamon
2 cups cold water

2 tablespoons lime juice
1½ teaspoons grated orange zest
1 teaspoon cornstarch
Pastry for 2-crust pie (your favorite
   recipe, or Quick Tender Food
   Processor Pie Crust [see *index*]

Combine apples, pears, apricots, raisins, brown sugar, cinnamon, and cold water in a saucepan. Cover and bring to boil. Lower heat and simmer 10 minutes, stirring once or twice. Remove from heat. Add lime juice and grated orange zest. Turn into a bowl and allow to cool. Cover and chill several hours.

Preheat oven at 400°F. (204°C.). Drain a tablespoon of liquid from the chilled fruit into a small saucepan. Combine with the cornstarch. Drain the balance of the liquid from the fruit into the saucepan and combine. Bring to a boil, stirring. Pour over the fruits and mix well. Roll the pastry and fit the bottom crust into a 9-inch pie pan. Spoon the fruit into the pie shell, spreading out evenly. Cover with the top crust.

Trim the crust and seal around the edges with the tines of a fork. Slash the top crust in several places for steam vents. Bake 40 to 45 minutes. Cool on a wire rack. Serve at room temperature or chilled.

Makes 1 9-inch pie.

COLONIAL VIRGINIA THANKSGIVING DINNER

* Crab Bisque

* Plantation Roast Turkey with Virginia Ham Stuffing and

* Currant Sauce

* Onion Spoon Bread   * Asparagus with Buttered Crumbs

* Rice with Pine Nuts and Pistachios

* Fig Pudding

In the 1700s glasses of fine Sherry would have preceded a dinner such as this one, and it would still be nice to serve today. Crab and other seafoods were abundant in Virginia's coastal waters, and crab dishes such as bisque were often served at special dinners. Turkey and ham, typical foods of the period that were available in November, combine in this menu as flavorful roast stuffed turkey. Onion Spoon Bread is a pleasing modern version of oldfashioned Southern spoon bread, while Asparagus with Buttered Crumbs is one of the ways this vegetable was served. Rice with Pine Nuts and Pistachios was a favorite of Thomas Jefferson, who prepared the dish himself. Fig Pudding, which is English in origin, was the appropriate ending to many a wintertime Colonial dinner.

OVEN TEMPERATURE AND USE. Unless you have two ovens, one to use for the turkey and the other for the Onion Spoon Bread, you will need to turn up the oven temperature as soon as the turkey is removed and left to stand on the carving board covered with aluminum foil, shiny side in, while the Onion Spoon Bread is baking.

* Recipes follow for asterisked items.

CRAB BISQUE

2 tablespoons margarine or butter
3 tablespoons grated onion
2 tablespoons flour
3½ cups half and half (milk and
    cream dairy product)
½ pound lump crabmeat (picked
    over and all shell and cartilage
    bits removed)

⅛ teaspoon mace
½ teaspoon salt
Freshly ground pepper to taste
¼ cup sherry
Paprika

Sauté the onion in margarine or butter in a heavy saucepan until soft but not brown. Add flour and cook for a minute. Add 2 cups of the half and half and cook, stirring with a wire whisk until thickened. Remove from heat. Add the crabmeat, mace, salt, and pepper. Put through a food processor fitted with a steel blade or through an electric blender until puréed. Pour the mixture back into the saucepan. Add the sherry and the remaining half and half. Bring to simmer, lower heat, cover, and simmer 15 minutes. Ladle into soup cups and sprinkle lightly in center with paprika.

Makes 8 or more servings.

PLANTATION ROAST TURKEY WITH VIRGINIA HAM STUFFING

1 12-pound turkey, giblets reserved
    for another use
1 recipe Old-Fashioned Bread
    Stuffing (see index)

1½ cups finely diced Virginia ham
1 recipe Currant Sauce (below)

Prepare turkey as directed in Chapter 2, Roast Turkey. Prepare the Old-Fashioned Bread Stuffing, adding the diced Virginia ham to the ingredients when adding the breadcrumbs. Stuff, truss, and roast the turkey. Serve with Currant Sauce.

CURRANT SAUCE

1 small garlic clove, finely minced	1 tablespoon lemon juice
¼ cup currant jelly	½ cup sherry
½ cup butter or margarine	½ teaspoon salt
2 tablespoons prepared mustard	Freshly ground pepper to taste

Place the garlic, currant jelly, and butter or margarine into a small saucepan and place over very low heat. Cook, stirring, until the jelly and butter or margarine are melted. Add the mustard, lemon juice, sherry, salt, and pepper and heat just to simmer, but do not allow to boil. Transfer to a heated sauce boat.

Makes 1¼ cups, or enough for 8 servings.

ONION SPOON BREAD

3 cups milk	2 tablespoons grated onion
1 cup corn meal (preferably stone ground corn meal)	3 tablespoons finely sliced scallions
1 teaspoon salt	¼ cup melted margarine or butter
½ teaspoon baking powder	3 eggs, beaten

Preheat oven at 350°F. (177°C.). Heat the milk slightly in a saucepan. Add the corn meal and cook, stirring constantly, for several minutes until thickened. Remove from heat. Transfer to a bowl. Add the salt and baking powder and mix well. Add half of the melted margarine or butter and mix well. Pour the other half into a 1½ quart baking dish. Stir the grated onion and scallions into the batter. Add the beaten eggs and pour into the baking dish. Bake 35-40 minutes, or until a knife inserted in the center comes out clean. Serve immediately, spooning out portions from the baking dish.

Makes 8 servings.

ASPARAGUS
WITH BUTTERED CRUMBS

Asparagus goes very nicely with this menu, but since it is out of season at Thanksgiving time frozen asparagus must be used instead of fresh. Should you make this dish when asparagus is in season allow 3 or 4 thick asparagus spears per person, or 24 to 32 spears.

3 10-ounce boxes frozen asparagus (preferably jumbo size spears)	1 tablespoon chopped parsley
¼ cup margarine or butter	½ teaspoon savory
¾ cup fine dry bread crumbs	½ teaspoon salt
	Freshly ground pepper to taste

Cook asparagus according to package directions until just tender. Meanwhile melt the margarine or butter in a skillet. Add the bread crumbs and sauté for several minutes, stirring with a wooden spoon. Add the parsley, savory, salt, and pepper, and heat a few more minutes, stirring. Drain the asparagus and place on a heated serving dish. Sprinkle the breadcrumb mixture over the asparagus.

Makes 8 servings.

RICE WITH PINE NUTS
AND PISTACHIOS

1½ cups rice	½ cup unsalted blanched pistachio
6 tablespoons butter	nuts
½ cup pine nuts (pignolias)	½ teaspoon mace

Cook rice in a covered saucepan in boiling water to cover by 1 inch for about 20 minutes or until just tender.

Melt butter in a skillet. Add the pine nuts and sauté over medium heat, stirring, until golden. Add to the rice along with the pistachio nuts and combine gently but thoroughly. Spoon into a heated serving dish and sprinkle with the mace.

Makes 8 servings.

FIG PUDDING

½ pound dried figs
¼ cup molasses
½ cup brown sugar, firmly packed
½ cup finely chopped suet
   (preferably beef kidney suet)
4 eggs
1 cup peeled, cored, chopped, tart
   apples
¼ teaspoon salt

1 teaspoon cinnamon
½ teaspoon nutmeg
3 cups slightly dry crumbled white
   bread crumbs
½ cup flour
1 cup milk
½ cup chopped pecans
1 cup heavy cream

Place figs into a saucepan and add enough cold water to cover them generously. Bring to boil and simmer 30 minutes, or until tender. Drain and chop the figs. Combine in a bowl with the molasses, brown sugar and suet. Add the eggs, one at a time, combining thoroughly after each addition. Add the apples, salt, cinnamon and nutmeg. Add the bread crumbs alternately with the milk. Add the pecans and mix well.

Spoon the mixture into a buttered and sugared 1½ quart pudding mold. Cover the mold with a lid or with aluminum foil tied on securely. Set the mold on a rack in a pot and pour boiling water into the pot to a level halfway up the side of the mold. Cover the pot and steam the pudding over low heat for 5 hours, checking the water level occasionally and adding more boiling water if necessary. Remove the pudding and unmold on a serving plate. Spoon onto individual serving dishes and pour a little cream over each serving.

Makes 8 or more servings.

COUNTRY THANKSGIVING DINNER

* Pumpkin Soup

* Roast Turkey with Oyster-Lemon Stuffing (see index)

* Classic Giblet Gravy (see index)   Fluffy Mashed Potatoes

* Whipped Turnip Casserole

* Green Beans with Dill-Parsley Butter

* Cranberry-Walnut Bread

Apple-Raisin Pie with Sharp Cheddar Cheese

This is a hearty and earthy dinner like those made long ago in farm kitchens from the bounty of fall harvests. Golden pumpkins would have been gathered in from the fields to make soul-satisfying soup. Potatoes and turnips would have been brought up from the root cellar, the former to be cooked and mashed to a fluffy consistency ready to soak up lots of luscious giblet gravy, and the latter converted into a light-as-a-feather casserole dish. Roast turkey would be stuffed with oysters, an oldtime all-time favorite. The aroma of freshly baked Cranberry-Walnut Bread and apple pies would fill the air.

Even though you'll probably be taking the easier way out by getting your pumpkin from a can and your vegetable from the local market, you can still feel you've gone "back to the farm for Thanksgiving" with this country flavor menu. The oyster stuffing for the turkey is given a new twist with the addition of lemon. If Thanksgiving doesn't seem like Thanksgiving without mincemeat pie, have that instead of apple, or better still, have both.

OVEN TEMPERATURE AND USE. Unless you have two ovens, one to use for the turkey and one for the Whipped Turnip Casserole, you will need to turn up the oven temperature as soon as the turkey is removed and left to stand on the carving board covered with aluminum foil, shiny side in, while the turnip casserole bakes. The Cranberry-Walnut Bread can be baked early in the day, or the day ahead.

* Recipes follow for asterisked items.

PUMPKIN SOUP

2 cups milk
1 bay leaf
2 slices onion
3 sprigs parsley
1 29-ounce can pumpkin
⅛ teaspoon nutmeg
Pinch of ginger
½ teaspoon cinnamon

Pinch of coriander
1 tablespoon lemon juice
2 tablespoons brown sugar
1 tablespoon grated onions
1 teaspoon salt
Freshly ground pepper to taste
1 cup cream

Scald the milk with the bay leaf, onion slices, and parsley. Combine with the pumpkin. Place into top of double boiler and add the nutmeg, ginger, cinnamon, coriander, lemon juice, brown sugar, grated onions, salt, and pepper. Set over simmering water and heat 30 minutes, stirring occasionally. Scald the cream and add to the soup. Taste and adjust seasoning if necessary. Serve in soup cups.

Makes 8 servings.

WHIPPED TURNIP CASSEROLE

1 yellow turnip, about 3½ pounds
¼ cup margarine or butter
¼ cup finely chopped onions
1 teaspoon chicken broth
    concentrate

Freshly ground pepper to taste
1 tablespoon lemon juice
2 eggs, lightly beaten

Peel turnip and cut into small cubes. Place into a large saucepan and add cold water to just cover. Bring to boil, lower heat, cover, and simmer until very tender when pierced with a fork, 30 minutes or longer.

Meanwhile melt the margarine or butter in a small skillet and sauté the onion until soft. Set aside.

Preheat oven at 375°F. (191°C.). When the turnips are cooked, drain and mash them. Add the chicken broth concentrate, the sautéed onion with the margarine or butter in the skillet, the pepper and lemon juice. Add the beaten eggs and combine thoroughly, transfer to a greased casserole and bake about 45 minutes.

Makes 8 servings.

GREEN BEANS WITH
DILL-PARSLEY BUTTER

2 pounds green beans, ends   ½ cup finely chopped parsley
    removed   1 teaspoon dillweed
6 tablespoons butter, melted

   Cook green beans in 2 inches of boiling water until just tender.
Drain. Place in a heated serving dish. Combine the melted butter, parsley, and dillweed. Pour over the green beans and toss.

Makes 8 or more servings.

CRANBERRY WALNUT BREAD

3 cups sifted flour   1 cup milk
4 teaspoons baking powder   2 tablespoons melted butter or
½ cup sugar   margarine
1 teaspoon salt   1 teaspoon vanilla extract
½ cup chopped walnuts   1 cup cranberries
1 egg

   Preheat oven at 350°F. (177°C.). Sift together flour, baking powder, ¼
cup sugar, and salt. Add the walnuts and toss together. Beat the egg and
add the milk to it. Add the melted butter. Add half of the flour mixture
and beat until smooth. Add the vanilla extract. Chop the cranberries, or
put them through a food processor using the slicing blade. Combine the
cranberries with the remaining ¼ cup sugar. Add to the batter and mix
well. Add the remaining flour mixture and combine thoroughly. Turn
the mixture into a greased 5-inch by 9-inch loaf pan and bake 50 to 60
minutes, or until a cake tester inserted into the center comes out clean.
Turn out on wire rack to cool. Wrap tightly in aluminum foil if storing
overnight. Slice thinly to serve.

Makes 1 loaf.

CITY THANKSGIVING DINNER

* Sorrel Soup

* Boneless Turkey Breast with Savory Mushroom Filling (see index)

* Straw Potato Nests with Glazed Minted Peas and Baby Carrots

* Cranberry Sauce with Orange Liqueur

* Pecan Bread

* Pumpkin Parfait

Although this City Thanksgiving Dinner has an air of sophistication it still retains all the essential parts of a traditional Thanksgiving feast. The boneless turkey breast is outstanding, easy to serve, and takes up little space in the refrigerator. Straw Potato Nests are simple to make and look really charming when served. Cranberry sauce achieves new heights when made with orange liqueur, and the nutty goodness of Pecan Bread rounds out the meal. Pumpkin takes the form of a frozen dessert rather than a heavier one such as pie.

OVEN TEMPERATURE AND USE. Unless you have two ovens, one for the turkey breast and the other for the Straw Potato Nests, you will need to raise the oven temperature as soon as the turkey breast is taken from the oven, and left to stand on the carving board covered with aluminum foil, shiny side in, while you bake the nests. Bake the Pecan Bread the day before the dinner so that its flavor will have time to develop.

* Recipes follow for asterisked items.

SORREL SOUP

1 medium onion, grated
3 tablespoons butter or margarine
1 13-ounce jar sorrel
2 egg yolks, lightly beaten
1 cup light cream

4 cups chicken broth
1 teaspoon salt
Freshly ground pepper to taste
1 tablespoon lemon juice

Sauté the onion in butter or margarine until it becomes transparent. Stir in the sorrel. Remove from heat. Combine the egg yolks and cream. Heat the chicken broth in a heavy saucepan to the boiling point, lower heat, and add the cream and egg mixture all at once, stirring briskly with a wire whisk. Add the sorrel mixture along with the salt and pepper, and heat, stirring occasionally, until very hot, but not boiling. Stir in the lemon juice and serve in soup cups.

Makes 8 or more servings.

STRAW POTATO NESTS WITH GLAZED MINTED PEAS AND BABY CARROTS

2 or 3 large Maine potatoes (do not
    use new potatoes)
1 egg
Salt
1 pound fresh peas
1 teaspoon dried mint

2 cups cooked baby carrots cut into
    1½ inch lengths, or 1 can (about
    14 ounces) extra small baby
    carrots
¼ cup butter or margarine
3 tablespoons brown sugar
Paprika

Peel the potatoes, one at a time, and slice as thin as possible (paper thin is the goal). Cut the slices into paper thin strips and plunge them into a bowl of cold water to prevent discoloration. Make enough of these potato strips to measure 6 cups (drained).

Preheat oven at 425°F. (218°C.). Remove the potato strips from the water and spread out on paper towels. Pat them thoroughly dry. Beat the egg. Add the potato strips to the egg and mix well. Divide the strips equally among 8 10-ounce greased custard cups. Spread the strips out across the bottoms and up the sides of the custard cups. Bake 40 minutes until partially browned at the bottom and on the sides. Remove from custard cups and sprinkle lightly with salt.

While the potato nests are baking, shell the peas and cook them with the mint in boiling water to cover for 5 minutes, or until just tender. Drain. Cook the carrots in boiling water until just tender, or remove from the can and drain.

Melt the margarine or butter in a skillet. Add the drained peas and carrots and toss to coat. Add the brown sugar and paprika and toss again. Cook over medium heat until lightly glazed, tossing frequently. Fill the potato nests with the glazed peas and carrots, dividing equally. (The potato nests cannot be reheated.)

Makes 8 servings.

CRANBERRY SAUCE WITH ORANGE LIQUEUR

1 cup sugar
1½ cups water
4 cups (1 pound) cranberries
1 teaspoon grated orange zest

½ teaspoon grated lemon zest
2 tablespoons Grand Marnier or
    other orange liqueur

Combine the sugar and water in a saucepan and heat to boiling, stirring constantly to dissolve the sugar. Boil a few minutes. Add the cranberries and boil until the skins pop open, stirring occasionally. Remove from heat and stir in the grated orange zest and lemon zest and the Grand Marnier or other orange liqueur. Allow to cool. Transfer to a glass or ceramic bowl. Cover and chill 24 hours. Transfer to a serving dish.

Makes about 8 servings.

PECAN BREAD

1 egg, lightly beaten
1 cup milk
3 cups sifted flour
¾ cup sugar
½ teaspoon salt

3 teaspoons double-acting baking
   powder
3 tablespoons melted margarine or
   butter
½ cup chopped pecans
½ cup ground pecans

Combine the egg and milk with an egg beater. Sift the flour, sugar, salt, and baking powder into a bowl and add the egg-milk mixture. Add the melted margarine or butter and the pecans and allow to stand 30 minutes undisturbed.

Preheat the oven at 300°F. (149°C.). Turn the batter into a greased 5-inch by 9-inch loaf pan and smooth the top with a rubber spatula. Bake 1¼ to 1½ hours, or until a cake tester inserted into the center comes out clean. Remove from the baking pan and cool on a wire rack. If making the day ahead, which is preferable, allow to cool completely, wrap tightly in aluminum foil and store in a cool place. Slice thinly to serve.

Makes 1 loaf.

PUMPKIN PARFAIT

2 cups pumpkin (canned or
   homemade thick mashed
   pumpkin)
½ cup brown sugar, firmly packed
1 teaspoon cinnamon
½ teaspoon ginger
¼ teaspoon nutmeg
⅛ teaspoon allspice

Pinch of salt
1 quart eggnog ice cream (if not
   available use French vanilla ice
   cream which is richer than plain
   vanilla)
Sweetened whipped cream
   (optional)
Crystallized ginger strips (optional)

Combine the pumpkin, brown sugar, cinnamon, ginger, nutmeg, allspice and salt. Soften the ice cream in a ceramic or glass bowl using a wooden spoon and working as quickly as possible. Stir the pumpkin mixture into the ice cream. Transfer to a plastic container, cover tightly and place in freezer immediately. Freeze until firm.

To serve, spoon into parfait glasses. If desired top each glass with a dollop of whipped cream and strew a few crystallized ginger strips over the top.

Makes 8 servings.

TURKEY LOVER'S THANKSGIVING DINNER

* Turkey-Oyster Stew (see index)

* Roast Turkey with Cornbread and Turkey Sausage Stuffing (see index)

* Turkey Pan Gravy (see index)   * Giblet Stuffing Balls (see index)

* Fluffy Pumpkin and Cannellini Bean Casserole

* Broccoli in Brown Butter Sauce

* Calico Cranberry Mold   * Whole Wheat Popovers

* Gobbler Mincemeat Pie

Turkey is the star of this Thanksgiving Dinner, starting with the first course where it lends a subtle flavor to Turkey-Oyster Stew. The grand bird is beautifully roasted as the main course and has a mildly spicy stuffing with turkey sausage as the main ingredient. Giblet Stuffing Balls, in which the turkey giblets and neck are used, accompany the roasted bird. To fill in around the turkey, the main course includes a mellow combination of pumpkin and cannellini beans in a casserole, broccoli with a quick but enticing Brown Butter Sauce, and a Calico Cranberry Mold so laden with cranberries, nuts, apples, and walnuts that there's only enough gelatin used to hold it together. You can really consider it a salad rather than a relish. Whole Wheat Popovers are a welcome and tasty change from the usual white ones.

If you thought you'd never have turkey for dessert you'll be pleasantly surprised by Gobbler Mincemeat Pie, one of the best mince pies you're ever likely to taste. The mincemeat is made with cooked turkey (all genuine mincemeat is made with meat) and you can make it weeks or months in advance. If you choose to use the accompanying pie crust recipe you'll find it one of the fastest and most tender of crusts, but you do need to have a food processor to make it.

OVEN TEMPERATURE AND USE. Turn up the oven temperature when the turkey is removed. If you want to bake the Fluffy Pumpkin and Cannellini Bean Casserole at the same time as the Whole Wheat Popovers, you can put them both in a preheated 450°F. (232°C.) oven and turn the oven down to 350°F. (177°C.) after 10 minutes. The casserole and popovers will then be finished at about the same time. Bake the Gobbler Mincemeat Pie ahead of time unless you have two ovens to use and want to serve the pie warm.

* Recipes follow for asterisked items.

FLUFFY PUMPKIN AND CANNELLINI BEAN CASSEROLE

½ cup very finely chopped onions
½ cup very finely chopped carrot
½ cup very finely chopped celery
3 tablespoons margarine or butter
1 garlic clove, finely minced
1 teaspoon salt
Freshly ground pepper to taste
Pinch of thyme
Pinch of oregano

1 29-ounce can pumpkin or 3 cups thick, cooked, mashed pumpkin
1 20-ounce can cannellini beans or 2⅓ cups cooked drained cannellini beans
2 eggs, lightly beaten
½ cup milk or cream
½ cup shredded Gouda cheese

Cook the onions, carrots, and celery in the margarine or butter in a heavy covered saucepan over low heat about 10 minutes, stirring occasionally. Do not allow the vegetables to brown. Stir in the garlic and cook another minute, stirring. Remove from the heat.

Preheat the oven at 350°F. (177°C.). Add the salt, pepper, thyme, oregano, and pumpkin to the sauce and mix well. Drain and rinse the cannellini beans and purée them in a food processor fitted with a steel blade or put them through a food mill. Add the puréed beans to the saucepan and mix well. Stir in the eggs and the milk or cream. Transfer to a greased casserole or baking dish. Sprinkle the grated cheese over the top. Bake 30 minutes or until top is brown. If necessary run under the broiler a minute or two to brown the top.

Makes 8 servings.

BROCCOLI IN BROWN BUTTER SAUCE

2 bunches broccoli   6 tablespoons butter

Wash and trim broccoli. Cook on a steamer rack with 1 inch of boiling water in the bottom of the pot, covered, or cook in a small amount of boiling water, covered, until just tender. Drain.

Meanwhile melt the butter over very low heat in a small saucepan. Allow to cook until a medium brown color. Remove from heat. Place drained broccoli in a heated serving dish and pour the brown butter over it.

Makes 8 servings.

CALICO CRANBERRY MOLD

4 cups (1 pound) cranberries   1 or 2 tart apples
½ cup sugar   1 cup chopped celery
1 envelope plain gelatin   1 cup chopped walnuts
½ cup orange juice

Put cranberries through food processor fitted with steel blade until well broken up but not at all puréed, or put through food grinder using blade that will give you the coarsest result. Place in a bowl and stir in the sugar. Allow to set 15 minutes, stirring occasionally. Meanwhile soften the gelatin in the orange juice in a small saucepan. Place over low heat and heat, stirring, until the gelatin is completely dissolved. Set aside.

Meanwhile peel, core, and chop enough apple to make 1 cup, and add to the cranberries immediately, whether or not 15 minutes has passed. After the 15 minutes has passed add the celery and walnuts and mix well. Add the orange juice mixture and mix well. Turn the mixture into a plain 5-cup ring mold which has been lightly oiled. Pack down well and smooth the top with the back of a spoon. Cover and refrigerate until firm, 6 hours or more. Unmold onto a chilled serving plate.

Makes 12 servings.

WHOLE WHEAT POPOVERS

2 eggs at room temperature
1½ cups milk at room temperature
½ teaspoon vegetable oil
1 cup whole wheat flour
 Preheat oven at 450°F. (232°C.). Beat the eggs. Add the milk and vegetable oil. In a larger bowl place the flour and salt. Grease muffin tins and place them in the oven. Add about one-third of the liquid mixture to the flour and mix until smooth. Add the remaining liquid mixture gradually and beat just until smooth. Remove the muffin tins from the oven and fill about one-half full. Put them back in the oven. Bake 10 minutes. Reduce oven temperature to 350°F. (177°C.) and continue baking 25 minutes or more. Do not open oven door during baking time.

Makes 12.

Note: These popovers will not "pop over" quite as much as popovers made with white flour, but their flavor is superior.

GOBBLER MINCEMEAT PIE

You'll want to start the mincemeat at least three weeks before you plan to bake the pies, so that it can age and mellow properly. The mincemeat keeps beautifully in the refrigerator for at least six months in the event you only want to bake one pie for Thanksgiving and the balance at a later time.

For the mincemeat:
1 pound coarsely chopped cooked
  turkey
½ pound coarsely chopped suet
  (preferably beef kidney suet)
1 cup raisins
1 cup Sultanas or white raisins
1 cup cut-up figs
1 cup cut-up preserved pineapple
  slices or candied pineapple
2 ounces or ¼ cup candied lemon
  peel

2 ounces or ¼ cup candied lemon
  peel
2 ounces or ¼ cup candied red
  cherries
1 cup currants
1½ cups dark brown sugar, loosely
  packed
1 cup chopped blanched almonds
2 cups apple juice or cider
1½ teaspoons cinnamon
1½ teaspoons nutmeg
1 teaspoon mace

1 teaspoon cloves
1 teaspoon ground coriander
½ teaspoon salt
1 cup or more brandy
Dry sherry (if required)

For the pie:
For each 9-inch pie:
4 cups of above mincemeat

2 cups peeled, chopped, tart apples
3 tablespoons lemon juice
Pastry for 9-inch 2-crust pie (Quick
    Tender Food Processor Pie Crust,
    below, or your own favorite
    recipe)
1 egg yolk combined with 2
    tablespoons water (optional)

FOR THE MINCEMEAT:

Three weeks or longer before ready to use the mincemeat, grind together the turkey, suet, raisins, Sultanas, figs, pineapple, orange peel, lemon peel, and cherries. Put into a large saucepan. Add the currants, almonds, brown sugar, apple juice or cider, cinnamon, nutmeg, mace, cloves, coriander and salt, and mix well. Heat to steaming over medium heat and simmer a few minutes, stirring constantly. Turn the mixture into a crock and allow it to cool. Stir in 1 cup brandy. Cover the crock and place it in the refrigerator or a cold dry cellar. Stir every few days, and if mixture is dry add some sherry to moisten it. Be sure to stir all the way to the bottom of the crock each time. The week before using the mincemeat add brandy, rather than sherry, if it needs moistening.

FOR THE PIE:

Preheat oven at 400°F. (204°C.). For each 9-inch pie combine 4 cups of the mincemeat with the chopped apples and lemon juice. Roll out the pie crust on a floured board and line the pie tin. Spoon in the mincemeat mixture and smooth with the back of a spoon. Place the top crust over it. Trim the edges and press together all around with the tines of a fork. Slash the top in several places for the steam to escape. Bake 20 minutes. If desired brush top with egg yolk mixture. Bake 20 to 25 minutes longer. Cool partially or completely before serving.

Makes enough mincemeat for 2 9-inch pies and 1 8-inch pie or some tarts.

QUICK, TENDER, FOOD PROCESSOR PIE CRUST

2 cups flour
1 tablespoon sugar
Pinch of salt
6 tablespoons cold butter or
  margarine

4 tablespoons cold vegetable
  shortening
¼ cup ice water

Place flour, sugar, and salt in food processor fitted with a steel blade. Turn the machine on and off. Add the butter or margarine and the vegetable shortening all cut into small pieces. Turn the machine on for 5 seconds. Then turn the machine on again and add the ice water in a thin steady stream. Turn off the machine when dough forms a ball. Wrap in waxed paper and place in freezer 15 to 30 minutes.

Divide into two parts and roll out on floured board.

Makes pastry for 1 9-inch 2-crust pie.

THANKSGIVING DINNER ELEGANTE

* Scotch Smoked Salmon

* Clear Turtle Soup with Madeira or Sherry

* Caviar Crêpes

* Roast Turkey with Twice-Wild Stuffing (see index)

* Classic Giblet Gravy (see index)

* Braised Boston Lettuce   * Featherbed Anchovy Potatoes

* Orange-Pickled Walnut Chutney   * Ultra Lemon Bread

* Frosty Cranberry Sherbet Mold

California Chardonay

You may have to empty out your purse to have this Thanksgiving dinner, but you won't be sorry, because it's a gourmet's treat from beginning to end and something to really inspire thanks. Another thing to be thankful for is that the first three courses, while really the ultimate in fine eating, require very little effort to prepare. Beyond that, the chutney can and should be made well ahead of Thanksgiving time, and the really lemony bread and tangy cranberry dessert mold are made the day ahead. The turkey is sumptuously stuffed with wild rice and wild mushrooms, Boston lettuce is treated as a braised vegetable, and Feather-bed Anchovy Potatoes are almost light enough to be called a souffle.

This dinner deserves a fine white wine, and since Thanksgiving is an American celebration a fine California wine seems in order. Select a California Chardonay in the style of a Puligny Montrachet or Macon Blanc as discussed in the French Thanksgiving Dinner to follow. Your wine dealer should be able to help you with a selection.

OVEN TEMPERATURE AND USE. The oven is used for the roast turkey and the Featherbed Anchovy Potatoes. Raise the oven temperature as soon as the turkey has been removed, and the potatoes can then be baked about 25 minutes.

* Recipes follow for asterisked items.

SCOTCH SMOKED SALMON

Boston or other buttery type lettuce
  leaves
16 slices (more or less) Scotch
  smoked salmon

8 lemon wedges
Capers
Freshly ground pepper to taste

Arrange a leaf or two of lettuce on each salad-size plate. Arrange 2 slices salmon over the lettuce on each plate. You may use more or fewer slices depending on the size of the salmon. Arrange a lemon wedge on each plate. Sprinkle some capers over the salmon. Let each person grind his own pepper. (If desired serve with thinly sliced bread.)

Makes 8 servings.

CLEAR TURTLE SOUP WITH MADEIRA OR SHERRY

2 cans clear turtle soup (not mock turtle soup)

2 or 3 tablespoons Madeira or Sherry

Heat the turtle soup in a saucepan with the Madeira or Sherry. Serve in small soup cups.

Makes 8 servings.

CAVIAR CREPES

16 5-inch crêpes (your own recipe, bought crêpes, or Basic Crêpes, below)
1 pint sour cream

4 ounces Beluga, Sevruga, or pressed caviar (do not substitute lumpfish caviar)
Lemon juice
Snipped chives

Prepare crêpes. Spread each with sour cream. Sprinkle with the caviar, dividing equally among the crêpes. Sprinkle the caviar with a little lemon juice. Roll up the crêpes. Arrange two on each plate. Put a dollop of sour cream on each pair of crêpes and strew some chives over the sour cream. Serve immediately.

Makes 8 servings

BASIC CREPES

1 cup instant or quick-mixing flour	Pinch of salt
⅔ cup cold milk	2 tablespoons melted butter
⅔ cup cold water	Melted butter or oil for greasing
3 eggs	crêpe pan

Combine the flour, milk, water, and eggs in a bowl using a wire whisk. Add salt and melted butter. Heat a 6½-inch (top measurement) crêpe pan over medium heat and brush inside the pan with melted butter or oil. Pour in a small ladleful of batter and tilt the pan immediately to make the batter cover the entire bottom of the pan thinly. After you make the first crêpe you can judge the right amount to use. If there is excess batter pour it back into the bowl immediately, before it has time to set, but it is preferable to measure out the right amount each time.

When the crêpe has browned on one side, turn it over with a spatula, or if you're adept at making crêpes, flip it over. Brown the second side briefly. The first side that was browned is the "outside" of the crêpe. Continue making crêpes, arranging them on a plate as you make them. They will not stick together so it's not too important how you stack them. Brush the crêpe pan with the melted butter or oil as often as necessary until all the batter has been used. Use immediately or freeze with a sheet of aluminum foil between each crêpe and the entire lot wrapped tightly in plastic wrap. Thaw overnight in refrigerator or until the crêpes can be separated easily without tearing. Warm in a 300°F. (149°C.) oven for several minutes before filling and serving.

Makes about 2 dozen.

BRAISED BOSTON LETTUCE

6 small firm heads Boston lettuce,
  washed in several changes of
  cold water
3 slices bacon
½ cup finely chopped onions
⅓ cup finely chopped carrot

Freshly ground pepper to taste
½ cup turkey stock or chicken broth
½ cup turkey gravy (homemade or
  canned)
3 tablespoons butter

Trim bottoms of lettuce straight across and remove any outside leaves that are not close to the head. Place the heads of lettuce in a pan of cold water. Cover and bring to boil. Boil 2 or 3 minutes. Remove the lid, and remove from heat. Place the pan under cold running water so that cold water replaces the boiling water and cools the lettuce heads. Remove the lettuces and remove as much water from them as possible either by spinning them in a salad dryer, or by squeezing each lettuce from stem end to the opposite end and patting with paper towels.

Preheat oven at 350°F. (177°C.). Arrange the bacon in a greased shallow baking dish. Sprinkle the onions, carrots, and pepper over the top. Arrange the lettuces on their sides over the bacon in a single layer. Combine the turkey stock or chicken broth and turkey gravy and pour over the lettuces. Cover with aluminum foil. Bake 45 minutes. Remove the lettuces and cut in half lengthwise. Arrange on a heated serving platter. Boil down the sauce slightly. Swirl in the butter and strain the sauce over the lettuces.

Makes 8 to 12 servings.

FEATHERBED ANCHOVY POTATOES

3 or 4 medium size potatoes
8 anchovy fillets cut into small
   pieces
3 tablespoons butter or margarine
3 eggs
¾ cup cream
¾ cup freshly grated Emmenthal,
   Gruyère or Jarlsberg cheese

Freshly ground pepper to taste
   (preferably white pepper)
2 tablespoons fine dry bread
   crumbs
2 tablespoons melted butter or
   margarine

Peel, cut up, and boil the potatoes in salted water until tender. Meanwhile work half of the anchovy fillets into a paste along with 2 tablespoons butter or margarine with a mortar and pestle, or put through an electric blender or a food processor fitted with a steel blade.

Preheat the oven at 375°F. (191°C.). When the potatoes are done, drain and mash them. Measure enough of the mashed potatoes to make 3 cups. Reserve the balance for another use. Combine the hot mashed potatoes with the cream. Separate the eggs and beat the yolks lightly. Add them to the potatoes. Add the anchovy-butter mixture along with the remaining anchovy pieces, the cheese, and pepper. Beat the egg whites until stiff but not dry and fold them into the potato mixture. Transfer to a well-buttered souffle dish or straight-sided casserole. Sprinkle the top with the bread crumbs. Bake 25 minutes until brown and slightly puffed. If the top has not browned run under the broiler a minute or two until brown. Melt the remaining tablespoon of butter and pour over the top.

Makes 8 servings.

ORANGE-PICKLED WALNUT CHUTNEY

Make this at least a week before Thanksgiving, and the longer beforehand the better. It keeps for months and is nice to have in any season.

3½ cups (approximately) malt
    vinegar and liquid from pickled
    walnuts * combined
1 12-ounce package pitted prunes
1 12-ounce package pitted dates
3 pounds firm tart apples
4 to 5 medium onions

4 juice oranges (not navel)
1 lemon
2 cups dark brown sugar
8 to 10 pickled walnuts *, drained
    and crushed
4 garlic cloves, bruised
1½ ounces mixed pickling spices

Drain the liquid from the pickled walnuts and add enough malt vinegar to measure 1½ cups liquid. Place in a saucepan and bring to boil. Add the prunes and simmer 5 minutes, covered. Set aside.

Chop the dates. Core the apples and chop them coarsely. Peel and coarsely chop enough onions to measure 4 cups.

Drain the prunes and pour the vinegar into a large measuring cup. Add enough additional malt vinegar to measure 3½ cups. Set aside.

Combine prunes, dates, apples, and onions in a large pot or kettle. Cut off any letter stamping on the orange and lemon rinds, and cut off the stem ends. Cut each orange and the lemon into quarters lengthwise, and in half crosswise. Remove any seeds. Put the pieces briefly through a food processor fitted with a steel blade so that they are still quite coarse, or put through a meat grinder fitted with a coarse blade. Add the orange and lemon mixture to the pot, along with the measured vinegar. Add the brown sugar and pickled walnuts. Tie the garlic and pickling spices in a clean cloth and drop into the pot. Bring to a boil and simmer until the apples have disintegrated, 3 to 3½ hours, stirring often. Remove the spice bag and discard. Pack the chutney in sterilized jars. Seal, cool and refrigerate.

Makes 7 pints.

* Jars of pickled walnuts are imported from England and are available in specialty food stores, grocery stores, and supermarkets.

ULTRA LEMON BREAD

2¾ cups flour
½ teaspoon baking soda
3 teaspoons baking powder
½ teaspoon salt
⅓ cup margarine or butter
1 cup brown sugar, loosely packed

½ cup wheat germ
2 tablespoons grated lemon zest
2 eggs, lightly beaten
½ cup lemon juice combined with
  ½ cup water

Preheat oven at 350°F. (177°C.). Grease a 9-inch by 5-inch loaf pan. Sift the flour, baking soda, baking powder and salt together into a bowl. Cut the margarine or butter into small pieces and drop into flour mixture. Work in with the fingers or pastry blender. Add the brown sugar, wheat germ, and grated lemon zest, and combine with the fingers. Stir in the eggs with a spoon, adding the lemon juice-water mixture gradually. Mix until smooth and turn into the greased loaf pan. Smooth the top with a rubber spatula. Bake 1 hour or until a cake tester inserted into the center comes out clean. Turn out on a wire rack to cool completely before slicing.

Makes 1 loaf.

FROSTY CRANBERRY SHERBET MOLD

1 pound (4 cups) cranberries
5 cups water
2 cups sugar
⅔ cup lemon juice
⅓ cup orange juice

Frozen whole cranberries for
    garnish (optional)
Crystallized mint leaves for garnish
    (optional)

In a stainless steel or enamel saucepan combine the cranberries and 2 cups water. Bring to boil, add ¼ cup sugar and stir until dissolved. Lower heat and simmer 10 minutes, stirring occasionally. Put the mixture through a food mill fitted with a fine mesh disc (do not use food processor) into a bowl. Cool, cover and chill 2 hours or longer.

Meanwhile combine the remaining 3 cups water and 1¾ cup sugar in a saucepan and bring to boil, stirring. Simmer 3 minutes. Transfer to a bowl and allow to cool. Cover and chill 2 hours or longer.

Add the lemon juice and orange juice to the cranberry purée. Add the syrup and freeze in an ice cream freezer according to manufacturer's instructions, or pour the mixture into a rectangular pan or freezer tray and freeze until it becomes mushy (about 2 hours). Transfer the mixture to a chilled bowl and beat with an electric beater until smooth. Return the mixture to the pan and place it in the freezer again. When the mixture is almost firm, break it up and, preferably, put it through a food processor fitted with a steel blade, or put it in a chilled bowl and beat with an electric beater until smooth. Spoon into a mold (preferably a melon mold or a plain round mold or bombe mold) and pack down well. Cover with plastic wrap and then with aluminum foil. Lay a flat plate over the top so it covers the mold completely, and weigh it down with a heavy object. Freeze for 8 hours or overnight.

Unmold by running a thin knife around the edge, dipping the mold in cool water for a few seconds, and inverting it over a serving plate. Decorate, if desired, with frozen whole cranberries and crystallized mint leaves attractively arranged.

Makes 8 or more servings.

SPEEDY BUT SMART THANKSGIVING DINNER

* Madeira Mushroom Soup

Roast Turkey with Prepared Chestnut Stuffing   * Turkey Pan Gravy (see index)

* Flageolets in Cream   ** Orange Sweet Potatoes*

* Hearts of Palm Salad   *Whole Cranberry Sauce*

Fruit Bread

Pumpkin Pie with Brandied Whipped Cream

Here's a dinner that can be put together in no time, with no sacrifice to flavor or appearance. It's a very smart dinner and one you can be proud of. The secret of this dinner is to buy a number of the main ingredients canned or packaged and to lend some fine touches to them to disguise their origin. The flavor of canned mushroom soup, for example, is enhanced by bits of sautéed onion and a splash of Madeira, flageolets are drained and gently simmered in cream, and canned sweet potatoes are the basis of the potato dish. In the event you aren't familiar with flageolets, they're lovely little green beans that look somewhat like thin baby lima beans, but their flavor is very distinctive; it's unlike that of any other bean. (Substituting lima beans will not give you even remotely the same result.) For the turkey, follow the general directions for Roast Turkey in Chapter 5, and stuff the bird with already-prepared chestnut stuffing. Look for this product, which is canned, in specialty food stores and some supermarkets. Brands most often seen are Clement Faugier, imported from France, and Raffetto, and the cans generally contain 10 ounces. Serve a can of whole berry cranberry sauce, but break it up so it isn't in the shape of a can, and spoon it into your prettiest glass serving dish. Buy a nice fruit bread. Date nut bread is easy to find, but with a little more hunting in bakeries or specialty shops you can find other more interesting kinds of bread such as banana-nut or lemon marmalade. Another time saver is to buy a ready-made pumpkin pie from a good bakery. You can make it look and taste special by whipping some heavy cream until stiff, stirring in a spoonful or two of sugar and brandy to taste, and spooning a dollop on each serving.

OVEN TEMPERATURE AND USE. The turkey and Orange Sweet Potatoes can share the oven since they both require the same temperature.

MADEIRA MUSHROOM SOUP

2 10¾-ounce cans condensed
   mushroom soup with sliced
   mushrooms (such as Campbell's
   Golden Mushroom)
3 cups milk

¼ cup Madeira wine
2 teaspoons plus 1 tablespoon
   butter or margarine
¼ cup finely minced onion
4 medium sized mushrooms, sliced

Place the soup into a heavy saucepan. Add the milk gradually and stir until smooth. Add the Madeira and stir. Cover and heat slowly, stirring occasionally.

Meanwhile melt the 2 teaspoons butter or margarine in a skillet and sauté the minced onion until soft. Stir into the soup. To the same skillet add the remaining tablespoon butter or margarine. Over high heat brown the sliced mushrooms in the skillet, turning once. Remove from heat.

When soup is well heated ladle into soup cups. Float 2 or 3 sautéed mushroom slices on top of each.

Makes 8 servings.

FLAGEOLETS IN CREAM

3 15-ounce cans Green Flageolets
   Beans
⅔ cup heavy cream

2 tablespoons butter
Dash of nutmeg

Drain the flageolets and place in a saucepan with the cream, butter and nutmeg. Cover and heat slowly. Transfer to a heated serving dish.

Makes 8 servings.

HEARTS OF PALM SALAD

3 14-ounce cans hearts of palm
Vinaigrette dressing or oil and
   vinegar dressing

1 tablespoon snipped chives
Boston or other buttery type lettuce
   leaves

Drain the hearts of palm. If the pieces are thick split them in half lengthwise. Cut all the hearts of palm into 1-inch pieces, crosswise. Place in a bowl and cover with the dressing. Add chives and toss. Cover and refrigerate 1 or more hours. To serve, arrange lettuce leaves on each salad plate and spoon the drained hearts of palm over the lettuce, dividing equally.

Makes 8 servings.

ORANGE SWEET POTATOES

2 1-pound cans sweet potatoes
1½ tablespoons grated orange peel
¼ cup brown sugar
Salt to taste
Freshly ground pepper to taste

1 cup orange juice
2 tablespoons brandy
3 tablespoons melted butter or
   margarine

Preheat oven at 325°F. (163°C.). Drain the sweet potatoes and cut them lengthwise in ¼ to ½ inch slices. Arrange them in slightly overlapping rows in a baking dish about 8 inches by 12 inches. Sprinkle them with the orange peel, brown sugar, salt, and pepper. Combine the orange juice and brandy and pour over the potatoes. Cover the baking dish and bake 30 minutes, basting once or twice. Remove the cover and pour the melted butter or margarine over the potatoes. Bake uncovered another 30 minutes, basting once or twice.

Makes 8 servings.

FRENCH THANKSGIVING DINNER

* Escargots Bourguignonne with French Bread

Lobster Bisque

* Roast Turkey with Brandied Chestnut Stuffing (see index)

* Classic Giblet Gravy (see index)

* Brussels Sprouts with Almond Butter   * Salade Composée

Brie de Meaux

Apple Tart

Demi-Tasse

French White Burgundy

Whether you're in France or the U.S.A. at Thanksgiving time, this Gallic dinner is bound to please you as a lover of good food. Start with a favorite French first course, escargots, and move on to a smooth lobster bisque, which can be made by using a good brand of canned bisque (preferably one imported from France), adding a bit of Sherry when heating it up, and sprinkling each serving with finely chopped parsley or chervil. Prepare your roast turkey with chestnut stuffing, just as Frenchmen have probably been doing for hundreds of years, but include brandy for extra fine flavor. Brussels sprouts taste special when served with almond butter, and Salade Composée, a salad of potatoes, artichoke bottoms, and celery hearts, is truly exquisite.

A French white burgundy would be right with this dinner. Select a Puligny Montrachet or Macon Blanc or Macon Blanc Villages, about in the four dollar range. These are relatively substantial wines, with nice roundness but fairly intense fruitiness.

Have some nice ripe Brie de Meaux to finish off your meal, and rather than making an apple tart (not apple pie please) buy the genuine article at a good French bakery. Demitasse tops it all off.

OVEN TEMPERATURE AND USE. When the turkey is removed from the oven turn up the oven temperature to 350°F. (177°C.) for the escargots. Heat the escargots in the oven about 10 minutes before you're ready to serve them. Don't forget to pop the French bread into the oven for a few minutes too.

* Recipes follow for asterisked items.

ESCARGOTS BOURGUIGNONNE

4 dozen snails (canned)
Dry white wine
1 cup salted butter
4 large cloves garlic
½ cup finely chopped parsley

Very generous pinch of nutmeg
Freshly ground pepper to taste
Pinch of salt
4 dozen snail shells

Drain snails well. Place in a bowl. Cover with wine. Cover the bowl and refrigerate 8 hours or overnight. Drain.

Cream the butter until very soft. Chop the garlic very fine or put it through a garlic press. Add it to the butter, along with the parsley, nutmeg, pepper, and salt, and mix well. Put a tiny dab of the butter inside each snail shell. Insert a snail in each shell, pointed end in. Fill the space at the end of the shell with the butter mixture, using it all up by mounding it if necessary. Set the snails in 8 6-place snail plates with the buttered sides up and perfectly level.

Preheat oven at 350°F. (177°C.). Place the snails in the oven for about 10 minutes, or until the butter melts and bubbles. Serve immediately with French bread. Supply each person with snail tongs and a snail fork.

Makes 8 servings.

BRUSSELS SPROUTS IN ALMOND BUTTER

2 pounds Brussels sprouts or 3 10-
ounce boxes frozen Brussels
sprouts

6 tablespoons margarine or butter
½ cup sliced unblanched almonds

Trim Brussels sprouts and soak in lightly salted water 15 minutes. Rinse. Boil in a saucepan containing a small amount of water, or preferably with a steamer rack set into the saucepan over an inch of boiling water. Cook, covered, 10 to 15 minutes until just tender. Drain. (If using frozen Brussels sprouts cook according to package directions and drain.)

In a skillet melt the margarine or butter. Add the almonds and sauté a minute, stirring. Add the drained Brussels sprouts and sauté until the almonds are browned and the Brussels sprouts are well heated. Transfer to a heated serving dish.

Makes 8 or more servings.

SALADE COMPOSEE

1¼ pounds small waxy type
potatoes
1 cup (approximately) dry white
wine
1 14-ounce can artichoke bottoms,
drained, sliced crosswise in ¼-
inch slices
1 celery heart, thinly sliced
crosswise
1 tablespoon snipped chives
1 teaspoon chervil

1 tablespoon finely chopped parsley
¼ teaspoon tarragon
½ cup vegetable oil (preferably a
French or light Italian olive oil)
3 tablespoons red wine vinegar
(preferably French)
1 teaspoon salt
Freshly ground pepper to taste
1 teaspoon dry mustard
1 small head Boston lettuce or other
buttery type lettuce

Scrub the potatoes and place into a saucepan. Cover with cold water. Bring to boil and cook until potatoes are just tender. Drain and peel off the skins immediately. Slice in ¼ inch slices and place into a bowl. Pour enough wine over the slices to just cover them and allow to stand until cool. Drain off the wine and discard or reserve it for another cooking purpose. Add the sliced artichoke bottoms, sliced celery heart, chives, chervil, parsley, and tarragon to the potatoes and toss lightly. Place the oil, vinegar, salt, pepper, and dry mustard in a glass jar. Cover and shake well. Pour enough of this dressing over the potato mixture to coat well, tossing gently but thoroughly. Cover and chill well.

At serving time add the lettuce and toss again, adding more of the dressing if required.

Makes 8 servings.

MIDDLE EASTERN
THANKSGIVING DINNER

Calamata Olives   *Salted Pistachio Nuts*

Stuffed Vine Leaves with Lemon   *Feta Cheese*

Wheat Crackers (optional)

* *Egg-Lemon Soup*

* *Roast Turkey with Cracked Wheat-Ground Veal Stuffing (see index)*

* *Artichokes and Rice*   * *Turkey Pan Gravy (see index)*

* *Zucchini au Gratin*   *Broiled Tomato Halves*

* *Greek Holiday Bread*

* *Honey Fig Pastries*

Retsina, or a non-resinous Greek dry white wine

Featured here are specialties of Greece and other Middle Eastern countries that team up to make a fantastic dinner of exotic flavors. Start off with an arrangement of cold appetizers to nibble on. These include Calamata olives, which are black olives packed in olive oil and vinegar; they've a flavor like no other black olives. Pistachios, which are native to Turkey, are a fine nut to include in this course. Those from Turkey are light green in color, and darker green ones come from Italy and Afghanistan, but they are all delicious. If you have trouble locating nice pistachios, substitute salted mixed nuts without peanuts. Serve some Greek Feta cheese, which can be bought in bulk or in glass jars. Whichever way you buy it, it's packed in brine, and you will need to drain it before serving if you buy it in the jar. You may want to serve some crackers to accompany the Feta. The final appetizer item is Stuffed Vine Leaves. You can buy them canned. Chill them well, arrange them on a serving plate and sprinkle them liberally with lemon juice.

On to the main course, where the turkey gets stuffed with that Middle Eastern favorite, cracked wheat (bulgur wheat), as well as with ground veal. Vegetables are very much loved in the Middle East, and three delicious recipes are included in this menu. Make the Greek Holiday Bread and the Honey Fig Pastries the day before Thanksgiving so that you can concentrate on the main course on the festal day. If you like the resinous wines of Greece, have retsina with your dinner, but since this is an acquired taste, you may prefer one of the other Greek dry white wines of a non-resinous type.

OVEN TEMPERATURE AND USE. As soon as the turkey is removed from the oven, set it on a carving board to await carving. Then turn up the oven temperature and bake the zucchini for 15 minutes. Then turn the oven to broil and broil the tomato halves, running the zucchini under the broiler for a minute to brown the tops if desired.

* Recipes follow for asterisked items.

EGG-LEMON SOUP

¼ cup orzo (rice-shaped pasta)   2 eggs
4 cups chicken broth   3 tablespoons lemon juice.

Cook the orzo *al dente* in boiling salted water according to package directions. Drain. Heat the chicken broth to boiling and remove from heat. Meanwhile beat the eggs well. Add the lemon juice to the eggs and beat again. Add a little of the hot chicken broth to the egg mixture. Then add the egg mixture to the chicken broth along with the drained orzo. Serve in heated soup cups.

If made ahead, reheat, covered, in the top of a double boiler over simmering water, but do not allow the soup to boil.

Makes 8 servings.

ARTICHOKES AND RICE

6 small artichokes	1 tablespoon dillweed
6 tablespoons lemon juice	3 cups boiling chicken broth
½ cup plus 3 tablespoons olive oil	1½ cups rice
¾ cup chopped onions	½ teaspoon salt
¼ cup chopped parsley	Freshly ground pepper to taste

Cut the stems off the artichokes. With scissors trim the pointed ends off the leaves. Wash the artichokes well. Fill a bowl three quarters full of cold water. Add 2 tablespoons of lemon juice to the water. Cut the artichokes into quarters. With a small spoon scoop out the thistles (fuzzy center part) and discard. Place the artichoke quarters in the lemon water.

In a casserole sauté the onions in ½ cup olive oil until soft. Shake the water from the artichokes and drain in a colander. Add the artichokes to the onions along with the parsley and dillweed. Sauté about 10 minutes, tossing. Add the boiling chicken broth, cover, and simmer 20 minutes.

Bank the artichokes to one side of the casserole and add the rice, salt, and pepper to the liquid. Stir so that the rice is distributed evenly throughout the liquid. Rearrange the artichoke quarters. Cover the casserole and simmer 20 minutes, or until the rice is tender. If necessary add a little boiling water during cooking. Sprinkle with ¼ cup lemon juice and 3 tablespoons olive oil. Simmer 5 minutes longer, covered.

Makes 8 to 12 servings.

ZUCCHINI AU GRATIN

1 tablespoon plus 1 teaspoon
  margarine or butter
1 tablespoon plus 1 teaspoon flour
⅔ cup milk, or half and half, or light
  cream
½ teaspoon salt

Freshly ground pepper to taste
Pinch of nutmeg
2 pounds small zucchini
½ cup freshly shredded Gruyère or
  Swiss cheese

Melt margarine or butter in a small saucepan. Stir in the flour and cook, stirring with a wooden spoon for a minute or two. Remove from heat and add milk all at once, beating with a wire whisk. Return saucepan to heat, stirring constantly with the wire whisk until mixture thickens. Add the salt, pepper and nutmeg and continue to cook for a few minutes. Remove from heat and set aside.

Remove and discard ends of zucchini. Cut in half lengthwise. Place on steamer rack and steam in covered pot containing an inch of boiling water until just tender, about 10 minutes. Preheat oven at 350°F. (177°C.)). Arrange the zucchini in a single layer, flat side up, in a greased baking dish. Spoon the sauce evenly over the zucchini. Sprinkle with the shredded cheese. Bake 15 minutes. If top is not browned, run under the broiler for a minute or two until browned.

Makes 8 or more servings.

GREEK HOLIDAY BREAD

1 package active dry yeast
¼ cup warm water (about 115°F. 46°C.)
1 teaspoon sugar
½ cup butter
¼ cup milk
3 eggs
¾ cup sugar

¼ teaspoon salt
½ teaspoon cinnamon
¼ teaspoon nutmeg
2 teaspoons grated orange rind
3½ or more cups flour
1 egg yolk mixed with 1 tablespoon cold water
1 tablespoon or more sesame seeds

Sprinkle the yeast over the warm water in a small bowl. Add the teaspoon of sugar and stir until the yeast is dissolved. Set in a warm place until the mixture begins to become foamy, about 5 minutes. Meanwhile melt the butter and remove from heat. Combine with the milk. In another bowl beat the eggs. Add the ¾ cup sugar, salt, cinnamon, nutmeg, and orange rind to the egg and combine. Add the butter mixture to the egg mixture and mix well. When the yeast mixture is ready add it to the butter-egg mixture and combine well. Sift the flour into a bowl. Make a well in the center and pour in the butter-egg mixture. With a spoon or your fingers work the flour into the liquid mixture until thoroughly blended. Turn out on a floured board and knead 10 minutes, kneading in more flour if required. Place the dough in a greased bowl. Turn the dough over so it is greased on top. Cover the bowl with plastic wrap and set in a warm place to rise for 2 hours or longer, or until doubled in bulk.

Punch down dough. Knead lightly for a minute. Shape into a round loaf and set on a greased 8-inch round cake pan or pie plate (top measurement). Cover loosely and set in a warm place to rise again for 1 hour or longer, until it has almost doubled in bulk.

Preheat oven at 350°F. (177°C.). Bake 20 minutes. Brush the top with the egg yolk and water mixture and sprinkle with the sesame seeds. Continue baking for another 25 to 30 minutes, or until the loaf sounds hollow when tapped on the bottom. Turn out on a wire rack to cool. If storing overnight wrap tightly in aluminum foil.

Makes 1 loaf.

FIG HONEY PASTRIES

8 ounces dried figs
¼ cup honey
½ teaspoon cinnamon
½ cup (approximately) butter

5 sheets filo (phyllo) pastry leaves
(if frozen, thaw at least 8 hours
before using)

Remove and discard stems from the figs. Grind the figs. Combine them in a bowl with the honey and cinnamon. Melt the butter.

On a work table unroll the filo so that it lies flat. Remove one sheet of filo and place on work table. Cover remaining filo sheets with a damp (not wet) towel. Brush the filo sheet with melted butter. With scissors cut the filo lengthwise into 4 strips about 3¼ inches wide.

Place 2 teaspoons of the fig filling at the bottom of one strip and spread it out a little crosswise. Fold the strip up over itself to encase the filling. Fold over the two outer edges of the strip about ½ inch, folding toward the center of the strip. Then fold up the encased filling, keeping a rectangular shape, until you reach the end of the strip. Brush all over with melted butter and arrange on an ungreased baking sheet. Continue in this manner until all the strips have been prepared, working with one sheet of filo at a time and keeping the balance covered with the damp towel. Do not worry if the filo breaks or cracks as you work with it. Just keep forming the rectangles. It will not make any difference in the finished product.

Preheat the oven at 350°F. (177°C.) about 10 minutes before you are ready to bake. Bake the pastries about 12 minutes until golden brown. Remove with a spatula and cool on a wire rack.

Store in an airtight metal box overnight if making the day ahead.

Makes about 20.

FAR EAST THANKSGIVING DINNER

* Winter Melon Soup

* Braised Ginger-Scallion Turkey Breast (see index)

* Bacon Fried Rice   ** Oriental Vegetable Mélange*

* Peppery Red Cabbage Salad   ** Crisp Shrimp Cakes*

* Two Tone Fruited Holiday Dessert

You may never have thought of turkey and Thanksgiving in relation to Chinese cooking, but Braised Ginger-Scallion Turkey and its accompaniments are likely to give you a new outlook. Add to the turkey some oriental treats such as Bacon Fried Rice, Crisp Shrimp Cakes, a Peppery Red Cabbage Salad, and a medley of vegetables that includes snow peas, broccoli, cabbage and mushrooms, and you have a really glorious Oriental meal. Steaming bowls of Winter Melon Soup start off the dinner and Two Tone Fruited Holiday Dessert lends a South East Asian touch to the finale.

OVEN TEMPERATURE AND USE. In true Far Eastern style, no oven is required for the preparation of this dinner.

* Recipes follow for asterisked items.

WINTER MELON SOUP

¼ cup dried Chinese black
  mushrooms
1 pound winter melon
6 cups chicken broth
Salt to taste

Freshly ground pepper to taste
⅓ cup thinly sliced ham (preferably
  Smithfield ham) cut into 1-inch
  squares

Place mushrooms in a small bowl and cover with hot water. Allow to soak about 30 minutes. Drain and cut each mushroom into quarters, or if large into eighths.

Meanwhile peel the winter melon. Remove the pulp and seeds. Rinse the melon and cut it into ¼ inch slices. Cut the slices into pieces about 1 inch square. Place them in a saucepan with the chicken broth, mushrooms, salt, and pepper, and bring to a boil. Lower the flame, cover, and simmer 10 minutes. Add the ham and cook another minute or two. Ladle into soup cups.

Makes 8 servings.

BACON FRIED RICE

1½ cups rice
6 ounces bacon cut crosswise into
  ½-inch slices
½ cup thinly sliced scallions
2 eggs, lightly beaten

3 tablespoons oil, preferably peanut
  oil
¼ cup soy sauce, preferably tamari
  soy sauce

Place rice into a heavy saucepan. Cover with boiling water to a level 1 inch above the rice. Cover. Bring to boil, lower heat and simmer about 20 minutes, or until rice is just tender. Transfer to a bowl. Allow to cool, fluffing with a fork several times to keep grains separated. Cover and chill.

Cook the bacon in a wok or skillet, tossing until lightly browned. Remove with a slotted spoon and drain on paper towels. Pour off all but about 2 tablespoons of the bacon fat. Add the scallions to the wok or skillet and cook a minute or two, stirring until lightly browned. Remove with a slotted spoon and set aside. Add the beaten eggs to the wok or skillet and scramble the eggs, stirring to break them up into small bits. Remove and set aside. (If you wish to make this dish ahead of time the bacon, scallions and scrambled eggs can be combined at this point, placed in a bowl, covered, and refrigerated until time to combine with the rice.) In a clean wok heat 3 tablespoons oil until hot. Add the rice and toss and stir it so that all the rice is coated with oil. Continue tossing and stirring until the rice is well heated. Add the soy sauce and continue stirring. When combined, add the bacon, scallions, and egg, and toss until well combined and heated through. Arrange in a serving dish.

Makes 8 to 12 servings.

ORIENTAL VEGETABLE MELANGE

1 6-ounce box frozen snow peas
3 tablespoons vegetable oil,
   preferably peanut oil
1 garlic clove, mashed
¼ teaspoon salt
1 cup chopped onions
2 cups broccoli flowerettes

2 cups shredded cabbage
½ pound mushrooms, sliced
½ cup turkey stock or chicken broth
2 tablespoons soy sauce (preferably
   tamari soy sauce or Indonesian
   ketjap manis)

Pour boiling water over the snow peas in a colander to remove ice. Set aside. Heat a wok slightly over high heat and add the vegetable oil, garlic, and salt, and stir for a few seconds. Add the onion and stir fry for about 2 minutes. Add the broccoli flowerettes and stir-fry another minute. Add the snow peas, cabbage, and mushrooms and stir fry a few minutes more. Add the turkey stock or chicken broth and soy sauce, lower heat, and cover. Simmer 2 minutes. Transfer to a heated serving dish.

Makes 8 servings.

PEPPERY RED CABBAGE SALAD

1 small red cabbage
2 tablespoons oil, preferably peanut
   oil
2 tablespoons vinegar

2 tablespoons ketjap manis
   (Indonesian soy sauce), or if not
   available substitute 2
   tablespoons ordinary soy sauce
   and 1 tablespoon brown sugar
½ teaspoon red pepper flakes

Cut cabbage in half, remove core and cut halves into ¼ inch slices, and pull apart loosely. Heat the oil in a wok and stir fry the cabbage over high heat for 2 minutes. Lower heat. Remove the cabbage and place into a bowl. Combine the remaining ingredients and heat for a minute in the wok. Pour over the red cabbage and mix well. Cover with a plate and weigh down with a heavy object. Cover all with plastic wrap or aluminum foil and refrigerate for 12 to 24 hours.

Transfer to a chilled serving dish.

Makes 8 servings.

CRISP SHRIMP CAKES

1 pound shrimp in shells
3 tablespoons or more vegetable oil
3 to 4 tablespoons cut-up scallions
¼ cup coarsely chopped water
    chestnuts
2 eggs
2 tablespoons grated lemon zest
2 tablespoons lemon juice
1 tablespoon chopped fresh ginger
    root or canned green ginger root

½ teaspoon salt
Freshly ground pepper to taste
1 cup (approximately) dry bread
    crumbs
¼ cup flour
1 teaspoon ground coriander
Pinch of cayenne
1 tablespoon or more margarine or
    butter

Wash the shrimp and pat them dry with paper towels. Heat 2 tablespoons oil in a wok and stir fry the shrimp for two minutes. Remove from heat. Remove the shells from the shrimp and discard. Remove the veins from the shrimp. Chop the shrimp coarsely and combine with the scallions, water chestnuts, eggs, lemon zest, lemon juice, ginger, salt, and pepper. Add 1 cup bread crumbs. Put through food processor briefly, or put through an electric blender briefly in small batches, taking care not to purée the mixture. The mixture should just hold together nicely. If necessary add a little more of the bread crumbs. Cover and chill 1 or 2 hours.

Shape into 8 flat cakes. Combine the flour, coriander and cayenne and roll the shrimp cakes into the mixture. Brown slowly in a skillet on both sides, 4 at a time, in 1 tablespoon each margarine or butter and vegetable oil, adding more if necessary.

Makes 8.

TWO-TONE
FRUITED HOLIDAY DESSERT

1 11-ounce can mandarin orange
   segments
1 11-ounce can peeled seedless
   lichees (available in Oriental
   groceries or in specialty food
   stores or some supermarkets)
1 package frozen melon balls,
   thawed
1 15-ounce can guava shells
1 15-ounce can mango slices, or 1
   fresh mango, peeled and sliced
1 large sliced banana
2 packages lime gelatin dessert

1 tablespoon lemon juice
3 tablespoons crème de menthe
2 envelopes plain gelatin
2 cups canned sweetened coconut
   cream
2 cups coconut milk (canned, or see
   directions below *)
Pinch of salt
3 drops rose essence (if not
   available, use 1 teaspoon
   rosewater)
1 drop red food coloring (optional)
¼ cup grated coconut

Drain orange segments, lichees, melon balls, guava shells, and mango slices, reserving all liquid. Place the fruits in a large fancy glass serving bowl along with the sliced banana. Boil 2 cups of the reserved liquid and pour over the lime gelatin in another bowl, stirring until dissolved. Pour the lemon juice, crème de menthe, and any remaining reserved liquid into a 2-cup measuring cup. Add enough cold water to fill the cup and pour into the bowl with the lime gelatin. Stir. Add the gelatin to the fruit, stirring gently. Cover and refrigerate until set.

Meanwhile soften the plain gelatin in ½ cup sweetened coconut cream. Heat the coconut milk almost to boiling, and pour over the gelatin, stirring until completely dissolved. Add the remaining coconut cream, salt, rose essence or rosewater, and food coloring if desired. And mix well. Pour carefully over the set fruit mixture. Sprinkle the grated coconut over the top. Cover and refrigerate until set. To serve, spoon into individual dessert glasses at the table.

Makes about 12 servings.

* To make coconut milk, combine 1 cup (3 ounces) unsweetened grated coconut and 2 cups warm water in a bowl. Allow to sit at room temperature from 30 minutes to 2 hours, the longer the better. With your hands press and squeeze the coconut in the water for several minutes. Strain through a fine strainer or through a double thickness of cheesecloth into a bowl, pressing down the coconut in the strainer with the back of a wooden spoon to extract as much liquid as possible from the coconut, or squeeze the cheesecloth until no more liquid runs out. Repeat this process two more times, squeezing the coconut in the water and then pressing out as much liquid from it as possible. After the last squeezing or pressing discard the dry coconut. Measure the liquid and if necessary add a little water to make 2 cups.

7

Main Dishes From the Luscious Leftovers

No man can say a harsh thing with his mouth full of turkey, and disputants forget their differences in unity of enjoyment.

—CAPT. THOMAS HAMILTON,
Men and Manners in America, 1833

Leftover turkey has caused generations of desperate cooks to invent thousands of recipes for turkey hash, most of them pretty similar. It also once inspired F. Scott Fitzgerald to write a series of intentionally crazy and unworkable post-Thanksgiving turkey cooking ideas, including one that calls for ham sandwiches to be kept standing by in case things go wrong. Through the years deciding what to do with the remains of the roast bird seems to have presented many a household with difficulty.

Hopefully all of that is past, for if you look through this chapter you'll find myriad ideas for making great main dishes from the leftovers, with not a recipe for turkey hash or turkey à la king in sight. There really are so many good ways to utilize cooked turkey that you may very well find yourself buying an extra large bird just so that you can have leftovers to work with. Besides the main dishes in this chapter, there are salubrious salads, saporous sandwiches, savory soups, and extraordinary hors d'oeuvres and appetizers by the score in other chapters. I'm certain you'll find that turkey leftovers can and should be luscious.

If you've skipped Chapter 2, please consult it for suggestions on handling and storing cooked turkey, stuffing, and gravies.

TURKEY IN CARDAMOM-YOGURT SAUCE

1 cup chopped onions
2 tablespoons vegetable oil
1 tablespoon margarine or butter
1 small garlic clove, crushed
1 tablespoon flour
¾ cup turkey stock or chicken broth
¼ teaspoon cinnamon

Pinch of ground aniseed (optional)
½ teaspoon ground cardamom
⅛ teaspoon ground ginger
Dash of Tabasco sauce
2 cups diced or slivered cooked turkey
1 cup plain yogurt

Sauté the onions in a skillet in the vegetable oil and margarine or butter until lightly browned. Add the garlic and stir for a few seconds. Add the flour and stir for a minute. Add the turkey stock or chicken broth and continue to cook, stirring, until mixture thickens. Reduce heat and stir in the cinnamon, aniseed, cardamom, ginger, Tabasco sauce, and turkey meat. Cover and simmer 5 minutes until heated through. Remove cover, turn off heat, and stir in the yogurt. Mix well, re-cover, and allow to sit a minute or two before serving.

Makes 4 servings.

NEW MEXICO TORTILLA BAKE

2½ cups turkey stock or chicken
  broth
1 10-ounce can enchilada sauce
  (mild or hot, according to taste)
1 5-ounce can evaporated milk
12 corn tortillas
2½ cups shredded or diced cooked
  turkey

1 cup freshly shredded Monterrey
  Jack, Cheddar or other fairly firm
  cheese
1 4-ounce can green chilies,
  drained, seeded and chopped
½ cup chopped onions

Preheat oven at 350°F. (177°C.). Combine the turkey stock or chicken broth, enchilada sauce, and evaporated milk in a bowl. Arrange 6 of the corn tortillas in a greased 9½-inch by 13-inch baking pan. Arrange the turkey over the tortillas. Sprinkle with about two-thirds of the cheese. Scatter the chilies and chopped onions over the cheese. Arrange the remaining 6 tortillas over the top. Sprinkle with the remaining cheese. Pour the enchilada sauce mixture evenly over everything. Bake for about 1 hour, or until the sauce is absorbed, basting with the sauce after 30 minutes, and pressing down any tortilla that curls up.

Makes 6 servings.

RIBBON TURKEY LOAF WITH MUSHROOM SAUCE

1 10-ounce package frozen chopped
  broccoli
1½ teaspoons plus 6½ tablespoons
  margarine or butter
1 teaspoon plus 1½ tablespoons
  grated onions
2 teaspoons plus 6 tablespoons flour
½ cup milk
2 tablespoons freshly grated
  Parmesan, Romano or Sardo
  cheese

½ teaspoon savory
4 eggs
½ teaspoon or more salt
Freshly ground pepper to taste
4 cups ground cooked turkey
4½ cups turkey stock or chicken
  broth
¼ to ½ pound mushrooms, sliced
¼ cup cream or milk

Cook broccoli according to package directions just until broken apart. Drain in a colander. Meanwhile melt 1½ teaspoons margarine or butter in a small saucepan. Add 1 teaspoon grated onions and stir for a minute. Add 2 teaspoons flour and stir for another minute. Add the ½ cup milk and stir with a wire whisk until thick and smooth. Continue to simmer 5 minutes, stirring constantly. Combine with the well-drained broccoli. Add the cheese, savory, 1 of the eggs, beaten lightly, ½ tea-spoon salt, and pepper. Stir and set aside.

Preheat oven at 350°F. (177°C.). In a saucepan melt 4½ tablespoons margarine or butter. Add 1½ tablespoons grated onions and stir for a minute. Add 6 tablespoons flour and stir for 2 minutes. Add the turkey stock or chicken broth gradually, stirring constantly with a wire whisk. Heat until thickened and continue simmering 5 minutes, stirring. Taste, and add salt and pepper as needed. Combine 1⅓ cups of this sauce with the ground turkey. Cool the remaining sauce, cover, and refrigerate. Beat the 3 remaining eggs and stir into the turkey mixture. Add salt and pepper to taste. Divide the turkey mixture into two parts, one a little larger than the other. Spoon the smaller part into a greased 4¼-inch-by-8¼-inch loaf pan and smooth the top with a rubber spatula. Spoon the broccoli mixture on top and smooth with the rubber spatula. Spoon the remaining turkey mixture on top and smooth with the rubber spatula. Cover the loaf pan with aluminum foil, and set it in a baking pan. Pour hot water in the baking pan to reach two-thirds of the way up the sides of the loaf pan. Bake 1½ hours.

Shortly before the turkey loaf is finished baking, sauté the mush-rooms in 2 tablespoons margarine or butter over medium-high heat for 2 or 3 minutes. Combine the mushrooms with the reserved sauce from the refrigerator, and heat gently. Add the ¼ cup cream or milk and heat gently. Taste, and adjust seasoning if necessary.

Remove the loaf pan from the oven and let stand 5 minutes on a rack. Run a knife around the sides of the pan. Unmold the loaf on a serving platter. Spoon a little of the sauce over the loaf and serve the balance in a heated sauce boat.

Makes 6 to 8 servings.

EGGPLANT-TOMATO-CHEESE TURKEY BAKE

For the tomato sauce: *
1 garlic clove, chopped
2 tablespoons vegetable oil,
    preferably olive oil
1 cup finely chopped onions
1 2-pound 3-ounce can Italian
    tomatoes
1 bay leaf
½ teaspoon oregano
½ teaspoon basil
½ teaspoon salt, or to taste
Freshly ground pepper to taste

For the turkey mixture:
1 cup chopped onions
2 tablespoons vegetable oil
2 to 2½ cups ground cooked turkey
¾ cup ground ham
½ teaspoon basil

½ cup turkey gravy, or ½ cup turkey
    stock or chicken broth mixed
    with 2 teaspoons cornstarch and
    brought to a boil
1 garlic clove, finely chopped
¼ teaspoon salt
Freshly ground pepper to taste
1 egg, beaten
¼ cup chopped parsley

For the eggplant:
1 large or 2 medium eggplants
    (about 2 pounds)
1 tablespoon salt
2 to 5 tablespoons vegetable oil

For assembling:
1 cup whole wheat bread crumbs
2 tablespoons margarine or butter
1 cup shredded Gouda cheese

For the tomato sauce: Sauté the garlic lightly in the vegetable oil. Remove the garlic and discard. Add the onions to the oil and sauté over gentle heat until soft and very lightly browned, about 10 minutes. Drain the tomatoes, discarding the liquid or reserving it for another use. Put the tomatoes through a food mill using a disc fine enough to keep the tomato seeds from passing through. Add the tomato pulp to the onions along with the bay leaf, oregano, basil, salt and pepper. Cover and simmer over low heat for 15 minutes, stirring occasionally. Meanwhile start to prepare the eggplant (see below). Cover and simmer the sauce 45 minutes longer, stirring occasionally. Remove from heat and set aside.

For the turkey mixture: Sauté the onion in vegetable oil over low heat until soft but only lightly brown. Add the ground turkey, ground ham, basil, turkey gravy or thickened broth, garlic, salt and pepper. Cook for several minutes, stirring, until well-combined and heated through. Remove from heat and cool slightly. Add the egg and parsley and mix well. Set aside.

For the eggplant: Cut the eggplant(s) into quarters lengthwise, and then into ½ inch slices. Drop into boiling salted water and allow to cook for 2 minutes, pushing down the eggplant pieces with a spoon. Drain in a colander. Lay out the slices on paper towels. Pat dry with more paper towels. Sauté the slices in vegetable oil for about 1 minute on each side, adding more oil as necessary, until all the slices have been sautéed.

For assembling: Preheat oven at 375°F. (191°C.). Dividing the eggplant, turkey mixture and tomato sauce each into 3 equal parts, arrange 3 layers of eggplant, turkey mixture and tomato sauce in a greased casserole, sprinkling ⅓ cup cheese over the tomato sauce on the first two layers. Toss the bread crumbs with the melted margarine or butter and toss with the remaining cheese. Sprinkle over top of the casserole and bake for 1 to 1¼ hours.

Makes 6 servings.

* Note: 2 cups good quality spaghetti sauce that is not heavily spiced can be substituted for the tomato sauce if you wish, although the freshly made tomato sauce is preferable.

CRISPY WHISPER
OF CURRY CROQUETTES

3 tablespoons margarine or butter,
  melted
2 tablespoons grated onion
½ cup milk or cream
1 cup cooked hominy grits (about 5
  tablespoons before cooking)
1 cup finely ground cooked turkey
2 tablespoons chopped parsley

½ teaspoon curry powder
½ teaspoon salt
Freshly ground pepper to taste
2 eggs
1 cup fine dry bread crumbs
¼ cup wheat germ
Vegetable oil

In a saucepan sauté the onion in 1 tablespoon margarine or butter for several minutes, but do not brown. Add the milk or cream, grits, turkey, remaining margarine or butter, parsley, curry powder, salt, and pepper, and mix well. Heat well, stirring. Remove from heat and add 1 egg which has been beaten, stirring in quickly. Cook for another minute, stirring constantly. Remove from heat and spread out on a plate or board to cool.

When they are firm divide into 8 equal parts and shape each part into a cylinder about 1¼ inches in diameter. Beat the remaining egg lightly in a flat soup plate. Combine the bread crumbs and wheat germ in another flat soup plate. Roll the croquettes in the crumb mixture, then in the beaten egg, and again in the crumbs. Heat the vegetable oil in a deep fryer or wok until hot but not smoking. Fry the croquettes until golden. Drain on paper towels.

Makes 4 servings.

STIR-FRIED TURKEY WITH SNOW PEAS

3 dried black mushrooms (size of a
   50¢ piece or larger)
1 6-ounce package frozen snow pea
   pods
1 tablespoon cornstarch
1 tablespoon sherry
2 tablespoons vegetable oil
½ cup finely chopped onions
1½ teaspoons fresh ginger root or
   canned green ginger root, finely
   chopped
1 cup turkey stock or chicken broth
3 tablespoons soy sauce (preferably
   tamari soy sauce)
4 cups diced or shredded cooked
   turkey

Place mushrooms in a small bowl, cover with hot water and allow to soak 20 to 30 minutes. Meanwhile remove the snow peas from the package and allow to thaw. Drain and chop the mushrooms. Combine the cornstarch and sherry and set aside.

Heat a wok and add the vegetable oil. Add the onions and stir-fry 1 or 2 minutes until lightly browned. Add the snow peas and stir-fry another minute. Add the chopped mushrooms and ginger root and stir-fry another minute. Add the turkey stock or chicken broth and soy sauce and continue stirring until the mixture boils. Add the cornstarch mixture and stir until the mixture thickens. Add the turkey and stir until heated through. Serve immediately on heated platter.

Makes 4 servings.

TURKEY·BREAST CORDON BLEU

2 tablespoons margarine or butter
¼ cup minced onions
1 tablespoon flour
2 tablespoons grated carrot
1 cup turkey stock or chicken broth
¼ teaspoon thyme
Salt to taste
Freshly ground pepper to taste
1 tablespoon sherry

¾ pound (approximately) cooked
   turkey breast slices ¼-inch thick
   (6 or more slices, depending on
   the size of the turkey breast cut
   from)
½ pound (approximately) thinly
   sliced ham
¼ pound (approximately) thinly
   sliced Jarlsberg or Swiss cheese
2 tablespoons chopped parsley

Melt margarine or butter in a small skillet or saucepan. Add the onions and sauté gently until transparent. Add the flour and stir a minute. Add the carrot and stir another minute. Add the turkey stock or chicken broth gradually, stirring constantly, and cook until thickened. Add thyme, salt, pepper, and sherry. Remove from heat.

Preheat oven at 400°F. (204°C.). Place a slice of turkey at one end of a buttered baking dish (a 7-inch by 10½-inch oval baking dish is a good size to use). Arrange a slice of ham on the turkey, not quite covering the edge. Arrange a slice of cheese on the ham. Continue with the overlapping row of turkey, ham and cheese until the baking dish is full. You can cut the pieces to fit as you go along, and exact proportions are not important. Pour the reserved sauce over all. Bake 12 to 15 minutes until the cheese is melted and the top is lightly browned. Sprinkle chopped parsley over the top.

Makes 6 servings.

COUSCOUS A LA TURK

1½ cups chopped onions
1 tablespoon margarine or butter
1 tablespoon vegetable oil
1 medium carrot, scraped and
  coarsely shredded
1 medium tomato, chopped
3¼ cups turkey stock or chicken
  broth
½ cup dry white wine
1 15-ounce can chick peas
  (garbanzos), drained, or 1½ cups
  cooked, drained, chick peas

1 or more small dried hot red
  peppers, crumbled (with or
  without seeds, according to
  taste)
1 tablespoon turmeric
1 teaspoon cumin
⅛ teaspoon cinnamon
Dash of cloves
Freshly ground pepper to taste
2 cups cooked turkey strips about ½
  inch by ½ inch by 2 inches
1 cup couscous

Sauté the onions in margarine or butter and vegetable oil until soft. Add the carrot and tomato and cook a few minutes, stirring. Add the turkey stock or chicken broth, wine, chick peas, dried pepper(s), turmeric, cumin, cinnamon, cloves, and pepper, and bring to boil. Simmer 15 minutes, covered. Add the turkey strips and cook about 5 minutes more until heated through. Add the couscous, mix thoroughly, cover, and turn off heat. Allow to sit 10 to 15 minutes. Stir before serving.

Makes 6 servings.

TURKEY TETRAZZINI
WITH LINGUINE

4 ounces linguine (pasta)
¼ pound mushrooms, sliced
4 tablespoons margarine or butter
2 tablespoons flour
1½ cups milk or half and half (milk
    and cream dairy product)
Salt to taste
Freshly ground pepper to taste

Dash of cloves
Dash of nutmeg
1 tablespoon grated onions
2 tablespoons chopped parsley
2 cups cooked turkey cubes
3 tablespoons wheat germ
¼ cup freshly grated Parmesan,
    Romano, or Sardo cheese

Cook the linguine *al dente* in boiling salted water according to package directions. Drain. Cut into 2 or 3-inch lengths and set aside.

Preheat oven at 350°F. (177°C.). Sauté the mushrooms in 1 tablespoon margarine or butter until lightly browned. Set aside.

Melt remaining 3 tablespoons margarine or butter in a saucepan. Stir in the flour and cook a minute, stirring. Add the milk or half and half gradually, stirring constantly until thickened. Add the salt, pepper, cloves, nutmeg, onions and parsley, and cook a minute longer. Transfer to a bowl. Add the linguine and toss. Add the mushrooms and turkey and toss again. Transfer to a shallow greased baking dish. Bake about 20 minutes until bubbly and lightly browned on top.

Makes 4 servings.

TURKEY CUTLETS WITH LEMON SAUCE

For the sauce:
2 eggs, separated
¼ cup lemon juice
½ cup turkey stock or chicken broth
2 teaspoons cornstarch combined
 with 1 tablespoon cold water

For the turkey cutlets:
2 eggs
3 tablespoons milk

¾ cup fine dry bread crumbs
6 tablespoons wheat germ
½ teaspoon salt
Freshly ground pepper to taste
4 slices cooked turkey breast ¼-inch
 thick by about 4 inches by 5
 inches per slice (about ¾ pound)
Vegetable oil
1 tablespoon chopped fresh mint

For the sauce: Beat the egg whites until stiff but not dry. Add the egg yolks one at a time and continue beating. Add the lemon juice gradually and continue beating. Meanwhile heat the turkey stock or chicken broth to boiling. Stir in the cornstarch mixture and heat just until thickened. Remove from heat and add to the egg mixture gradually, beating constantly. Set aside.

For the turkey cutlets: Beat the eggs lightly in a flat soup plate. Add the milk and mix. Combine the bread crumbs, wheat germ, salt, and pepper in another flat soup plate. Pour vegetable oil into a skillet to a depth of ¼ inch and heat until quite hot, but do not allow to smoke. Dip cutlets one at a time in the egg mixture, then in the crumb mixture, again in the egg mixture, and finally in the crumb mixture. Brown quickly, 1 minute or less on each side, in the skillet. Drain on paper towels.

Arrange the cutlets on a heated serving platter. Spoon some of the sauce over the cutlets and pour any remaining sauce into a heated sauce boat. Sprinkle the chopped mint over the cutlets and over the top of the sauce in the sauceboat.

Makes 4 servings.

TURKEY PANUCHOS

For the pickled onions:*
2 medium size red onions, thinly
  sliced
10 peppercorns
¼ teaspoon oregano
2 garlic cloves, sliced
½ teaspoon salt
¾ cup or more white vinegar

For the tortillas:
1 cup masa harina (such as Quaker

Oats brand, available in Spanish-
  American grocery stores and
  some supermarkets)
½ cup or more warm water

For assembling:
1 16-ounce can refried beans
2 hard-cooked eggs, sliced
1½ to 2 cups shredded cooked
  turkey
Lard or vegetable oil

* *For the pickled onions:* These must be started at least 2 days before you plan to serve Turkey Panuchos, but you can make them as far as 2 or 3 weeks ahead if you wish. They can be stored in a tightly closed glass jar and any leftovers can be used with other foods as you would use pickles. To make them, combine the onion slices, peppercorns, oregano, garlic and salt in a glass or ceramic bowl. Add just enough vinegar to cover the onions. Cover and allow to marinate in the refrigerator 48 hours or longer, turning once or twice every 48 hours.

For the tortillas: These are much smaller than standard tortillas. They can be made just before you are ready to use them (they take about 35 minutes to make), or they can be made several hours ahead. Do not substitute store-bought tortillas, as you need freshly made tortillas that puff and form a space in the center for stuffing.

Mix the masa harina and ½ cup warm water together in a bowl. The mixture should be slightly moist and soft and yet hold together well. If a little dry, add water 1 tablespoon at a time until it is of proper consistency. Divide into 12 equal parts. Form into 12 balls by rolling and shaping in the palms of your hands.

To cook, work with one ball at a time and keep the remaining balls in the bowl, covered with plastic wrap. Heat an iron griddle or shallow skillet over moderately high heat, then regulate the heat so that the griddle is moderately hot, but not hot enough to scorch or burn. While the skillet is heating cut 2 pieces of plastic wrap about 10 inches square. (Exact size is not important.) Lay one square on the work table. Put the ball of masa harina in the center, and lay the other square of plastic wrap on top. With a small flat board or piece of wood press down firmly on the ball until it is flattened to a circle less than ⅛-inch thick and between

3 and 3½ inches in diameter. It does not have to be exactly the same thickness all over. One side may be a little thinner than the other. Peel off the top layer of the plastic wrap. Pick up the remaining piece of plastic wrap with the dough (the tortilla) and place the dough on your hand. Peel the plastic wrap off the dough and place the dough on the heated griddle. When steam begins to appear (in 10 to 15 seconds) turn the tortilla over with a pancake turner. Allow to cook about 1½ minutes until lightly browned on the bottom. Turn over and cook about 30 seconds longer. The tortilla will puff up when turned over. If it does not, press down on it lightly with your fingers or a paper towel. If it still does not puff, turn it over again and it should puff, as it probably was not thoroughly cooked on the first side. The entire operation of cooking the tortilla takes about 2 minutes. Remove the tortilla from the griddle and with a sharp pointed knife slit it around the edge ¼ to ⅓ of the way around. Run the smooth handle of a plastic or wooden spoon all around inside the tortilla to make sure it is completely open inside. You will not tear the tortilla at this point. Place the slit tortilla inside a fold of aluminum foil and keep it covered.

Continue pressing, cooking and slitting tortillas until all have been made, stacking them inside the aluminum foil as they are made to keep them moist. If you are not using them immediately, seal the edges of the foil until you are ready.

To assemble: At serving time spread a tablespoon or so of refried beans in each tortilla. Place a hard-cooked egg slice on top of the refried beans. Press the open edges of the tortilla together. When all the tortillas are filled, fry them briefly on both sides in a skillet in about ¼ inch melted lard or vegetable oil. Drain on paper towels. Arrange on a heated serving plate and put some shredded turkey on top of each tortilla, dividing it equally. Arrange some drained pickled onions over each tortilla and serve the balance of the pickled onions separately for those who may wish more.

Makes 12. Allow 3 panuchos as a main dish serving. May also be served as a snack, or with cocktails, allowing 1 or 2 per serving.

BAKED TURKEY MOUSSE MARSALA

2 tablespoons margarine or butter
2 tablespoons flour
¾ cup turkey stock or chicken broth
¼ cup Marsala wine
Salt to taste
Freshly ground pepper to taste,
  preferably white pepper

Generous pinch of nutmeg
1 cup heavy cream
2 tablespoons lemon juice
4 cups ground cooked turkey
2 tablespoons finely chopped
  parsley
3 eggs

Melt the margarine or butter in a small saucepan. Add the flour and cook a minute, stirring. Add the turkey stock or chicken broth and the Marsala all at once, beating with a wire whisk. Cook until thickened and simmer several minutes more, stirring constantly. Remove from heat. Add salt, pepper, nutmeg, and 3 tablespoons heavy cream. Mix in the lemon juice. Add to the ground turkey along with the parsley, and mix well.

Preheat the oven at 325°F. (163°C.). Separate the eggs and beat the yolks. Add them to the turkey mixture. Whip the remaining heavy cream until stiff. Beat the egg whites until foamy. Add a pinch of salt and beat until soft peaks form. Fold the beaten egg whites into the turkey mixture, a third at a time, alternating with the whipped cream, using a rubber spatula for the folding. Transfer to a well-greased 6-cup ring mold. Set into a pan of hot water to a level halfway up the sides of the mold. Set in oven and bake about 45 minutes or until a sharp knife inserted into the center comes out clean. Unmold onto a heated serving dish.

Makes 8 servings.

TURKEY PUFFOVER

¼ cup dried mushrooms
2 tablespoons plus ¼ cup margarine
  or butter
½ cup chopped onions
2 tablespoons plus ¾ cup flour
¾ cup turkey stock or chicken broth
Salt to taste

Freshly ground pepper to taste
2 cups cooked slivered turkey breast
2 eggs
¾ cup milk
3 or 4 tablespoons freshly grated
  cheese (any kind)

Cover the mushrooms with hot water and set aside for 10 minutes or more. Preheat oven at 425°F. (218°C.). Sauté onions in 2 tablespoons margarine or butter until softened. Drain the mushrooms and add them to the onions. Stir for a minute. Add 2 tablespoons flour and stir for another minute or two. Add the turkey stock or chicken broth and cook, stirring, until thickened. Add salt and pepper to taste. Stir in the turkey meat and remove from heat.

Beat eggs lightly. Add the milk and beat again. Add ¾ cup flour and ½ teaspoon salt and stir and beat until smooth. Set the ¼ cup margarine or butter in a 9-inch pie pan and place in the oven until melted and bubbly. Remove from the oven and pour the batter into the pie pan immediately. Spoon in the turkey mixture, keeping it towards the center. Sprinkle with cheese. Place in oven immediately and allow to bake undisturbed for 25 minutes. Remove and cut into wedges. Serve immediately.

Makes 4 or 5 servings.

TURKEY PILAF WITH ALMONDS

2 tablespoons margarine or butter
1 cup bulgur wheat
¼ cup finely minced onions
2 cups turkey stock or chicken
    broth
¼ cup whole blanched, slivered or
    sliced almonds

2 tablespoons sultanas or golden
    raisins
½ teaspoon oregano
Salt to taste
Freshly ground pepper to taste
2 cups diced cooked turkey

In a skillet melt the margarine or butter over medium to low heat. Add the bulgur wheat and onions and sauté, stirring, until lightly browned. Add the turkey stock or chicken broth, almonds, raisins, oregano, salt, and pepper, and bring to boil. Lower heat, cover, and simmer 10 minutes. Add the turkey and combine thoroughly. Cover and cook 5 minutes longer.

Makes 6 servings.

TURKEY AVOCADO CREPES

12 crêpes 6 or 6½ inches in
   diameter (see index for Basic
   Crêpes or use frozen crêpes,
   completely thawed)
2 tablespoons vegetable oil
1½ cups chopped onions
1 17-ounce can Italian tomatoes
½ teaspoon salt

Freshly ground pepper to taste
2 tablespoons chopped parsley
1 cup half and half (milk and cream
   dairy product) or milk
3½ to 4 cups cooked turkey in
   julienne strips or shredded
1 avocado
1 cup or more sour cream

Sauté onions in vegetable oil for 5 minutes. Meanwhile drain the Italian tomatoes and cut them up. Add the tomatoes to the onions along with the salt, pepper, and parsley, and sauté 5 minutes longer. Lower heat, cover, and simmer 20 to 25 minutes, stirring occasionally.

Preheat oven at 350°F. (177°C.). Put the onion-tomato mixture through a food processor fitted with a steel blade, or put through an electric blender. Add half and half or milk and blend again. Transfer to a bowl. Add the turkey and toss well. Lay the crêpes out on a work table. Spoon some of the turkey mixture down the center of each crêpe, dividing equally. Peel the avocado and cut into 12 slices, reserving the balance of the avocado for another use. (Leave in the pit, cover the avocado tightly with plastic wrap, refrigerate, and it will not discolor overnight.) Lay one avocado slice over the filling of each crêpe. Roll up and arrange crêpes, seam side down, in a greased baking dish. Bake about 15 minutes until heated through. Serve with sour cream.

Makes 6 servings.

TURKEY TAMALE PIE

1½ cups corn meal, preferably stone
   ground
2 teaspoons salt
4 cups boiling water
2 tablespoons margarine or butter
1 cup chopped onions

1 garlic clove, minced
½ cup chopped green pepper
2 tablespoons vegetable oil
5 cups ground cooked turkey
1 tablespoon or more chili powder
1 teaspoon cumin

Freshly ground pepper to taste
1 12-ounce can Italian tomatoes
¾ cup corn kernels

⅓ cup cut-up black olives
(preferably imported black
olives)

Add corn meal and salt to the boiling water in a saucepan, stirring constantly, until smooth and thickened. Remove from heat and stir in the margarine or butter. Spoon half of the corn meal into a greased 2-quart shallow casserole. Keep the remaining corn meal covered.

Preheat oven at 350°F.(177°C.). In a skillet sauté the onions, garlic, and green pepper in vegetable oil until lightly browned. Add the remaining ingredients and mix well, breaking up the tomatoes with a fork. Heat a few minutes. Turn into the casserole over the corn meal and smooth the top with the back of a spoon. Spoon the remaining corn meal on top and spread out evenly with a rubber spatula. Bake about 1 hour.

Makes 6 servings.

TURKEY COLUMBO

2 ribs celery, thinly sliced
1 cup chopped onions
2 tablespoons vegetable oil
1 tablespoon margarine
½ pound mushrooms, thinly sliced
2 tablespoons flour
1½ cups milk
½ teaspoon salt

½ teaspoon ground cumin
Freshly ground pepper to taste
1 2½-ounce pepperoni, thinly sliced
3 cups cooked turkey cut into thin
    strips
¼ cup freshly grated Parmesan,
    Romano or Sardo cheese

Preheat oven at 375°F. (191°C.). Sauté celery and onions in 1 tablespoon vegetable oil and margarine or butter until lightly browned. Add 1 more tablespoon vegetable oil and the mushrooms and sauté a minute or two, tossing. Add the flour and cook for another minute, tossing. Add the milk gradually and cook, stirring, until thickened. Add the salt, cumin, pepper, pepperoni, and turkey. Remove from heat. Combine gently but thoroughly and transfer to a shallow greased baking dish. Sprinkle with the cheese. Bake 10 minutes. Run under the broiler for a minute or two to brown the top.

Makes 6 servings.

INDIA TURKEY CURRY

3 tablespoons margarine or butter
½ cup chopped onions
1 tart apple, seeded and chopped
2 ribs celery, thinly sliced
3 tablespoons flour
2 tablespoons curry powder, or
    more to taste

1 teaspoon cumin
¼ teaspoon ginger
1⅓ cups turkey stock or chicken
    broth
2 cups diced cooked turkey

Melt the margarine or butter in a skillet and sauté the onions, apple,
and celery until soft but not brown. Add the flour and stir for a minute.
Add the curry powder, cumin, and ginger and stir for another minute.
Add the turkey stock or chicken broth gradually, stirring constantly,
until the mixture thickens. Add the turkey and mix well. Lower heat and
simmer gently about 5 minutes until heated through.

Makes 4 servings.

TACCHINO E CANNELLINI
CON VERMICELLI

1 cup chopped onions
1 garlic clove, minced
2 tablespoons olive oil
1 35-ounce can Italian tomatoes
½ teaspoon basil
¼ teaspoon oregano
Pinch of sugar
Pinch of salt
½ cup red wine

1 20-ounce can cannellini beans,
    drained and rinsed under cold
    water
1 cup (2 ounces) 2-inch pieces
    vermicelli (preferably whole
    wheat vermicelli)
2 cups cooked turkey cut into small
    pieces

Sauté the onion and garlic in the olive oil until the onion is soft. Add
the tomatoes with their liquid, basil, oregano, sugar, salt, and wine and
simmer, covered, for 30 minutes, stirring occasionally and breaking up
the tomatoes. Add the cannellini beans and simmer briskly uncovered 10
minutes. Meanwhile cook the vermicelli in boiling salted water *al dente*

according to package directions. Drain the vermicelli and add it to the tomato-bean mixture, along with the turkey pieces. Simmer, stirring, until well heated through.

Makes 4 to 6 servings.

BACON AND TURKEY STUFFED EGGPLANT HALVES

2 medium eggplants
Vegetable oil
4 slices bacon, sliced crosswise into
    1-inch pieces
1 garlic clove, finely minced
¼ cup finely chopped parsley
¼ cup chopped black olives
    (preferably Greek or French
    olives)

2 tablespoons pine nuts (pignolias)
1 cup diced cooked turkey
¼ teaspoon salt
Freshly ground pepper to taste
¼ cup freshly grated Parmesan,
    Romano or Sardo cheese

Preheat oven at 375°F. (191°C.). Cut the eggplants in half lengthwise. Scoop out the flesh, leaving the shells about half an inch thick. Brush the cut sides with vegetable oil. Place the shells into a baking dish into which they just fit comfortably, cut sides up. Pour about half an inch of boiling water in the bottom of the baking dish around the eggplant shells. Bake for 30 minutes.

Meanwhile sauté the bacon and garlic in a skillet until the bacon is brown. Remove the bacon and garlic with a slotted spoon and place in a bowl. Chop the eggplant which was scooped out of the shells and sauté it in the skillet for 5 minutes, turning continually with a pancake turner. Combine the sautéed eggplant in a bowl with the bacon and garlic. Add the parsley, olives, pine nuts, turkey, salt, and pepper and combine well. When eggplant shells have baked for 30 minutes remove from oven and fill them with the bacon mixture, dividing equally. Sprinkle with the grated cheese, dividing equally. Return to oven and bake 20 minutes longer.

Makes 4 servings.

SPAGHETTI SQUASH
AND TURKEY AU GRATIN

1 2-to-2½ pound spaghetti squash
2 tablespoons margarine or butter
2 tablespoons flour
1 pint sour cream
1 tablespoon paprika
1 teaspoon salt

Freshly ground pepper to taste
3 tablespoons snipped chives
2 cups cooked julienne turkey strips
⅓ cup freshly grated Parmesan,
   Romano or Sardo cheese

Wash squash and plunge into a pot of boiling water. Boil 20 minutes or more or until tender when pierced with a fork. Remove from water. Cut in half. Scoop out and discard seeds. Scrape out the flesh of the squash with a fork and discard the shell. The squash will fall into spaghetti-like strands when scraped from the shell. Set aside.

Preheat oven at 350°F. (177°C.). Melt the margarine or butter in a saucepan, add the flour and cook for a minute, stirring. Remove from heat and mix in the sour cream. Add the paprika, salt and pepper. Return to heat and bring just to boil, stirring constantly. Remove from heat. Add chives and turkey strips and mix well. Add the spaghetti squash and stir until well combined.

Transfer to a greased shallow baking dish and smooth out with a rubber spatula. Sprinkle the cheese over the top. Bake 15 minutes until bubbly. If not browned, run under the broiler for a minute or two to brown.

Makes 8 servings.

8

Turkey Appetizers and Hors D'Oeuvres

A large cold bottle, and a small hot bird!
—EUGENE FIELD, *"The Bottle and the Bird"*

There's a nice collection of recipes in this chapter that you can serve at cocktail time or as a first course. Some can be used for either purpose, and in each case the recipe specifies its most appropriate use. A number of these piquant little dishes are made from leftover turkey, others from smoked turkey, and still others from turkey liver, turkey sausage, or raw turkey breast.

POMMERY HORS D'OEUVRES
(for cocktail time)

Pommery Turkey Roulades (see index)
¼ cup butter
1 tablespoon Pommery mustard

Round cocktail toasts (or toasted bread cut into rounds with a small biscuit cutter)

Prepare Pommery Turkey Roulades and chill, or use leftover Pommery Turkey Roulades that have been chilled. Slice thinly. Cream the butter until soft. Add the mustard and mix well. Spread on cocktail toasts and place a slice of the roulade on each. Arrange on hors d'oeuvre tray or chilled serving plate.

STUFFED PARTY RYE SLICES
(for cocktail time)

1 1-pound loaf party rye, about 2½ inches square
2 cups (12 ounces) whipped cream cheese
2 cups ground cooked turkey
1 tablespoon finely snipped chives
1 teaspoon oregano
1 teaspoon basil
½ teaspoon salt
Freshly ground pepper to taste
2 tablespoons finely chopped sour pickle
½ small garlic clove, finely minced
2 tablespoons or more milk or cream

With a sharp knife cut out centers of all bread slices except the crusts, leaving about ¼ inch all around. This can be done most easily by stacking and cutting about 4 slices at a time. Reserve center part of bread for another use.

Combine the cream cheese with the remaining ingredients except the milk or cream. Add enough milk or cream to make an easily workable mixture. Place in a pastry bag fitted with a large plain tip. Fill the center of the bread by piping the filling into about 6 stacked-up slices at a time, adding 6 more slices and filling them, and so on. Pack filling tightly so there are no air spaces. Place a crust at either end. Wrap the filled loaf tightly in plastic wrap or aluminum foil and chill for several hours.

To serve, cut in between the slices with a sharp knife and arrange the filled slices in overlapping rows on an hors d'oeuvre tray.

Makes about 40.

TURKEY-CHEESE TRIANGLES
(for cocktail time)

1 large egg
1 cup ground cooked turkey
2 tablespoons freshly grated Parmesan, Romano or Sardo cheese
Pinch of sage
¼ teaspoon salt
Freshly ground pepper to taste
½ cup (approximately) butter
5 sheets or more filo (phyllo) pastry (if frozen, thaw for at least 8 hours before using)

Beat the egg in a small bowl. Add the turkey and combine. Add the grated cheese, sage, salt, and pepper and mix well. Set aside. Melt the butter.

On a work table unroll the filo so that it lies flat. Remove one sheet of filo and place it on the work table. Cover the remaining filo sheets with a damp (not wet) towel. Brush the filo sheet with melted butter. With scissors cut lengthwise strips about 2½ inches wide. You should get 5 strips per sheet. Place about a teaspoon of the turkey filling in the lower corner of one strip. Fold over the end of the filo to enclose the filling in an open trangle. Fold the triangle upward and continue folding over and up in exact triangles until you come to the opposite end. Brush on all sides with butter and arrange on an ungreased baking sheet. Continue in this manner until all the triangles have been filled, working with one sheet of filo at a time and keeping the balance covered with the damp towel. Do not worry if the filo cracks or breaks as you work with it. Just keep forming it into triangular shapes. It will not make any difference in the finished product.

Preheat oven at 350°F. (177°C.) about 10 minutes before you are ready to bake. Bake for about 10 to 12 minutes until golden brown. Remove with spatula to hors d'oeuvre tray or heated serving plate. Serve while still warm.

If you wish you can form the triangles, butter them on the outside, wrap in plastic wrap in separate layers in a flat freezer container, and freeze them until ready to use. Bake them frozen for 15 minutes or until golden.

Makes about 25.

RUTH'S COCKTAIL SQUARES
(for cocktail time)

Whipped cream cheese
Small white toast squares

Thinly sliced cooked turkey breast
cut to fit toast squares
Green hot pepper jelly

Spread cream cheese on toast squares as thickly as desired. Cover with a turkey slice. Place ½ teaspoon pepper jelly on top of each square.

PIQUANTS
(for cocktail time)

¾ cup ground cooked turkey
1 tablespoon soft butter or
    margarine
1 tablespoon capers
1 teaspoon green peppercorns

1 teaspoon anchovy paste
2 tablespoons or more Port wine
6 or more cocktail onions
12 or more pumpernickel rounds

In a food processor or electric blender combine the ground turkey, margarine or butter, capers, green peppercorns, anchovy paste, and 2 tablespoons Port. Add a little more Port if necessary to make a spreadable mixture. Spread on pumpernickel rounds. Cut the cocktail onions in half lengthwise and decorate each pumpernickel round with half a cocktail onion, cut side down.

Makes 12 or more.

FONDS D'ARTICHAUTS DINDE
(for cocktail time)

1 cup finely chopped cooked turkey
    breast
6 tablespoons mayonnaise
4 teaspoons snipped chives

1 teaspoon or more curry powder
4 large canned artichoke bottoms (5
    to 7 count per 15-ounce can)

Combine turkey, mayonnaise, chives, and 1 teaspoon curry powder. Drain artichoke bottoms and pat dry with paper towels. Cut each into 4 pieces, pie fashion. Cut each piece in half horizontally. Place a heaping half teaspoon of the filling on each artichoke piece. Sprinkle tops lightly with curry powder. Serve immediately or cover and chill until serving time.

Makes about 32.

TURKEY LIVER AND BACON BITES
(for cocktail time)

3 cups water
1 turkey liver (about 2 ounces)
¼ cup finely chopped onions
2 tablespoons margarine or butter
¼ of a beef bouillon cube
1 hard-cooked egg

2 slices bacon, cooked, drained and
  crumbled
Freshly ground pepper to taste
12 canapé shells
Parsley sprigs

Bring the water to boil in a small saucepan. Drop in the turkey liver, lower heat, and simmer for 5 minutes. Remove the turkey liver with slotted spoon and drain on paper towel.

Sauté the onions in margarine or butter until soft and lightly browned. Add the piece of bouillon cube and mash and stir until dissolved. Place the turkey liver in a chopping bowl or on a chopping board and chop with the hard-cooked egg until fine. Transfer to a ceramic or glass bowl and add the onion mixture. Add the crumbled bacon and pepper, mix, cover, and chill.

Stir and pack some of the turkey liver mixture into each canapé shell. Decorate each with a tiny parsley sprig.

Makes 12 or more.

TWO-ALARM TURKEY SQUARES
(for cocktail time)

1 4-ounce wedge ripe brie (left at
  room temperature 2 hours)
2 tablespoons butter or margarine
¼ cup finely chopped cooked
  turkey breast

2 tablespoons finely chopped
  jalapeño peppers, seeds removed
20 (approximately) 1½-inch square
  party toasts, or toast cut into 1½
  inch squares

With a sharp knife remove the rind from the brie and discard. Place the brie in a bowl and cream it with the butter or margarine until well combined. Add the turkey breast and jalapeño peppers and mix well. Spread on the toast squares.

Makes about 20.

SMOKED TURKEY CIGARETTES
(for cocktails or first course)

8 thin slices smoked turkey breast
   about 4 x 8 inches, slices
   separated and chilled, skin
   removed and discarded

1 5-ounce package Boursin cheese
   with garlic and herbs, left at
   room temperature for 1 hour
16 or more sprigs watercress or
   parsley

Spread one-eighth of the cheese on one slice of turkey breast. Starting at a narrow end roll up tightly to form a cigarette-like shape. Spread and roll up remaining slices.

If serving for cocktails, cut crosswise into thirds. Insert a tiny sprig of watercress or parsley in one end of each piece.

If serving as a first course, insert a tiny sprig of watercress or parsley in both ends of each "cigarette." Serve on individual plates, preferably on a small leaf of lettuce.

Makes 24 cocktail hors d'oeuvres or 8 first-course servings.

INDIVIDUAL SMOKED TURKEY IN ASPIC MOLDS
(first course)

2¾ cups chicken broth or turkey stock
2 onion slices
1 egg white, lightly beaten
1 egg shell, crushed
1 envelope plain gelatin
2 tablespoons Madeira wine

1 hard-cooked egg white
1 black truffle or a few black olives
½ pound (approximately) thinly sliced smoked turkey breast
16 cornichons (tiny French sour gherkins)

Put the chicken broth or turkey stock in a saucepan and add the onion slices, egg white and egg shell. Simmer, uncovered, for 10 minutes. Remove from heat and allow to stand undisturbed for 20 minutes. Strain the broth through several layers of cheesecloth and discard the material left in the cheesecloth. Pour about ¼ to ½ cup of the broth into a small saucepan and bring to a boil. Remove from heat, add the gelatin and stir until completely dissolved. Combine with the balance of the broth. Add the Madeira and stir. Allow to cool 10 minutes.

Lightly oil 8 individual ½ cup molds, preferably star-bottom oval shaped aspic molds. Spoon a thin layer of the aspic (the clarified broth) in the bottom of each mold and refrigerate for about 10 minutes until set. Cut small fancy shapes from pieces of hard-cooked egg white and from the sliced black truffle or black olive. Lay some of the black and white pieces in each mold to make an attractive decoration. Drizzle a few drops of aspic over the black and white pieces and refrigerate about 10 minutes until set and the pieces are held in place. Spoon a little more aspic into each mold and let set again for 10 minutes. Add a little more aspic until the decorations are completely covered. Refrigerate another 10 minutes or until firm. Cut pieces of the smoked turkey slices a little smaller than the molds, allowing 4 or 5 pieces per mold. Make alternating layers of smoked turkey slices and 1 to 1½ tablespoons of aspic in each mold, refrigerating about 20 minutes between each layer for the aspic to set. When molds are filled, cover and chill for several hours or overnight.

To serve, unmold on chilled individual serving plates. If there is any extra aspic it can be chopped and spooned around the molds, or used for another purpose. Arrange 2 cornichons beside each mold.

Makes 8 servings.

TURKEY QUENELLES WITH
SAUCE MICHEL
(first course)

Quenelles, when properly prepared, are delectable enough to die for. Carême, one of France's most famous chefs in days gone by, did just that. Once as he inspected the quenelles being made by one of his students, he advised that they were good, but they were being prepared too hastily. He instructed the student to shake the pan lightly as he cooked. As he raised the pan to demonstrate the proper movement, he fell to the floor dead.

In those days quenelles were difficult to make because the meat or fish from which they were made had to be pounded by hand and forced through fine sieves before being used. Today we simply pop the meat into a food processor and stand back while electricity and modern engineering do all the work. The recipe below should be made only with a food processor.

For the quenelles:
½ cup water
3 tablespoons margarine or butter
1¼ teaspoons salt
1 cup flour
2 eggs
1 pound raw turkey breast cut into pieces 1 inch square or smaller
Pinch of cayenne
Generous pinch of nutmeg
¼ cup softened margarine or butter
2 tablespoons or more cream
1 or 2 egg yolks (optional)

For the sauce:
¼ cup margarine or butter
2 tablespoons very finely minced onion
1 small garlic clove, finely minced
¼ cup flour
1 cup half and half (milk and cream dairy product)
1 cup chicken broth
1 cup chopped canned drained tomatoes
2 tablespoons chopped parsley
1 tablespoon brandy
¼ teaspoon salt, or to taste
White pepper to taste

For the quenelles: Combine the water, 3 tablespoons margarine or butter, and ¼ teaspoon salt in a saucepan, and bring to boil. Remove from heat and add the flour all at once, beating in with a wooden spoon. Continue beating for another minute. Add 1 egg and combine thoroughly. Return saucepan to heat and cook over medium heat, stirring constantly, until the mixture forms a ball and leaves the sides of the pan. Remove from heat and spread mixture in a flat greased soup plate. Cover closely with plastic wrap and refrigerate until well chilled.

Meanwhile place turkey pieces in the container of a food processor.

Add 1 teaspoon salt, cayenne, and nutmeg, and process until puréed. Add the softened margarine or butter and process until blended. Add the chilled flour mixture in bits and process until blended. Add 1 egg and blend again. Transfer the mixture to a bowl. Make certain that any streaks in the mixture are blended in with a wooden spoon. Add 2 tablespoons cream, 1 tablespoon at a time, and mix in well. Cover and chill for several hours or as long as 24 hours.

For the sauce: Melt margarine or butter in a small saucepan. Stir in the onions and garlic and cook over low heat, stirring, until onion is soft but not brown. Blend in the flour and cook for a minute, stirring. Add the half and half and cook over medium heat, stirring constantly, until the mixture thickens. Add the chicken broth gradually and cook, stirring, until thickened. Add chopped tomatoes, parsley, brandy, salt, and white pepper, and cook until well heated through. If not using immediately, cool, cover, and refrigerate. Sauce can be reheated in the top of a double boiler over simmering water.

To assemble the dish: Test the flavor and texture of the quenelle mixture by dropping a tablespoon of the mixture into a small pan of simmering water and poaching the quenelle about 3 minutes on each side, turning. Drain on a paper towel and taste the quenelle. Add salt, cayenne, or nutmeg to the quenelle mixture if necessary. If the texture seems too firm, mix in more cream, 1 tablespoon at a time. If the texture is so loose that it does not hold together during poaching, beat in an egg yolk or two. Butter a large skillet. Make quenelles into spoon shapes one at a time by scooping up some of the mixture with a large greased oval soup spoon. Invert the bowl of another greased large oval soup spoon over the first soup spoon with the handles in opposite directions to smooth and shape the top of the quenelle. Remove the excess mixture from around the sides of the spoons. With the top spoon, scoop under the quenelle to remove it, and place it in the buttered skillet. (You may need to use two skillets if you wish to prepare all the quenelles at once.) When all the quenelles have been shaped, pour boiling water into the skillet to come just to the top of the quenelles, making sure you do not pour water directly onto any of the quenelles. Poach 5 minutes, keeping the water just below simmering and shaking the pan now and again so that the quenelles do not stick to the bottom. Turn the quenelles with a slotted spoon and poach another 5 minutes. Remove with a slotted spoon and drain on paper towels.

Arrange the quenelles in a serving dish, spoon the heated sauce over them and serve immediately. Or, arrange the quenelles in a buttered baking dish. Spoon the sauce over them and bake 12 to 15 minutes in a preheated 375°F. (191°C.) oven.

If you wish to make this dish in advance, you may poach the quenelles, arrange them in a greased baking dish, and cover closely with plastic wrap. The sauce can be spooned on and the quenelles baked at the last minute.

Makes 12 or more servings, 2 quenelles per serving.

LUSCIOUS LITTLE QUICHES
(first course)

Pastry for 2-crust pie (your own
   recipe or Quick Tender Food
   Processor Pie Crust [see index]
½ cup shredded Swiss or Gruyère
   cheese
½ cup chopped mushrooms
2 slices bacon, fried, drained, and
   crumbled

1 cup cooked turkey breast cut in
   matchstick pieces
2 eggs
1 cup milk
¼ teaspoon salt
Freshly ground pepper to taste
Pinch of nutmeg
½ teaspoon chervil
1 teaspoon Dijon mustard

Preheat oven at 425°F. (218°C.). Divide the pastry into 8 equal parts. Roll each out separately and line 8 4-inch fluted edge individual quiche or tartlet pans. Trim the tops and press the dough to the sides of the pans all around. Prick the bottoms with a fork every half inch. Set the pans on a baking sheet and place in the oven 5 to 6 minutes. Remove from oven and pat down any bubbles that may have formed in the pastry.

Sprinkle a little of the cheese in each quiche pan, dividing equally. Cover with some of the chopped mushrooms, dividing equally. Sprinkle with crumbled bacon, dividing equally. Cover with the turkey pieces, dividing equally. Beat the eggs and add the milk, salt, pepper, nutmeg, chervil and mustard, and mix well. Pour over the turkey to nearly fill each quiche. Set baking sheet with the quiches on it back in the oven and bake 25 to 30 minutes longer until puffed and a knife blade inserted in the center of a quiche comes out clean.

Remove from pans and serve immediately.

Makes 8 servings.

GOBBLER MUSHROOM CAPS

12 mushrooms about 2½ inches in diameter
1 tablespoon margarine or butter
½ cup Turkey Breakfast Sausage (see index)*
1 small garlic clove, finely minced
1 tablespoon snipped chives
¼ teaspoon marjoram
¼ teaspoon salt, or to taste
Freshly ground pepper to taste
1 tablespoon Marsala wine
¼ cup (approximately) fine dry bread crumbs
Vegetable oil, preferably olive oil
Finely chopped parsley (optional)

Preheat oven at 375°F. (191°C.). Wash and dry mushrooms and trim the stems. Break off the stems and scoop out any mushroom where part of the stem is protruding. Finely chop the stems and any scooped out part of mushrooms. In a skillet sauté the chopped mushrooms in margarine or butter for 5 minutes. Add the sausage and garlic and cook for another 4 minutes, breaking up the sausage with a fork. Remove from heat and add the chives, marjoram, salt, pepper and Marsala wine. Mix in the breadcrumbs one tablespoon at a time until the mixture just holds together.

Brush the outside of the mushroom caps with the oil. Fill cavities of the mushrooms with the sausage mixture, rounding the stuffing on top. Sprinkle the filled mushroom caps lightly with bread crumbs. Arrange in a greased shallow baking pan. Drizzle a little oil over the bread crumbs. Bake for 15 minutes or until mushrooms are just tender when pierced with a fork. If desired sprinkle with parsley before serving.

Makes 6 servings as a first course.

* Gobbler Mushroom Caps may be made with mild turkey sausage if you do not want to make the Turkey Breakfast Sausage. In that case, reduce the quantity of turkey sausage to ⅓ cup and add another tablespoon of margarine or butter to the skillet when sautéeing the turkey sausage.

9

Turkey Soups

Of soup and love the first is the best.
—Proverb, from Dr. Thomas Fuller's
Gnomologia, 1732

Nothing could be more welcome on a nippy day than a hearty bowl of soup, and if it's turkey soup, there's even more cause for jubilation. Some of the most marvelous soups imaginable can be produced just from a collection of turkey bones with good bits of meat still attached, some fresh vegetables, and a few other taste-laden ingredients.

The basis for most turkey soups is good turkey stock, which can be made from the carcass of a cooked turkey or from turkey bones that remain after you've done some boning out of raw turkey. The first recipe in this chapter tells how to make turkey stock, which, incidentally, can be used in place of chicken broth in just about any recipe you can think of. Most of the soup recipes that follow use the stock as their base. Small amounts of stock can also be made from turkey giblets, but most often this stock or broth is used to make Giblet Gravy. If you wish to make some stock from giblets please see Giblet Gravy in the index.

There are two recipes in this chapter using smoked turkey that lends a nice hamlike flavor to soup. One is a split pea soup, and the other a minestrone thick with beans, vegetables and little tube-shaped macaroni.

BASIC TURKEY STOCK

Turkey stock can be made either from an assortment of carcass and other bones that remain after boning out a turkey, along with uncooked wingtips, tails, and perhaps a drumstick, or it can be made from the remains of a roast turkey. Either assortment of parts makes a delicious stock which can be used as turkey broth, as a substitute for chicken broth in cooking, or as the basis for one of the simple but flavorful soups that follow.

If you're using the bones from cooked turkey don't let the carcass get picked down to the bare bones before you whisk it off to the stock pot. The more bits of meat that are left clinging to the bones the better and more flavorful your stock will be.

Once the stock is made, either use it right away, or cool it quickly and refrigerate, or ladle it into plastic containers (a one pint size is usually most convenient) and freeze until needed.

If you want an extra rich stock you can boil down the strained stock to half the original quantity. If you plan to do this make sure to salt the stock lightly so that the finished product will not be too salty.

The meat that's left on the bones after making stock can easily be picked off and used in any recipe calling for cooked shredded turkey meat, such as salads or some of the main dishes in Chapter 7. Or it can be added back to the stock to make soups featured in this chapter.

1 roast turkey carcass, all skin removed and stuffing well scraped out, and thigh and drumstick bones if available, OR	1 large or 2 medium carrots, scraped
	1 onion, cut in half
	2 ribs celery, preferably with leaves, cut in half crosswise
1 boned turkey carcass with wingtips, tail, neck, or other parts such as a drumstick if available	2 or more teaspoons salt
	5 or 6 peppercorns
	3 parsley sprigs
	1 bay leaf
10 cups water	½ teaspoon thyme

Break up the turkey carcass and place it, along with any other available parts, in a tall narrow soup pot or stock pot. Add the water and bring to a boil, skimming off particles as they rise to the surface. Continue skimming until no more particles rise. Add the remaining ingredients, cover partially, reduce heat, and simmer 1½ to 2 hours.

Remove the carcass and bones, set aside, and when cool enough to handle, pick off all the meat and shred it. Use in any recipe calling for cooked shredded turkey.

Meanwhile strain the stock and discard the vegetables. If not using the stock immediately, cool as quickly as possible and store in a glass jar or a bowl, tightly sealed. Before using, remove any fat that forms on the top. If you will not be using the stock within a day or two, pour into a plastic container when cooled, cover tightly, and freeze until needed. Remove any fat that may form on the top before using, and use the frozen stock within one month

Makes 5 to 6 cups stock, plus some shredded turkey meat.

TURKEY NOODLE SOUP

5 or 6 cups Basic Turkey Stock with
    shredded turkey meat
4 medium carrots, scraped and very
    thinly sliced
1 cup broken up fine noodles

Generous pinch of saffron
Salt to taste
Freshly ground pepper to taste
2 tablespoons finely chopped
    parsley

Place the turkey stock with the shredded turkey meat in a saucepan and bring to boil. Add the carrots and noodles and bring to boil again, stirring. Add the saffron, stir, lower heat, and simmer 10 minutes or until noodles and carrots are tender. Taste and add salt and/or pepper as desired. Stir in the parsley. Serve in soup bowls.

Makes 4 to 6 servings.

WINTER HARVEST SOUP

1 cup dried pinto beans or dried
    cranberry beans
5 or 6 cups Basic Turkey Stock with
    shredded turkey meat
3 cups Hubbard squash cubes ½ to
    ¾ inch square (peel and seed
    squash before cubing)

⅓ cup grits
⅛ teaspoon nutmeg
½ teaspoon marjoram
2 tablespoons chopped parsley
Salt and freshly ground pepper, if
    required

Soak the dried beans in cold water to cover 8 hours or overnight, or place them in a saucepan, cover with cold water, bring to boil, turn off heat, and allow to stand for 1 hour.

Place the turkey stock in a soup pot. Drain the dried beans and add them to the soup pot along with the hubbard squash cubes. Bring to boil, lower heat, and simmer, partially covered, for 1 hour.

Add the grits, the shredded turkey meat, nutmeg, marjoram, and parsley and simmer 45 minutes to 1 hour longer, partially covered, stirring occasionally. Taste and adjust seasoning if necessary. Serve in soup bowls.

Makes 8 servings.

TURKEY GUMBO

5 or 6 cups Basic Turkey Stock with
   shredded turkey meat
2 tablespoons margarine or butter
1 garlic clove, minced
1 cup chopped onions
1½ cups chopped green pepper
5 cups sliced fresh okra (1 pound)
1 16-ounce can tomatoes, drained
   and chopped
1 cup chopped or slivered ham

½ teaspoon thyme
1 bay leaf
Generous pinch of cayenne pepper,
   or to taste
4 tablespoons Roux (see recipe
   below)
Salt if required
2 cups or more cooked brown or
   white rice (optional)

Place the turkey stock in a soup pot. Melt the margarine or butter in a skillet and sauté the garlic, onions, green pepper, and okra over low heat about 25 minutes until the okra stops stringing. Add to the soup pot along with the tomatoes, ham, thyme, bay leaf, and cayenne pepper. Bring to boil, reduce heat, cover, and simmer 30 minutes. Meanwhile, prepare the Roux.

After the gumbo has cooked 30 minutes add the shredded turkey meat and 4 tablespoons of the Roux. (Store the balance of the Roux in the refrigerator for another use.) Allow the gumbo to simmer for 30 minutes more. Taste and adjust seasoning if necessary. Serve in soup bowls, if desired with a mound of rice in the center of each bowl.

Makes 8 or more servings.

ROUX

¼ cup vegetable oil   ½ cup unbleached flour

Heat the vegetable oil slightly in a heavy saucepan over medium heat. Stir in the flour. Cook over medium to low heat, adjusting heat as necessary, and stirring constantly until mixture becomes a dark golden brown. Do not allow to scorch or burn. Remove from heat and set aside. Stir before using if the oil begins to separate. When cooled, any unused portion may be stored in the refrigerator in a tightly capped glass jar. It will keep for several weeks and can be used to flavor and thicken soups and other dishes.

TURKEY-MUSHROOM-BARLEY SOUP

⅓ cup barley
¼ cup dried mushrooms
5 or 6 cups Basic Turkey Stock with
    shredded turkey meat
Generous pinch of sage
Generous pinch of thyme
1 teaspoon salt

Freshly ground pepper to taste
2 tablespoons margarine or butter
1 cup milk, half and half (milk and
    cream dairy product), or cream
2 or more tablespoons instant or
    quick-mixing flour (optional)

Soak the barley in cold water to cover well for 2 to 3 hours, or overnight. Soak the dried mushrooms in warm water to cover for 30 minutes. Bring the turkey stock with the shredded turkey meat to simmer in a soup pot. Add the drained barley and the drained mushrooms along with the sage, thyme, salt, and pepper. Adjust heat, cover, and simmer 1 hour.

Add the margarine or butter and stir until melted. If a thicker soup is preferred, add the instant or quick-mixing flour and stir until thickened. Add the milk or half and half or cream and heat but do not boil. Taste and adjust seasoning if necessary. Serve in soup bowls.

Makes 8 servings.

TURKEY-OYSTER STEW

2 cups thinly sliced celery
1 bunch scallions, thinly sliced,
    including some of green part
1 garlic clove, minced
4 tablespoons margarine or butter
¼ cup flour
5 or 6 cups Basic Turkey Stock with
    shredded turkey meat

2 cups milk or half and half (milk
    and cream dairy product)
Generous pinch of nutmeg
½ teaspoon salt
Freshly ground pepper to taste
    (preferably white pepper)
1 teaspoon lemon juice
2 cups (1 pint) oysters, drained of
    liquid

In a skillet sauté the celery, scallions and garlic in 3 tablespoons margarine or butter for 5 minutes without allowing to brown. Sprinkle the flour over the vegetables and cook, stirring, for 3 minutes.

Meanwhile, boil down the turkey stock rapidly until it measures 3 cups.

Add the turkey stock to the skillet gradually, stirring constantly, and removing briefly from the heat if necessary to prevent lumping. Transfer the mixture to a saucepan. Bring to boil, stirring. Add the shredded turkey meat along with the nutmeg, salt, pepper, and lemon juice, and allow to simmer gently.

Meanwhile, heat the oysters in a skillet in 1 tablespoon margarine or butter until the oysters begin to curl at the edges. Add the oysters to the soup and serve immediately in soup bowls.

Makes 8 servings.

FRAGRANT CREAM OF TURKEY SOUP

Prepare Turkey-Oyster Stew, omitting the oysters and 1 tablespoon of the margarine or butter.

Makes 8 servings.

TURKEY TORTELLINI EN BRODO

For the filling:
1½ cups ground cooked turkey
⅓ cup ground prosciutto ham
1 egg yolk, beaten
1 tablespoon freshly grated
   Parmesan, Romano or Sardo
   cheese
Freshly ground pepper to taste
Pinch of nutmeg
Pinch of cinnamon

For the pasta:
1¾ cups flour
½ teaspoon salt
1 egg, lightly beaten
1 teaspoon vegetable oil
4 or more tablespoons warm water

For serving:
7 cups rich turkey stock or chicken
   broth

For the filling: You may use either a food processor or a meat grinder. If you are using a food processor, after grinding and measuring the turkey and the prosciutto, put them back in the food processor fitted with a steel blade, and blend until very fine. Add the egg and blend again. Add the remaining ingredients and blend again. If using a meat grinder, after grinding and measuring the turkey and the prosciutto, regrind them together, using a fine blade. Transfer to a bowl in which the egg yolk has been beaten. Add the remaining ingredients, mixing well. Work with your hands until all ingredients are blended well.

For the pasta: Sift the flour and salt together into a bowl. Make a well in the center and put the egg and the vegetable oil in the well. Draw the flour into the egg and mix well. Add 3 tablespoons water and mix well. Add another tablespoon of water if necessary to make a medium firm dough. If necessary add warm water, a teaspoonful at a time, until the dough can be kneaded. Turn out on an unfloured board and knead for 10 minutes. Cover with a bowl or plastic wrap and allow to sit for 30 minutes. Roll out less than ⅛ inch thick, rolling from the center outward with the rolling pin. The dough should be at least 13 or 14 inches in diameter when rolled out, and preferably larger. Cut into 2-inch circles with a biscuit cutter. There should be at least 36 circles. Remove and discard excess dough.

Spoon ¼ teaspoon filling into the center of each circle. Put some water into a cup and with a finger moisten the edges of one circle. Fold in half to form a half circle. Pick up the half circle and press the edges firmly together with the fingers. Then place the half circle, seam side up, near the end of the index finger of the left hand. With the right hand turn down seam edges slightly, and at the same time wrap the half circle around the index finger and stretch and overlap the ends to form a ring.

Place on a tray or baking sheet lined with a clean dish towel. Continue forming the tortellini until they all have been arranged on the towel. Cover with another clean towel. Allow to sit for 2 hours. Turn each tortellini over and allow to sit for another 2 hours to dry.

For serving: Heat the turkey stock or chicken broth to boiling. Add the tortellini, stirring gently so that they do not stick to the bottom of the pot. After a minute or so the tortellini will rise to the surface. Simmer gently for 10 minutes or longer until the tortellini are done. Test with a fork for tenderness. Place 6 tortellini in each of 6 soup plates. Ladle the broth equally into the soup plates with the tortellini.

Makes 6 servings of soup, enough pasta for 6 servings, and enough filling for 18 servings. Extra filling can be tightly wrapped and frozen for use within 1 month.

TURKEY SOUP WITH CHINESE CABBAGE AND CELLOPHANE NOODLES

1 1⅞ ounce package cellophane noodles

1 pound Chinese cabbage (celery cabbage)

1 tablespoon vegetable oil

4 cups turkey stock or chicken broth

2 cups julienne strips cooked white meat turkey

2 tablespoons soy sauce (preferably tamari soy sauce)

Soak the cellophane noodles in hot water to cover for 10 minutes. Drain and cut into 2-inch lengths.

Meanwhile cut the Chinese cabbage into 2-inch lengths. Cut these into ½-inch wide strips.

Heat the vegetable oil in a wok. Stir-fry the cabbage strips for 2 minutes. Add the turkey stock or chicken broth and bring to a boil. Add the turkey strips, cellophane noodle pieces, and soy sauce. Simmer for 3 minutes and serve immediately in soup bowls.

Makes 4 to 6 servings.

TURKEY MINESTRONE

1 cup dried white beans	3 cups chopped cabbage
1 smoked turkey drumstick (1 to 1½ pounds)	1 garlic clove, finely minced
	2 teaspoons basil
1 cup chopped onions	Pinch of sage
2 tablespoons vegetable oil	1 teaspoon salt
2 cups diced scraped carrots	Freshly ground pepper to taste
1 cup diced peeled white turnips	½ cup tubetti, ditali, or ditalini pasta
2 cups diced small zucchini	¼ cup chopped flat leaf parsley
1 1-pound can Italian tomatoes, broken up	½ cup freshly grated Parmesan, Romano, Sardo, or Asiago cheese

Wash the beans and place them in a large pot. Cover well with cold water and bring to boil. Turn off heat, cover and allow to stand 1 hour. Drain. Add 2½ quarts fresh cold water to the beans. Add the turkey drumstick and bring to a boil. Lower heat and simmer 1½ hours or until the beans are tender.

Meanwhile sauté the onions in vegetable oil until soft. Add the carrots, turnips, and zucchini, and sauté for 5 minutes longer, adding a little more oil if necessary.

When the beans are tender add the vegetable mixture to them. Add the tomatoes, cabbage, garlic, basil, sage, salt, and pepper, and simmer another hour. Remove the drumstick. Pull off the skin. Pull off the meat and cut it up or shred it, discarding the tendons, bone and skin. Add the meat to the soup.

Meanwhile cook the pasta *al dente* in boiling salted water according to package directions. Drain. Add to the soup along with the parsley and simmer 5 minutes. Add the grated cheese and mix well, or sprinkle the cheese over the soup after ladling into soup bowls. Serve immediately.

Makes 8 or more servings.

SMOKY SPLIT PEA SOUP

2 cups green split peas	1 garlic clove, smashed
2 smoked turkey drumsticks, about	4 parsley sprigs
1 pound each	1 bay leaf
8 cups cold water	1 teaspoon marjoram
1 medium onion	8 peppercorns
2 whole cloves	Salt and pepper if required

Wash and soak the split peas in cold water to cover 8 hours or overnight. Soak the smoked turkey drumsticks in cold water to cover for 2 or 3 hours. Drain the split peas and the drumsticks and place them in a soup pot. Add the 8 cups of cold fresh water. Bring to boil, skimming particles or froth as it rises to the surface. When there is no more froth add the onion, which has been stuck with the whole cloves, the garlic, parsley, bay leaf, marjoram, and peppercorns. Lower heat, cover, and simmer about 2 hours or until the peas are tender and broken up completely. Remove the turkey drumsticks and peel off the skin, pull out the tendons and remove the bones. (Wear rubber gloves to protect your hands from the heat if necessary.) Pull the turkey meat into shreds or cut it into small pieces. Remove and discard the onion and the bay leaf from the soup pot. Put the soup through a food mill or sieve. Return it to a clean soup pot. Add the shredded turkey. Heat to boiling. Taste and adjust seasoning if necessary.

Makes 6 to 8 servings.

10

Cold Turkey

TURKEY SALADS AND SANDWICHES

Ho! 'tis the time of salads.
—LAURENCE STERNE, *Tristram Shandy*

What better way to have cold turkey than in a cool salad or tempting sandwich? Turkey salad has been a favorite in America since Colonial days when a salad was sometimes called salmagundi and contained a variety of good things besides greens. Look for an authentic Williamsburg version of the dish in this chapter, along with interesting new flavor partners for turkey in salads that include macadamia nuts, chutney, and sesame seeds.

Among the sandwiches are pita bread stuffed with turkey, feta, and Greek olives, and tacos stuffed with tomatoes, chilies, turkey, walnuts, and Monterey Jack cheese. There are also some hot sandwiches such as Sloppy Gobblers and Croque Monsieur à la Dinde. For little open-faced cocktail sandwiches featuring turkey, look in Chapter 8, Turkey Appetizers and Hors d'Oeuvres.

Salads

TURKEY SALAD SAO PAULO

½ cup mayonnaise
2 tablespoons lemon juice
Freshly ground pepper to taste
1 cup finely sliced celery, preferably from inner ribs, including some chopped leaves
⅓ cup sliced Brazil nuts

2½ cups cooked turkey, cut in julienne strips
1 11-ounce can Mandarin orange segments, well drained
1 medium banana
Lettuce leaves (optional)

Stir the mayonnaise in a bowl until smooth. Add the lemon juice, one tablespoon at a time. Add the pepper and stir. Add the celery and mix well. Add the Brazil nuts and mix well. Add turkey and Mandarin orange segments and toss well. Peel and slice the banana. Add it to the salad and mix well. Serve on lettuce leaves if desired.

Makes 4 to 6 servings.

TURKEY MACADAMIA MOUSSE (Salad)

1½ envelopes plain gelatin
½ cup cold turkey stock or chicken broth
2 cups boiling turkey stock or chicken broth
2 tablespoons lemon juice
½ teaspoon tarragon
¼ teaspoon salt
Freshly ground pepper to taste (preferably white pepper)

2 cups cooked shredded (or cut in julienne strips) turkey
1 cup finely sliced celery
3 hard-cooked eggs, chopped
½ cup Macadamia nuts, cut in half
⅓ cup mayonnaise
⅓ cup sour cream
Ripe olives for garnish (optional)

Soften the gelatin in the cold turkey stock or chicken broth. Add the boiling turkey stock or chicken broth and stir until the gelatin is dissolved. Add the lemon juice, tarragon, salt, and pepper. Add the turkey shreds or strips, celery, chopped eggs and Macadamia nuts, mixing gently.

Combine the mayonnaise and sour cream. Add a little of the liquid from the turkey mixture. Then add the mayonnaise mixture to the turkey mixture. Cover and chill for 1 to 1½ hours until slightly set. Mix gently but thoroughly. Pour into a lightly oiled 1½ quart mold, cover, and chill for about 12 hours, or until firm. Unmold onto a chilled serving plate. If desired decorate the top of the mousse with pieces of ripe olive cut into strips with a small sharp knife, or into various shapes with truffle cutters.

Makes 8 servings.

Variation: *Turkey Almond Mousse*
Substitute ½ cup slivered or sliced almonds for the Macadamia nuts.

SESAME TURKEY SALAD

1½ cups diced cooked turkey
1½ cups alfalfa sprouts, firmly
   packed
1½ cups diced tomatoes
1½ cups diced cucumbers
4 thinly sliced scallions, including
   some of green part

¼ cup tahini (ground sesame seeds)
1 tablespoon soy sauce (preferably
   tamari soy sauce)
¼ cup lemon juice
Lettuce leaves
Sesame seeds

Combine the turkey, alfalfa sprouts, tomatoes, cucumbers, and scallions in a bowl. Mix together the tahini, soy sauce, and lemon juice and pour over the turkey mixture. Toss. Serve on lettuce leaves. Sprinkle with sesame seeds.

Makes 4 servings.

TURKEY CHUTNEY SALAD

⅓ cup mayonnaise
½ cup Major Grey's chutney,
   chopped
1 tablespoon lemon juice
2 cups slivered or julienne strips
   cooked turkey

1 8-ounce can water chestnuts,
   drained and sliced
1 cup drained pineapple chunks
¼ cup coarsely chopped walnuts
Salt to taste
Freshly ground pepper to taste
Lettuce leaves

Combine the ingredients in the order listed, except for the lettuce leaves. Serve on lettuce leaves.

Makes 4 servings.

CHRISTIANA CAMPBELL'S TAVERN SALMAGUNDI*

16 cups salad greens
1 pound Virginia ham, thinly sliced and cut into strips
1 pound cooked turkey, thinly sliced and cut into strips
4 hard-cooked eggs, sliced

16 sweet gherkins (or other sweet pickles)
8 celery hearts (tiny center portions of the celery, split in half lengthwise)
16 sardines
16 anchovy fillets

Arrange the salad greens on a large platter or on individual salad plates. Distribute the remaining ingredients evenly over the top and around the greens. Sprinkle lightly with either of the following salad dressings.

Makes 8 servings.

WILLIAMSBURG OIL AND VINEGAR DRESSING*

¾ teaspoon salt
⅜ teaspoon white pepper

¼ cup cider vinegar
¾ cup vegetable oil

Dissolve the salt and pepper in the vinegar. Add the vegetable oil and shake vigorously in a covered jar.

* Recipe from *The Williamsburg Cookbook,* published by The Colonial Williamsburg Foundation.

BLUE CHEESE DRESSING

To ½ cup of the above dressing add 2 tablespoons crumbled blue cheese, 1 teaspoon dry mustard, ½ teaspoon tarragon, and a pinch of thyme. Combine well.

BENGAL CURRIED RICE
TURKEY SALAD

1¾ cup or more boiling turkey stock   ½ teaspoon curry powder
   or chicken broth   Freshly ground pepper to taste
1 cup rice (preferably basmatti rice   ¼ cup chopped pimiento
   from India)   ½ cup thinly sliced celery
⅔ cup mayonnaise   2 cups diced cooked turkey
2 tablespoons lemon juice

Add the boiling turkey stock or chicken broth to the rice in a heavy saucepan. There should be enough broth to come 1 inch above the level of the rice. Cover tightly, bring to boil, lower heat, and simmer 20 minutes or until rice is tender and broth is absorbed. Remove from heat and turn the rice into a bowl. Allow to cool, fluffing occasionally with a fork. Cover and refrigerate.

Several hours ahead or at serving time combine the mayonnaise and lemon juice in a bowl. Add the curry powder and pepper. Add the pimiento and celery and mix well. Add the turkey and toss well. Add the rice and toss gently but thoroughly. If not serving immediately cover and chill until serving time.

Makes 8 servings.

GRAPE-WALNUT TURKEY RING

2 envelopes plain gelatin   2 cups cooked turkey breast cut
4 cups celery tonic (such as Dr.   into thin strips
   Brown's Celray)   1 medium size tart apple, peeled,
1 cup walnut halves   cored, and diced finely
1 cup purple grapes, cut in half   ⅓ cup mayonnaise
   lengthwise, seeds removed   ⅓ cup plain yogurt

Soften the gelatin in ½ cup celery tonic. Pour 1 cup boiling celery tonic over the softened gelatin and stir until completely dissolved. Add the remaining celery tonic and allow to cool.

Oil a 6-cup plain ring mold lightly. In the bottom of the mold arrange some walnut halves, grape halves (round side down), and turkey strips to make an attractive design. Spoon in a layer of gelatin about ¼ inch thick.

Refrigerate until set. Spoon in another layer of gelatin about ¼ inch thick and refrigerate until set. (This may be done in the freezer very quickly.) Combine remaining gelatin mixture with the remaining walnut halves, grape halves, turkey strips, and apple. Pour into the mold. Cover and refrigerate until firm.

Unmold on a chilled serving dish. Combine the mayonnaise and yogurt and serve as a dressing to accompany the salad mold.

Makes 6 servings.

Sandwiches

TURKEY TACOS

Vegetable oil
10 to 12 corn tortillas
½ cup finely chopped onions
2 medium tomatoes, cored and
    chopped
1 to 4 tablespoons chopped green
    chilies, seeds removed (amount
depends on the strength of the
    chilies and your taste)
2 cups shredded cooked turkey
½ cup chopped walnuts
10 to 12 heaping tablespoons
    shredded Monterrey Jack cheese

Heat about 2 inches of vegetable oil in a wok or heavy sauté pan with high sides. With tongs dip a tortilla in the oil for about 3 seconds, then, with the tongs (or using two pairs of tongs if you find it easier) fold over the tortilla to shape it into a taco. Hold the taco open about 1 inch while you fry it in the oil until lightly brown, so that it can be filled later. The entire frying operation only takes about a minute or two. Drain the taco on a paper towel, then place between aluminum foil to keep warm while continuing to make the remaining tacos.

Sauté the onions in 2 tablespoons vegetable oil until lightly browned. Add the tomatoes and chilies and cook over high heat for several minutes, stirring. Add the turkey and walnuts, lower heat, and cook until heated through. Fill the tacos with this mixture, dividing equally. Place a heaping tablespoon of shredded cheese in each taco. Serve immediately.

Makes 10 to 12.

CRUNCHY CUCUMBER TURKEY SANDWICH ON FRENCH BREAD

1 loaf French bread or skinny Italian bread
Margarine or butter
1 or 2 cucumbers (peeled, if cucumber is waxed), thinly sliced
Salt to taste
Freshly ground pepper to taste
Mayonnaise
½ pound sliced cooked turkey
1 Bermuda onion, cut into paper-thin slices

Cut the French bread lengthwise into three slices. Butter all the cut sides lightly. On the bottom layer arrange a layer of cucumber slices. Sprinkle with salt and pepper. Spread with mayonnaise. Cover with second bread slice. Arrange the turkey on the bread and cover with a thin layer of onion slices. Spread the remaining bread with mayonnaise and arrange it on the sandwich. Wrap the sandwich tightly in plastic wrap or aluminum foil and chill.

To serve cut into wedges.

Makes 4 to 6 servings.

CROQUE MONSIEUR A LA DINDE

This long-popular French sandwich gets a new lease on life when we substitute delicate smoked turkey breast for the usual ham before sautéeing it.

For clarified butter:
½ cup butter

For each sandwich:
2 very thin slices firm white bread
2 thin slices Gruyère cheese (do not use processed Gruyère)
1 thin slice smoked turkey breast
Clarified butter

For clarified butter: Melt butter in a small saucepan without allowing it to brown. Remove from heat and allow to stand about 5 minutes. Skim off any skin that forms on the top, using a spoon. Pour off the clear butter (the clarified butter) and discard the milky sediment that remains in the pan.

For each sandwich: You can prepare as many sandwiches at a time as will fit into a large heavy skillet or frying pan. Prepare each as follows. Cover one slice of bread with a slice of Gruyère, then a slice of smoked turkey, and another slice of Gruyère. Cover with the remaining slice of bread. Trim off the crusts evenly, including any filling that may be sticking out. With the palm of your hand or with a small flat board, press down firmly on the sandwich. Brush the top of the sandwich with clarified butter. Coat the skillet heavily with clarified butter and place the sandwich, buttered side down, in the skillet. Brush the top with clarified butter. Place over low heat and sauté until crisp and nicely browned. Turn and brown the other side. Serve immediately.

CRANBERRY CREAM CHEESE TURKEY SANDWICHES ON ENGLISH MUFFINS

4 English muffins
Margarine or butter
Small container fluffy cream cheese

¼ to ½ pound cooked sliced turkey breast
½ cup or more whole berry cranberry sauce

Split and toast the English muffins. Butter them. Spread the bottoms of the muffins generously with fluffy cream cheese. Arrange turkey slices over the cream cheese. Spread 2 tablespoons or more cranberry sauce over the turkey. Close the muffins, cut in half, and serve immediately.

Makes 4 servings

SLOPPY GOBBLERS
(hot sandwich)

1 cup chopped onions
1 small green pepper, chopped
1 tablespoon margarine or butter
1 tablespoon vegetable oil
3 cups ground or minced cooked
   turkey
1 8-ounce can tomato sauce

½ cup chili sauce
2 teaspoons Worcestershire sauce
Pepper to taste
Dash of Tabasco sauce
1 tablespoon horseradish
6 round Italian rolls, split and
   toasted

Sauté the onions and green pepper in margarine or butter and oil until soft. Add turkey, tomato sauce, chili sauce, Worcestershire sauce, pepper, Tabasco sauce, and horseradish, and combine. Cook, stirring, until mixture comes to a simmer. Reduce heat and cook, covered, for 15 minutes, stirring occasionally. Spoon the mixture on the bottom halves of the rolls and cover with the tops.

Makes 6 servings.

TURKEY IN THE SLAW SANDWICHES

½ pound (2½ cups) cooked turkey
   breast cut into strips
¼ pound (1 cup) cole slaw, well
   drained
1 large dill pickle, thinly sliced
   crosswise

1 large red apple, cut crosswise into
   ¼ inch slices, core removed
8 to 10 slices whole wheat or other
   whole grain bread, buttered

Combine the turkey strips, cole slaw, and pickle slices. Arrange on 4 or 5 slices of buttered bread. Arrange the apple slices over the top. Cover with remaining bread slices. Cut in half and serve immediately.

Makes 4 or 5.

BROILED GOBBLER SANDWICH

Thickly sliced dark bread, 1 slice per
 serving
Cooked sliced turkey, 1½ to 2
 ounces per serving

Deviled Smithfield ham, 1½
 teaspoons per serving
Vermont cheddar cheese, 1 thick
 slice per serving

Arrange bread slices on a baking sheet and toast one side under the broiler. Turn the bread slices over and spread them with deviled Smithfield ham. Arrange the turkey slices over the Smithfield ham and top with a slice of Vermont cheddar. Place under the broiler until the cheese is lightly browned and bubbly. Serve immediately. To be eaten with knife and fork.

TURKEY SANDWICHES ATHENA
IN PITA BREAD

4 pita breads (preferably whole
 wheat) 6 inches in diameter
Margarine or butter
½ pound sliced cooked turkey
4 heaping tablespoons crumbled
 feta cheese

12 Greek olives (preferably
 Calamata olives), cut up and
 pitted
4 Salonika peppers (optional)
Lettuce

For each sandwich:
Slit the pita bread about one-third of the way around and open it up so that it can be stuffed. Butter the inside of the pita bread on the bottom. Arrange 2 ounces of sliced turkey on the butter. Arrange a heaping tablespoon of feta over the turkey. Arrange 3 cut-up olives over the feta. If using Salonika peppers cut up and arrange with the olives. Cover with a leaf or two or lettuce. Serve whole or cut in half crosswise if desired.

Makes 4 sandwiches.

PURIST'S TURKEY SANDWICH WITH RUSSIAN DRESSING

For the Russian dressing:
½ cup mayonnaise
1 tablespoon ketchup
2 tablespoons chopped sour pickle
1 tablespoon chopped parsley
1 teaspoon snipped chives
1 tablespoon chopped pimiento
½ teaspoon horseradish (preferably freshly grated)

¼ teaspoon Worcestershire sauce

For each sandwich:
2 slices firm white bread (homemade if possible)
Sweet butter, softened
Thinly sliced cooked turkey breast
Russian dressing

For the Russian dressing: Stir mayonnaise in a small bowl until smooth. Add remaining ingredients and mix well.

For each sandwich: Butter the bread generously. Cover one slice with turkey breast slices so that the meat is almost ½ inch thick. Spread generously with Russian dressing. Close and cut the sandwich in half.

Variations: If you don't want to be a purist, do any or all of the following:
   Substitute any kind of whole grain bread for the white.
   Toast the bread
   Add buttery type lettuce leaves.
   Substitute mayonnaise for Russian Dressing
   Add salt or pepper.
   Tuck in a bacon slice or two.
   Serve with olives, pickles, scallions, radishes, cherry tomatoes, or
      potato chips.

GRILLED TURKEY SANDWICHES WITH GORGONZOLA AND SALAMI

6 tablespoons margarine or butter, softened

6 tablespoons Gorgonzola cheese

8 slices cracked wheat bread

½ pound sliced cooked turkey breast

3 ounces thinly sliced hard smoked salami

Combine 2 tablespoons margarine or butter and the Gorgonzola and mix until creamy. Spread on the bread slices. Arrange the sliced turkey on 4 of the bread slices and arrange the salami over it. Cover with remaining bread slices, buttered side down. Butter the tops of the sandwiches and arrange the sandwiches buttered side down in a large cold skillet. Butter the top of the sandwiches. Cover the skillet and place over low heat. Allow to sauté until the sandwiches have browned. Turn and allow the other side to brown. Cut the sandwiches in half and serve immediately.

Makes 4.

11

Turkey Sausage and Turkey Ham Dishes

A rare bird on the earth.
—Juvenal, *Satires*

Two of the most useful products made from turkey are turkey sausage and turkey ham. Turkey sausage, which is usually displayed with other sausages in supermarkets, has several advantages over ordinary sausage. One is that it contains 50 percent less fat than the maximum government allowance for pork sausage. This is very noticeable when you cook turkey sausage, because very little fat exudes from it. It's a nice feature, since you can use turkey sausage in many recipes without fear of turning out a dish with a greasy quality. This sometimes occurs when using pork sausage.

You can use turkey sausage in place of pork sausage, which makes it possible to have sausage if you don't eat pork. There's a choice of flavors with turkey sausage, too, since it comes in both mild and hot styles. It generally is packaged in twelve ounce rolls and you can keep it either in the freezer or the refrigerator. You'll find some interesting recipes for using turkey sausage in this chapter, as well as a recipe for making your own fresh turkey sausage from ground raw turkey thigh meat. Other recipes using turkey sausage can be found in the index under "Sausage, Turkey", for example, Turkelettes a l'Orange, which are turkey thighs boned out and stuffed with a turkey sausage filling.

Turkey ham tastes very much like ordinary ham, and has a similar appearance. It's made in rolls about four or five inches in diameter, cut off in various lengths, and vacuum packaged. Like other ham type products it's smoked, and it's boneless. Although fully cooked, it must be kept refrigerated. You can substitute turkey ham for almost any recipe that calls for ham. Good ideas for using turkey ham, including a recipe for turkey ham muffins, are included in this chapter.

Other turkey products that you'll find at butchers and supermarkets are turkey frankfurters, which are used like any other frankfurters, and various types of turkey salami, which can be sliced up for snacks or sandwiches, or served with hors d'oeuvres.

GRATED SWEET POTATO-SAUSAGE BAKE

1 12-ounce package mild turkey
　sausage
½ cup finely chopped celery
½ cup chopped onions
Generous pinch or sage
Generous pinch of thyme
Freshly ground pepper to taste

1¾ to 2 pounds sweet potatoes or
　yams
1 cup soft rye with caraway seeds
　bread crumbs
2 tablespoons margarine or butter,
　melted

Sauté the sausage in a skillet over moderate heat, breaking up the sausage with a pancake turner or fork until it loses its pink color. Add the celery, onions, sage, thyme, and pepper, and continue to sauté, turning, about 10 minutes, without allowing the mixture to brown much. Remove from the heat.

Preheat the oven at 350°F. (177°C.). Peel the sweet potatoes or yams and immediately grate them by hand or in a food processor using a steel blade. Combine the grated sweet potatoes with the sausage mixture. Place in a 1½-quart greased baking dish. Cover and bake 30 minutes. Mix well, stirring up from the bottom. Bake 30 minutes more, uncovered, and mix again. Toss the bread crumbs with the margarine or butter. Sprinkle over top of the baking dish. Bake, uncovered, 30 to 45 minutes longer.

Makes 4 servings.

VEAL TURKEYBURGERS

1 pound ground veal
½ pound mild turkey sausage,
   broken up
1 egg
1 tablespoon tomato paste
1 tablespoon grated onions

2 tablespoons sesame seeds
2 tablespoons wheat germ
¼ teaspoon salt
Freshly ground pepper to taste
Vegetable oil

Combine ground veal and turkey sausage until well blended. This is easiest done with the hands. Add the remaining ingredients, except for the vegetable oil, and mix until well blended. Form into 6 patties. Brown the patties in one or 2 tablespoons vegetable oil over medium heat on one side. Turn and brown on the other side. Reduce the heat to low and cook until no red color remains in the center when one of the patties (burgers) is opened slightly with the tines of a fork. The pan may be covered during the last part of the cooking to hasten the meat cooking through if desired.

Makes 6 servings.

NIPPY TURKEY
SAUSAGE-BABY LIMA BEAN BAKE

2 10-ounce packages frozen baby
   lima beans
¾ cup water
½ teaspoon dry mustard
2 tablespoons dark brown sugar
⅓ cup seafood cocktail sauce (such
   as you might use in serving
   shrimp cocktail)

½ cup grated onion
¼ teaspoon salt, or to taste
Freshly ground pepper to taste
Boiling water or boiling tomato
   juice (optional)
1 12-ounce package hot style turkey
   sausage, cut crosswise into 8
   slices

Preheat oven at 400°F. (204°C.). Cook lima beans in the ¾-cup water for 5 minutes until just tender, or cook according to package directions. Remove frm heat but do not drain. Add the dry mustard, brown sugar, cocktail sauce, onion, salt and pepper to the lima beans. Transfer to a shallow greased casserole or baking dish. Arrange the turkey sausage slices on top of the lima beans. Bake 30 minutes. Reduce oven temperature to 325°F. (163°C.), stir the beans and bake 20 minutes longer. If the beans become too dry during baking, add a little boiling water or boiling tomato juice.

Makes 4 to 6 servings.

BEEF-TURKEY SAUSAGE-CHESTNUT LOAF

2 eggs
1 tablespoon tomato paste
½ cup fresh bread crumbs which have been allowed to stand until dry
¼ cup wheat germ
¼ cup very finely chopped onions
¼ cup chopped parsley
1 teaspoon salt

Freshly ground pepper to taste
¾ pound ground beef
1 12-ounce package mild turkey sausage
2 cups (approximately) leftover cooked Brandied Chestnut Stuffing (see index), loosely packed

Preheat oven at 350°F. (177°C.) Beat the eggs lightly. Add the tomato paste and bread crumbs and mix well. Add the wheat germ, onions, parsley, salt, and pepper and mix well. Crumble the ground beef into the egg mixture and mix until well blended. Break up the turkey sausage into small pieces and add to the beef mixture, combining with a spoon or with your hands until completely smooth. No lumps of turkey sausage should remain.

Divide the mixture into two parts, one slightly smaller than the other. Pack the smaller part into the bottom of a 5-inch by 9-inch loaf pan and smooth with a rubber spatula or with your hands. Break up the stuffing into small pieces. Arrange it evenly over the meat mixture in the loaf pan. Place the remaining meat mixture between two pieces of waxed paper or plastic wrap and pat and shape until the meat has taken on a rectangular shape that will fit over the stuffing. Remove one piece of waxed paper and invert the shaped meat rectangle over the loaf pan. Remove the second piece of waxed paper. With your fingers push the meat mixture so that it comes to the edges of the loaf pan all around, sealing in the stuffing. Bake 1 hour. Slice to serve.

Makes 6 or more servings.

FRESH TURKEY
BREAKFAST SAUSAGE

½ teaspoon each:
  crumbled bay leaf
  white peppercorns
  black peppercorns
  ground cloves
  mace
  nutmeg
  thyme
  paprika
1 teaspoon basil

¼ teaspoon each:
  cinnamon
  marjoram
  sage
  savory
2 pounds raw boneless turkey thigh
  cut into pieces
1 pound fatback cut into pieces
2 teaspoons salt
¼ teaspoon freshly ground pepper
Melted shortening

Place the crumbled bay leaf, white and black peppercorns, ground cloves, mace, nutmeg, thyme, paprika, basil, cinnamon, marjoram, sage, and savory in an electric blender. Process until all spices are thoroughly pulverized and blended. Transfer the mixture to a small jar or cup.

Grind the turkey thigh pieces with the fatback pieces twice through a meat grinder. Transfer to a bowl. Add the salt and pepper and 2 teaspoons of the spice mixture. Mix well, using your hands to combine the ingredients thoroughly. Sauté a teaspoon of the sausage mixture in a skillet and taste it. Add more salt, pepper, or spice mixture to the sausage according to taste, again mixing well with the hands. Any remaining spice mixture can be saved for use in making the sausage in the future, or in making paté, meatloaf, or other meat dishes. Divide the sausage mixture into two equal parts and shape them into cylinders about 2 inches in diameter.

Lay out two double layers of cheesecloth, each large enough to hold one of the sausage rolls. Brush the cheesecloth with melted shortening. Lay a roll of sausage on each cheesecloth. Roll up. Tie one end of each with kitchen string. Twist the other end to tighten the roll as much as possible. Then tie with string. Wrap each roll in aluminum foil and refrigerate for 24 hours.

Unwrap, slice, and sauté over low heat, turning once, until brown on both sides and cooked through. If desired use one sausage roll and freeze the remaining roll up to 2 to 3 weeks before using. Defrost thoroughly in refrigerator before cooking.

Makes about 14 servings.

HAMMY BUTTERMILK CORN MUFFINS

These are especially good at breakfast time. You may want to have some marmalade with them. To make a complete breakfast start off with tomato juice, have the muffins with scrambled eggs and top it off with a fragrant cup of freshly-brewed coffee.

1 cup flour	1 teaspoon chervil
¾ cup corn meal (preferably stone ground corn meal)	2 eggs
	1 cup buttermilk
2 teaspoons baking powder	¼ cup margarine or butter, melted
1 teaspoon baking soda	and cooled
1 cup finely diced turkey ham	

Preheat the oven at 425°F. (218°C.). Sift the flour, corn meal, baking powder and baking soda into a bowl. Add the turkey ham and chervil and toss. Beat the eggs lightly in another bowl. Add the buttermilk to the eggs and mix. Add the melted margarine or butter to the eggs and mix. Add the egg mixture to the flour mixture and mix just enough to combine. Spoon into greased muffin tins, filling them about ⅔ full. Bake for 20 to 25 minutes.

Makes 1 dozen.

TURKEY HAM GRENADINE

4 slices turkey ham, ½-inch thick	1 tablespoon vinegar
⅓ cup Grenadine syrup	1 teaspoon dry mustard

Preheat the oven at 325°F. (163°C.). Arrange the turkey ham slices in a shallow buttered direct heatproof baking dish. Combine the remaining ingredients and spoon over the turkey ham. Bake for 30 minutes, basting two or three times during the baking. Remove the turkey ham slices and arrange them on a heated serving plate. If the sauce is not thick, place the baking dish over medium heat and boil down slightly until thickened. Spoon the sauce over the turkey ham slices and serve.

Makes 4 servings.

PECAN PILAF WITH TURKEY HAM

¼ cup margarine or butter
1 cup finely chopped onions
½ cup chopped pecans
½ pound mushrooms, sliced
1 cup diced celery

2½ cups turkey stock or chicken
   broth
1 cup rice
Freshly ground pepper to taste
2 cups diced turkey ham
¼ cup chopped parsley

Sauté the onions in margarine or butter until soft. Add the pecans and sauté a few minutes longer until the pecans are lightly browned. Add the mushrooms and cook several minutes longer, stirring occasionally. Add the celery and turkey stock or chicken broth and bring to boil. Add the rice and pepper, stirring. Cover the pan, lower heat, and cook about 20 minutes, or until the rice is tender. Add the turkey ham and parsley and cook several minutes until heated through.

Makes 4 servings.

TURKEY HAM MOUSSE WITH PORT

1 envelope plain gelatin
1½ cups chicken broth
2 eggs, separated
¼ cup Port wine

4 cups finely ground turkey ham,
   loosely packed
Freshly ground pepper to taste
½ cup heavy cream
Parsley sprigs

Soften the gelatin in ¼ cup cold chicken broth. Add to 1¼ cups boiling chicken broth in a saucepan, stirring until the gelatin is dissolved. Beat the egg yolks lightly in a bowl and add the chicken broth mixture gradually, stirring constantly. Return the mixture to the saucepan and heat gently until hot but not boiling. Remove from the heat. Add the Port, ground turkey ham, and pepper, and allow to cool.

Whip the cream until thick and fold it into the ham mixture. Beat the egg whites until they form stiff peaks. Fold a little of the ham mixture into the egg whites. Then fold the egg whites into the ham mixture. Turn the mixture into a lightly oiled 5-cup ring mold. Cover with plastic wrap or aluminum foil and chill 8 hours or more.

Unmold on a chilled serving plate and garnish with parsley sprigs.

Makes 6 to 8 servings.

DOUBLE PERKY TURKEY LOAF WITH SWEET POTATO PECAN FILLING

2 eggs
⅓ cup wheat germ
2 tablespoons tomato paste
½ teaspoon marjoram
1 teaspoon salt
Freshly ground pepper to taste
1 pound raw ground turkey (ground twice)

¼ pound (1¼ cups) ground turkey ham
2 cups mashed cooked sweet potatoes
¼ cup margarine or butter, melted
2 tablespoons brown sugar
4 tablespoons (approximately) milk or cream
½ cup pecan halves

Preheat oven at 350°F. (177°C.). In a bowl beat the eggs lightly. Add the wheat germ, tomato paste, marjoram, salt, and pepper, and combine. Add the ground turkey and ground turkey ham and mix well. Divide the mixture into two parts, one slightly smaller than the other. Spoon the smaller portion into a 4½-inch by 8½-inch well-greased loaf pan and smooth with a rubber spatula. Place the remaining meat mixture between two sheets of waxed paper and shape into a rectangle about 4½ inches by 8½ inches. Set aside.

Combine the mashed sweet potatoes with most of the melted margarine or butter and the brown sugar. Add milk or cream, one tablespoon at a time, until of a nice spreading consistency. Spread over the meat mixture in the loaf pan. Arrange the pecan halves on top. Press the pecan halves into the sweet potatoes. Smooth over the top with a rubber spatula. Arrange the rectangular meat mixture over the sweet potato layer. Press around the edges of the meat so that it meets the sides of the loaf pan all around. Bake, brushing the top with the remaining melted margarine or butter after 30 minutes. Continue baking for a total of 1¼ hours. Allow to stand for 10 minutes before cutting.

Makes 6 servings.

12

The Wild Turkey

We thank thee for the bountiful supply of wildlife with which Thou has blessed our land; for the turkeys that gobble in our forests.
—ANDREW JACKSON, November 29, 1835

Unless you've spent a lot of time out in the woods in wild turkey country, chances are you aren't familiar with the bird and have probably never seen one face to face. They're scarce as pandas at zoos, so you can't even take a look at one there. For this reason, most of us know very little about the wild turkey, what it really looks like, what its behavior is like and how it lives. Most of us have probably never eaten wild turkey, either, but would like to if we only knew how to get one. The purpose of this chapter then is to take a look at the world of the wild turkey, to learn more about it, and find out how to go about getting this elegant bird onto the dinner table.

When we think of a turkey in its natural outdoor world, most of us envision a tom turkey, or gobbler as he's generally called, in full courting display. His irridescent velvety body feathers reflect bronze, purple, and green hues and are puffed out so that he appears much larger than he really is. His tail is smartly fanned out to reveal its impressive brown and white banding, and his wings are swung forward and down so that they scrape along the ground when he struts. His head is pulled back toward his body and the fleshy growths on his head, neck, and over his bill have swelled and turned a brilliant red. A long horsetail-like beard sprouts from the center of his breast. His long sturdy spurred legs move in short stiff strutting steps, and he makes a deep sound inside his throat followed by a gobble as he shows the wild turkey hen how attractive he is.

Contrary to most illustrations we see of the country gobbler surrounded by cornstalks, pumpkins, and other fall provender, in real life he only appears like this at those times of the spring when he's trying to add another turkey hen to his harem. The rest of the time wild turkeys are slender-bodied, deep-chested, long-tailed, and firm stepping. They are wary, resourceful, vigilant and hearty birds. Their keen vision, perhaps more acute than that of any wild creatures', is their most important tool of survival, and a wild turkey will disappear in the twinkling of an eye if it sees the slightest suspicious movement. They can travel long distances without tiring and are constantly on the move searching for food during fall and winter months. When deep snow covers the ground they can go for several days without eating. They have managed to survive a long list of predators that includes foxes, owls, coyotes, bobcats, dogs, weasels, snakes, hawks, eagles, skunks, and even an occasional house cat. Some of these are content to make off with the poults, as baby turkeys are called, while others, including squirrels, racoons, skunks, oppossums, and crows, add themselves to the long list of turkey egg stealers.

But somehow the wild turkey endures in the face of seemingly insurmountable odds. Toughness and independence begin from the day of hatching. A wild turkey gets its first view of the world from a nest which the turkey hen has built on the ground, and as soon as the poult has dried off after hatching it stands up and begins to peck at this and that in search of food. In a week to ten days its mother has it flying up into a tree to roost for the night, where she keeps it cozily tucked under her wing, along with her other poults, to protect it from chilly air or other dangers of the night. Sometimes two or more hens join forces so that they can help one another with baby-sitting and lookout chores. Both hens and poults busy themselves through most of the day nibbling on fresh grasses, grains, seeds and tidbits that are found in the spring. Their menu includes a few insects, and grasshoppers are a special favorite. If wild turkeys eat a certain food in abundance, such as wild onions or leeks, their flesh can assume a special taste, in this case a delicate oniony one. During the rearing season, the gobbler, who has assumed no parental responsibilities whatsoever, is off in the woods building himself up after his strenuous courting season and going through a complete moult, or change of feathers, to protect him through the winter.

What probably makes the wild turkey such a succulent bird for the table is the variety of food that it consumes not only during the verdant spring and summer months when the living is easy, but in the wintertime when foraging is a daylong occupation. Then most food is found by scratching up the ground or following the trail of deer who have already pawed the ground. Acorns are a favorite fall and winter food, and during these seasons wild turkeys also eat pine needles, pine seeds, sumac seeds, various tubers, roots, mosses, and other vegetable matter. When the snow freezes over and they can't scratch through it for food, they will usually remain in the trees and eat tree buds, which obviates any need to fly to the ground. Should you decide to go turkey hunting and spot a turkey roosting in a tree, it's considered poor sportsmanship to shoot it down when it is in such a vulnerable situation. What, then, is considered a fair shot, and how should one go about turkey hunting?

Turkey hunting takes place during two seasons, spring and fall/winter, and each season involves a different type of hunting. Turkey hunting in the spring, at which time only gobblers may be shot, is based on the well-proven theory that gobblers will answer the mating call of the hen and come to look for her. The call of the hen is imitated by the hunter, who uses a turkey caller for the purpose. A turkey caller is a device that imitates the call of a turkey, and while there are many types available, the most commonly used are box callers, which require two hands to operate, and the diaphragm caller, which is placed in the mouth and leaves the hands free for aiming a shotgun.

Turkey callers used hundreds of years ago were usually made of hollowed-out turkey bones, and Kit Carson is known to have used a quill for the purpose. A real woodsman in those days was able to use a leaf, or even a blade of grass in such a way as to imitate the call of a turkey, but there are probably few hunters who have such a skill today. In any case, when a gobbler comes near to what he presumes to be a waiting hen, he displays himself in all his colorful finery and moves in closer until at last he is within range of the hunter. This is the time, shotgun having been already properly positioned, that the hunter aims for the bird's neck, just below the head, hopefully to fell it with one clean shot. Some hunters prefer to use a double-barrelled shotgun as some assurance against a bird being merely wounded and going off into the woods to die.

If this description makes turkey hunting sound easy, you should know that it's not at all. Before you can shoot a turkey you must first find a turkey, and even before that you must find an area that turkeys are known to inhabit. The best bet is to contact county or state environmental conservation departments, state wildlife agencies, hunting organizations or turkey hunters, to learn where there are turkey hunting areas. At that same time you can inquire about season lengths and bag limits for wild turkeys, which vary from state to state or from county to county.

Go to the suggested area a day or two before the season opens and scout the woods to try to locate a gobbler or two. You can do this by looking for telltale signs of turkeys, the most definite of which are droppings beneath trees where the birds roost at night. Other signs are dust baths, which are rather oval-shaped depressions in dry ground where turkeys dust themselves. Often there will be feathers around such dust baths. If the ground is moist you can look for turkey tracks. Scratchings on the ground will also reveal that turkeys have been in the area searching for food. The deep V formations of their scratchings point in the direction in which they were traveling. You can often spot a turkey at sunset by locating the roost in which he sits and gobbles a little before settling down for the night. Gobblers dearly love to answer a variety of noises ranging from the slamming of a car door to the hooting of an owl, the falling of a dead tree in the woods, or the sound of a hunter's turkey caller, and their gobbling can be heard for at least half a mile.

Once you've located a gobbler you can be quite sure that you'll find him in the same vicinity on subsequent mornings. Return to the spot before sunrise and position yourself 150 yards or more from the roost, which will usually be a tall hardwood tree. Turkeys start gobbling at dawn and then fly down to start their breakfast search. When your bird flies down, try to attract him to you with the aid of a turkey caller. The rest is a matter of luck and good marksmanship.

Probably the best advice for a novice turkey hunter is to read one or two good books on the subject before getting started. There are several excellent ones available that make fascinating and instructive reading. You will learn, for example, that camouflage clothing is worn by turkey hunters, since turkeys are quick to spot any unusual color. They are, in fact, quite put off by the color red, which they apparently mistake for the neck growths of another tom turkey, and you can be sure they will not make an effort to come courting if you wear such a color. Take along a compass when you go into the woods and make sure you know how to use it before setting out. Chances are you'll do your turkey hunting solo, but if you do go out with another hunter don't talk or make any unnecessary noise. Wild turkeys have a highly developed sense of hearing and any strange sound will cause your prospective turkey dinner to be gone before you even have a chance to see it. Never shoot at a turkey unless you *can* see it, or you may end up shooting at another turkey hunter calling from a blind.

From the standpoint of turkey conservation, spring is the best time to hunt because only gobblers may be bagged then, and since turkeys are polygamous you will not be affecting future turkey generations by taking home a tom. From the standpoint of the novice hunter, spring is also more likely to be a better time to hunt since turkeys are continually on the move in the colder weather and are thus more difficult to locate.

However if fall or winter is the time you choose to go hunting, it may help you to know that there will be a greater number of wild turkeys around because the spring and summer broods will have been added to the population. In many states or counties, both male and female birds may be taken at this time of the year. Turkeys usually travel in flocks in the winter, and they can sometimes be followed by spotting their tracks in soft snow, or located by a few of the other methods already described.

Once you find a flock you can either scatter it with the help of a dog or by firing a gun. Then call to the scattered birds from a concealed place to lure them back toward you. Or you can try to get ahead of the flock and prepare an ambush. If you call to a scattered flock it's useful to know that very little gobbling is done in the fall and winter, and mating calls are completely out of order. Wild turkeys have a wide variety of calls and the one to use in this type of situation is the "lost call", which is the type used by a young turkey trying to get back to its flock. You can learn how to make several different calls with a turkey caller, and you can buy a record to learn how the sounds differ, or you can go to a wild turkey-calling contest to hear all the sounds first hand.

A rifle, rather than a shotgun, is usually used for fall turkey hunting, since shooting is generally done from a longer range.

Another type of turkey hunting can be pursued at private shooting preserves, where you hunt pen-reared wild turkeys. This is a kind of hunting which involves either going after birds which have been released an hour or two before the hunting begins (called "immediate release" hunting) or by tracking down birds that have been in the wild for a longer period (called "natural" hunting). A pen-reared wild turkey will generally not have the same quality of flesh as a true wild turkey since it has been fed corn and other nonwild foods while kept in captivity. It also is not as cautious a bird since it is used to being in the company of humans, and for this reason is generally easier to bag.

If you are worried that the hunting of wild turkeys will decimate turkey populations as it once did, you can relax. Due to some truly remarkable restoration programs conducted throughout many parts of the United States, there are now a great many more wild turkeys than there were 20 or 30 years ago. Nearly every state now has wild turkey populations, including states that originally had no turkeys, and those where the bird was wiped out in past centuries. Trap and transfer programs, which involve trapping and moving all or part of very large turkey flocks to new areas where conditions are good for survival and proliferation, are the principal means by which the turkey population of America has become so large. Game laws and hunters that respect them have also helped to keep wild turkey populations thriving.

Assuming now that you have bagged a wild turkey and have had the foresight to prepare a sling to carry the weighty bird, the next step is field dressing it. This should be done as soon as the bird has been shot, unless the weather is very cold.

First the crop should be removed, unless it is empty, because any strongly flavored food the turkey may have eaten will flavor the flesh if not removed, or the contents of the crop may sour. You can tell whether the crop is full by pinching the area at the base of the neck just where it enters the breast. The crop is underneath this area and can be as large as a fairsized fist when full. The skin over the crop should be slit for about four inches without cutting through into the crop itself, and the sac containing the food should be removed.

Next, eviscerate the bird by cutting a slit from the end of the breastbone to just above the vent. Slip two fingers into the opening and loosen the intestines just in front of the vent, and then cut around the end of the intestine with a knife. Remove the gizzard and intestines from the body cavity, then remove the liver and heart. Cut the gall bladder from the liver without spilling the contents of the gall bladder, which are very bitter. Cut the intestines away from the gizzard, open the gizzard, remove the contents, and pull out the inner lining of the gizzard.

Keep the turkey as cool as you can and refrigerate it as soon as possible. When you get home or back to camp, scald the bird in hot water to loosen the feathers. Remove them and cut off the head and lower legs. If there is any buckshot in the bird remove it if possible by using a small, sharp-pointed knife. Wash the bird well in cold water, drain and refrigerate it, covered, for at least twelve hours after the bird is shot. After dressing the turkey the amount you end up with will be about three quarters of the bird's original weight. Weights of wild turkeys vary according to age, sex, subspecies, and time of the year, and they are generally heaviest in late winter and early spring. Summer activities keep the weight of both the male and female turkey down. Weights average between approximately eight and fifteen pounds, and while there are turkeys twenty pounds or larger, not many hunters are successful in bagging them. It probably doesn't pay to get too concerned about whether you've come home with a really king-size bird, since any reasonably sized turkey is impressive enough. People can't seem to resist bragging about the size of the turkey they've bagged, though, and it might be wise to keep your trophy off the scale and heed the advice of a hunter in 1881 who said, "When you kill a gobbler of 25 or 30 pounds, do not weigh him: they generally resent such a proceeding by falling off from five to ten pounds."

Simple roasting or braising, as you will see in the recipes that follow, are the best ways to cook a wild turkey. They don't have a "gamey" taste, unless they're improperly attended to after they're shot, so there's no need to drench them in highly seasoned marinades or sauces. Some experienced turkey hunters who have eaten many wild turkeys say that most people, if blindfolded, would be hard pressed to differentiate between the taste of wild and domestic turkey. This is subject to debate, but it is at least accurate in the sense that the preparation of wild and domestic turkey is not very different.

If you aren't inclined to take gun in hand and tramp off into the forest, but you would still like to cook a wild turkey, you can buy one ready-to-cook at many fine butcher shops and specialty food shops in large cities. They can be bought fresh or frozen, but you will usually need to order a fresh-killed one several days in advance. You may also be able to buy a wild turkey at a game farm where they are raised for sale to restaurants, but it will probably take some searching to locate these places. You might inquire by phone or in person at feed stores, poultry farms and similar places.

Wild turkeys are not inexpensive, but they are worth buying for a special treat. Their flavor, I find, is more delicate than that of the domestic bird. In texture they're firmer and finer, and in body conformation quite streamlined. The breast is narrower, but the breast meat extends farther up the body toward the neck region. The bones are thinner and longer than those of the domestic bird, and are thus more easily broken if handled roughly during preparation.

In cooking wild turkey you'll notice that the flesh doesn't contain the amount of fat a domestic turkey does, so some precaution needs to be taken to keep the meat moist at all times during cooking. Strips of bacon or fatback, parboiled or not, as you prefer, can be laid over the breast and legs. Another method is to cover the breast and legs with a cloth, which should be basted often, or, as soon as the breast has browned lightly in the oven, it can be covered with aluminum foil for the balance of the roasting, lifting and replacing it after each basting. Roasting time is about the same as for domestic turkeys.

COLONIAL ROAST WILD TURKEY

1 10 to 12 pound wild turkey with
    giblets
Salt
¼ cup butter or margarine, softened
3 tablespoons flour

Freshly ground pepper to taste
2 tart apples
1 rib celery, cut into 3 or 4 pieces
½ cup peanut oil
½ cup strained lemon juice

Preheat the oven at 325°F. (163°C). Wash the turkey inside and out with cold water and pat thoroughly dry with paper towels. Rub lightly with salt in the neck opening and body cavity. Combine the softened butter or margarine with the flour and pepper. Set aside.

Peel and core the apples. Cut one apple in half and the balance into quarters. Place the half apple in the neck opening of the turkey, rounded side out. Close with a poultry pin. Place the remaining apple pieces, along with the celery, inside the body cavity. Spread or rub the butter-flour mixture all over the outside of the turkey. Truss the turkey.

Combine the peanut oil and lemon juice. Dip a thin clean white cloth or double thickness of cheesecloth large enough to cover the turkey breast and legs into the oil-lemon juice mixture. Lay the cloth over the turkey. Roast for 15 minutes. Pour the remaining oil-lemon juice mixture over the cloth on the turkey. Continue to roast, basting every 15 minutes with the pan juices.

While the turkey is roasting prepare Giblet Gravy (see index) with the giblets. Spoon off all fat from the roasting pan before finishing the gravy.

Roast 2½ hours, or until meat thermometer inserted in the center of inside thigh muscle adjoining the body registers 180°F. (82°C.), or until tender when pierced with a sharp-tined fork. Allow the turkey to stand for 15 to 20 minutes on a wooden carving board before carving.

An 11-pound turkey makes about 16 servings.

OVEN-BRAISED WILD TURKEY WITH HICKORY NUT STUFFING

Hickory nuts, which have a rich, haunting flavor that is especially appropriate with wild turkey, are used in the stuffing for this bird. They are very difficult to find, but it's worth the effort if you're successful. If you simply can't locate any, substitute half pecans and half walnuts for the hickory nuts.

1 9-pound wild turkey with giblets	Freshly ground pepper to taste
Salt	¼ teaspoon thyme
3 tablespoons (approximately) butter or margarine, softened	½ teaspoon chervil
½ cup melted butter or margarine	4 cups firm whole wheat bread crumbs
1 cup chopped onions	5 or more thin slices salt pork, rinsed and patted dry with paper towels
1 cup finely sliced celery	
¼ cup chopped parsley and celery leaves combined	1 cup dry white wine
¾ cup chopped hickory nuts	

Preheat the oven at 325°F. (163°C.). Wash the turkey inside and out with cold water and pat thoroughly dry with paper towels. Rub lightly with salt in neck opening and body cavity. Rub the turkey all over with the softened butter or margarine.

Sauté the chopped onions and celery in the melted margarine or butter just until the onions are soft. Remove from heat and transfer to a bowl. Add the parsley and celery leaves, hickory nuts, 1 teaspoon salt, pepper, thyme and the chervil, and mix well. Add the bread crumbs and toss lightly but thoroughly. Stuff the neck cavity loosely and close with a poultry pin. Stuff the body cavity loosely. Truss the turkey. Cover the breast and drumsticks with overlapping slices of salt pork. Place the turkey in a covered roasting pan without the lid and pour the wine over the turkey. Roast uncovered for 40 minutes, basting every 20 minutes with the pan juices. Cover the pan and continue roasting, basting every 20 minutes, until meat thermometer inserted in the center of inside thigh muscle adjoining the body registers 180°F. (82°C.) or until tender when pierced with a sharp-tined fork. Allow the turkey to stand for 15 to 20 minutes on a wooden carving board before carving.

While the turkey is roasting prepare Giblet Gravy (see index) with the giblets, increasing the rosemary to 1 teaspoon, reducing the cornstarch to 2 tablespoons, and reducing the Port wine to ¼ cup. Spoon off all fat from the roasting pan before finishing the gravy.

Remove the fatback from the turkey before carving.

Makes 8 servings.

PEANUT-STUFFED WILD TURKEY EN COCOTTE

1 12-pound wild turkey with giblets	1 egg, lightly beaten
Salt	Freshly ground pepper to taste
1 cup finely chopped onions	8 cups firm white bread crumbs
2 tablespoons butter or margarine	6 or more slices bacon
3 cups roasted salted peanuts	1 garlic clove, smashed
1½ cups dry white wine	Pinch of thyme
1½ cups turkey stock or chicken broth	1 bay leaf

Preheat the oven at 325°F. (163°C.). Wash the turkey inside and out with cold water and pat thoroughly dry with paper towels. Rub lightly with salt in neck opening and body cavity. In a skillet sauté the onions in butter or margarine until soft. Transfer to a bowl. Spread the peanuts on a baking sheet and place them in the oven for 10 to 12 minutes until lightly browned, stirring several times. Chop them finely, or put them briefly through a food processor fitted with a steel blade. Add the peanuts to the bowl. And ½ cup wine, ½ cup turkey stock or chicken broth, the egg, and pepper, and mix well. Add the bread crumbs, and toss lightly but thoroughly. Stuff the neck opening loosely and secure with a poultry pin. Stuff the body cavity loosely. Truss the turkey.

Lay the bacon slices over the turkey breast. Place the turkey in a cocotte, covered roasting pan, top-of-stove casserole (preferably oval-shaped), or Dutch oven. In a saucepan combine the remaining 1 cup wine, 1 cup turkey stock or chicken broth, the garlic, thyme, and bay leaf. Bring to simmer. Pour into the cocotte with the turkey. Cover and simmer gently 2¼ hours, or until meat thermometer inserted into the center of inside thigh muscle adjoining the body registers 180°F. (82°C.), or until tender when pierced with a sharp-tined fork.

Meanwhile prepare Giblet Gravy (see index) with the giblets, using 6 tablespoons cornstarch instead of 3 or 4, and mixing ¼ cup turkey stock or chicken broth with the cornstarch in place of the Port wine. Spoon off all fat from the roasting pan before finishing the gravy.

Allow the turkey to stand for 15 to 20 minutes on a wooden carving board before carving.

Makes 16 to 18 servings.

ROAST WILD TURKEY WITH HUNTER'S ONION SAUCE

For the turkey:
1 10 to 12 pound wild turkey
Salt
Freshly ground pepper to taste
2 navel oranges, peeled, and cut in half crosswise
¼ cup butter or margarine, melted
½ cup peanut oil
½ cup strained lemon juice

For the sauce:
2 navel oranges

1⅓ cups water
¾ cup sugar
6 medium onions, peeled and quartered
½ cup butter or margarine
1 cup orange juice
¾ cup currant jelly (preferably black currant jelly)
1 teaspoon salt
1 cup Sherry
2 tablespoons crème de cassis
2 tablespoons brandy

For the turkey: Preheat the oven at 325°F. (163°C.). Wash the turkey inside and out with cold water and pat thoroughly dry with paper towels. Rub lightly with salt and pepper in neck opening and body cavity. Place an orange half in the neck opening, rounded side out. Close with a poultry pin. Place the remaining orange halves in the body cavity. Truss the turkey. Brush the turkey all over with melted butter or margarine.

Combine the peanut oil and lemon juice. Dip a thin clean white cloth or double thickness of cheesecloth large enough to cover the turkey breast and legs into the oil-lemon juice mixture. Lay the cloth over the turkey. Roast for 15 minutes. Pour the remaining oil-lemon juice mixture over the cloth on the turkey. Continue to roast, basting every 15 minutes with the pan juices.

For the sauce: Meanwhile with a small sharp knife peel the zest (rind) from the oranges, making certain not to include any of the white part of the rind. Cut the orange zest into 2-inch pieces and cut the pieces into narrow strips like matchsticks. Place them in a small saucepan and add 1 cup water. Bring to boil, lower heat, and simmer for 5 minutes. Drain off the water and spread the orange strips on paper towels. Set aside.

Combine the remaining ⅓ cup water with the sugar in the saucepan and cook, stirring, to boiling point. Continue to boil to the soft ball stage, about 238°F. (114°C.), placing the lid on the saucepan to hasten the temperature rise. Remove from heat and stir in the orange strips. Set aside.

In a heavy sauté pan or skillet, sauté the onion quarters in butter or margarine, stirring often. Cover the pan when the onions begin to take on color. When completely soft, transparent and broken up, add the orange juice, currant jelly, and salt.

Continue cooking, stirring constantly, until the jelly has melted. Continue cooking, stirring frequently, until the mixture becomes slightly caramelized. Remove the orange strips from the sugar syrup and add them to the sauté pan, discarding the sugar syrup. Add the Sherry and heat to simmering. If the turkey has not finished roasting by this time, remove the sauce from the heat and set aside.

To serve: Roast the turkey 2½ hours or until meat thermometer inserted in the center of inside thigh muscle adjoining the body registers 180°F. (82°C.), or until tender when pierced with a sharp-tined fork. Allow the turkey to stand for 15 to 20 minutes on a wooden carving board before carving.

Meanwhile, skim off fat from the pan juices. Pour the remaining pan juices into the sauté pan with the sauce and bring to simmer. Add the crème de cassis and brandy. Taste and correct seasoning if necessary. Serve the sauce in a heated sauce boat or bowl.

An 11-pound turkey makes about 16 servings.

Index